P9-CJY-193

THE
BEN EAST
HUNTING
BOOK

THE
BEN EAST
HUNTING
BOOK

Foreword by
WILLIAM E. RAE
Editor-in-Chief, Retired
Outdoor Life

OUTDOOR LIFE

•

HARPER & ROW
New York, Evanston, San Francisco, London

Copyright © 1974 by Ben East
Published by Popular Science/Outdoor Life Book
Division, Times Mirror Magazines, Inc.

Brief quotations may be used in critical articles and re-
views. For any other reproduction of the book, however,
including electronic, mechanical, photocopying, record-
ing or other means, written permission must be obtained
from the publisher.

Library of Congress Catalog Card Number: 73-80715
SBN: 06-011237-9

Designed by Jeff Fitschen

Manufactured in the United States of America

THIS BOOK is dedicated to the memory of the men with whom I have shared the woods, fields and marshes for more than sixty years, with gratitude and with admiration for their unswerving sportsmanship.

CONTENTS

FOREWARD

by WILLIAM E. RAE
Editor-in-Chief, Retired
Outdoor Life

A great deal of headway has been made in this country in the last fifty years in the protection of wild lands and clean waters, and in the improvement of the habitat necessary for the survival of wildlife. In addition, many game species have been brought back from serious scarcity or the very threshold of extinction. Most of this has happened at the insistence of hunters and fishermen who were also the nation's pioneer conservationists.

Long strides have been taken to curb pollution of streams and lakes. Shelter belt and soil bank lands have been set aside to produce quail and rabbits and pheasants. Forest fires have been brought under control, and professional foresters have been weaned away from their earlier philosophy that timberlands should grow nothing but sawlogs, although it has to be admitted that in some parts of the country the multiple-use concept is still served more frequently by lip service than in actual practice.

Large areas of wetlands have been preserved, both in this country and in Canada. (Unhappily, in the same breath, larger areas have been lost to drainage and development.) The rules for hunting waterfowl have been linked to annual production. Deer and other big game have thrived as their habitat needs were recognized and met.

At the end of the last century, for example, it was estimated that the total remaining whitetail deer population of the United States was not more than 500,000. Today a number of the leading whitetail states have that many or more apiece. Fifty years ago, the western plains supported an estimated 12,000 antelope. The figure now stands at around a half million. The buffalo herds of this country had all but vanished by 1900. Today, with their Canadian counterparts, they number not fewer than 30,000. Almost forty states now have wild turkey populations big enough to support open hunting seasons.

Scientific wildlife management has largely replaced the unsound hit-and-miss controls of former years, and in virtually every state the game department has experienced enormous growth in size and funds and trained personnel. Major federal agencies likewise devote their efforts and big sums of money to the perpetuation of wildlife.

In many ways the future of hunting looks far brighter today than it did in 1920.

All this is the credit side of the ledger, and it has many encouraging entries. Unfortunately, however, there is another side as well. If much has been accomplished, much more remains to be done.

I dislike to dampen whatever enjoyment the reader may find in this book by talking about unpleasant subjects in advance. But there are clouds over the future of hunting in this country today, ominous clouds of which the great majority of hunters are only vaguely or not at all aware. If they are to be dispelled, the hunter must be told about them.

I served *Outdoor Life* as its Editor-in-Chief for twenty-two years. It was mainly in the last ten of those years that the author of this book and I worked together on a great many hard-hitting articles dealing with the things I want to talk about here.

The threats fall into two categories: First, the many abuses of the outdoors that, if continued, must greatly reduce or actually eliminate wildlife populations in the years ahead. Second, the activities of a hard-core group of fanatics who are determined to end all hunting by legal steps of one kind or another.

In my judgment, the direct threats to wildlife and hunting opportunities that merit the most serious consideration are channelization, strip mining, pesticides, oil spills, poaching, political administration of state game departments, and lack of access to public lands. Let me cite a few sample cases.

1. CHANNELIZATION

Channelization, at present the top-priority darling of the Soil Conservation Service and the U. S. Army Corps of Engineers, consists of ditching a free-flowing stream by dredging and straightening it, eliminating bends and pools, riffles and bottom snags, deep holes and overhanging banks. Along with this goes the stripping away of all streamside cover, and almost unfailingly this is followed by extensive drainage of the bottoms and the conversion of marsh and timber to cropland. The Obion River bottoms in western Tennessee provide a classic example.

Says John Madson of Winchester-Western, one of the country's leading conservation writers, in a biting attack on channelization: "The Obion used to loaf peacefully through a forested flood plain. Its bottoms once offered duck hunting that surpassed even the fabled green-timber areas of eastern Arkansas. Today the river is a barren shadow of what it was, much of it a sterile ditch, and the bottomland forests are vanishing."

An even more disastrous case is the Cache River and its tributaries in northeastern Arkansas, where in the summer of 1972 the Army Engineers began a dredging project that will cost close to $60,000,000, take 20 years to complete, ditch 230 miles of river and bayou, and drain 170,000 acres of bottomland. When those acres are put to soybeans the state's finest tract of wintering habitat for mallards and wood ducks, accommodating between 500,000 and 800,000 birds each year, will be destroyed. Where will the ducks go? No one knows, but waterfowl authorities say the mallard population of the Mississippi flyway will shrink accordingly.

The nationwide magnitude of the channelization threat is indicated by the fact that to date more than 8,000 miles of stream in 40 states have been ruined and 13,000 more are scheduled for "watershed improve-ment," the term by which the Soil Conservation Service attempts to disguise the destruction. SCS leaders estimate that in the entire country 175,000 miles of stream "need" channelization.

"Wherever a free stream runs it runs under threat of death," John Madson warns. "Natural streams do more than support wildlife," he adds. "They are wildlife."

2. STRIP MINING

Strip mining is an unruly eyesore industry that few Americans apart from those living in the affected areas know anything about. In the last fifty years, and mostly in the last thirty, its blighting scars have been left on not less than five thousand square miles of torn-up land, scattered from Florida to Alaska.

To understand the kind of destruction this mining leaves in its wake, you have to know something about how it is done. In strip mining for coal, for example, the overburden of soil and rock is scalped off and piled to the rear or dumped over a cliff, and the coal is then removed.

In level country, for each acre mined at least a second is left buried under subsoil, broken rock and sulphur-laden earth. In mountains or rugged hill country the destruction is even greater, since the overburden is dumped down the hillside and left to slide or wash down the steep slopes. Where one acre is laid waste, ten are likely to be disfigured.

This mining shocks the sensibilities. You have to see the tormented earth, the choked creek beds, the streams running lifeless from mine-acid poisoning to understand the magnitude of its blight on the land.

Today's foremost strip-mining threat is a project so huge that it boggles the imagination.

Mining and power interests are making plans for a complex of power-generation plants in eastern Montana and Wyoming that will produce 150 billion watts of electrical energy. The coal that will be needed to fuel them is to be extracted by strip mining.

The area involved stretches north and south for more than two hundred miles, from Colstrip east of Billings, Montana, to Casper, Wyoming. East and west it is a hundred miles across, bounded by the Bighorn Mountains and the Black Hills.

It covers twenty thousand square miles, of rolling sagebrush plains, vast grasslands and pine-clad hills. It is among the best hunting areas in the country, with antelope, mule deer, whitetails, sage hens, sharptail grouse, wild turkeys and waterfowl. In addition, it is veined with excellent fishing rivers.

Under the surface is the Fort Union Coal Basin, the world's largest known coal deposit. The coal seams vary from 25 to 150 feet in thickness and are covered with only 10 to 200 feet of overburden, making them ideal for strip mining.

If the power complex is built and the coal is stripped, Montana fish and game authorities warn that the face and character of that part of their state will be changed forever and fish and wildlife will be the losers.

In Montana alone the strip mining is expected to tear up almost 800,000 acres, and cooling water for the power plants threatens to leave the Yellowstone, Big Horn, North Platte and Tongue Rivers close to dry.

"Yellowstone River anglers may get an opportunity to walk across their favorite fishing hole without getting their socks wet," warns the Montana Fish and Game Department.

"We in Montana are not interested in becoming another Appalachia," U.S. Senator Mike Mansfield told a Senate Committee in March of 1963. Hunters and fishermen will hope that effective ways can be found to prevent that very thing, and found in time.

I know of no one who has summed up the ground rules that should govern strip mining—and that would go far to prevent its aftermath of ruin—better than the National Audubon Society, in a sharp warning it sounded in 1972.

America needs coal, the Society conceded, and then added that about two-thirds of the remaining coal seams could be strip-mined without lasting damage to the environment if three simple rules were enforced:

1) That the stripping be confined to areas that can be reclaimed, and prohibited on steep mountain slopes where reclamation is impossible.

2) That effective controls be enforced during the mining.

3) That the mining companies be compelled to carry out complete reclamation afterward.

Over the entire country, the strip mining done to date is no more than a drop in the bucket compared with what the future promises. The coal reserves in the state of Kentucky alone are estimated at 66-billion tons, for example. Much of it can be removed by surface mining. One county, Harlan, has sufficient coal to keep the stripping industry going for 150 years.

It is long past time that the rules advocated by the Audubon Society were put into effect, preferably at the national level.

3. PESTICIDES

Three weeks before the sixty-day season on pheasants and Hungarian partridge was due to open in the province of Alberta in September of 1969, the Provincial Cabinet issued an order cancelling the season. The action was taken when it was learned that pesticide residues five to ten times the level safe for human consumption had been found in the birds.

The primary offender was not DDT or any of the so-called hard pesticides, but poisonous mercury compounds widely used to treat seed grain before planting. Public-health authorities had sounded the chilling warning that a hunter taking home and eating two average pheasants would take in as much of these poisons as a human can safely tolerate in a period of one year.

It is hard to find proof of pesticide consequences in game birds and animals, but proven cases of kills are not lacking.

In the Western states over the last twenty years, for example, millions of acres of land have been sprayed with 2, 4-D to kill sagebrush, allowing grass to come in. A study in Wyoming proved conclusively what the results were for sage grouse.

On one thirteen-thousand-acre study area, in three years the grouse population plummeted from six hundred birds to twelve, and the following spring the strutting grounds were totally deserted.

Many states suspect that pesticide spraying is a major factor in the pheasant slump that has plagued most of the country's ringneck range in recent years, and state game authorities in many cases also believe that agricultural spraying largely accounts for a steady decline in the cottontail rabbit population.

For the hunter the most pressing

question raised by all this is the one raised in Alberta in 1969. Will the day come when hunting will have to be halted over large areas of this country because wild game is no longer safe to eat?

The threat today is probably not as grave as it was a few years ago, since the use of DDT has been phased out, but heavy spraying with other pesticides is still the rule in most farming areas and the hazard is still present. It will bear the most vigilant watching by every hunter-conservationist in the nation.

4. OIL

In February of 1970 floating patches and blobs of oil began to come ashore on the beaches of Kodiak and Afognak islands in Alaska, and the smaller islands around them. By mid-March it was known that more than a thousand miles of beach, mostly wild and unpeopled, on the islands and around the Kenai Peninsula to the north, were fouled with oil.

The total wildlife toll will never be known. Investigators estimated that ten thousand seabirds and waterfowl died, but admitted that that figure might be far below the actual loss. The bird kill was called the worst in Alaska's history, and hair seals and sea lions were found drenched with oil. How many died was not learned.

It was hardly a wonder that the editor of the Kodiak *Daily Mirror* cried in outrage, "I do not know how anyone, even the filthy rich oil industry, can begin to compensate the people of this region for the sickening disaster they have vomited upon us."

A month later disaster struck another time, in the form of a massive wildlife kill in Bristol Bay.

The chief victims were seabirds called murres. Several dead sea otters also were found, and state game men spotted four hundred seals in one band sick or dying, their eyes white, blurry and glazed, and rimmed with black corrosion. Oil sheens were reported offshore.

The toll of murres was fantastic. Officials estimated the loss at not fewer than 86,000, but admitted that as many as 800,000 to 1,000,000 might have perished.

No one has summed up the problems that go with Alaska's oil riches better than Tom Brown, a writer on the Anchorage *Daily News,* when he began an award-winning series of articles in that paper with the statement: "On the one hand Alaska possesses the richest pool of oil ever found in North America, and on the other hand the world's most magnificent wilderness. To avoid wrecking the scenic beauty of our state, to err on the side of conservation—that is the course Alaskans must chart."

To date, however, there is not much evidence that Alaska's political leaders or the oil interests intend to follow that course.

What happened in Alaska has happened on a smaller scale in many another state. Oil and oil operations, including pipelines and ocean shipment, pose a continuing threat to a clean outdoors and a wildlife population.

5. POACHING AND POLITICS

Perhaps the country's best example of a state failing to give its game populations adequate protection through strict enforcement of hunting laws is Alaska. Ironically, it is also the state that has the most to protect.

One scandal after another has broken there in recent years. In the summer of 1970, a ranking official of the Fish and Game Department admitted that his agency had lost control of the polar bear hunt completely the previous spring. Joe LaRocca, a resource writer on an Anchorage paper, estimated that the polar bear quota for the year had been exceeded by more than a third and that another hundred bears had been taken illegally.

LaRocca also exposed widespread illegal traffic in grizzly and brown bear hides. Other Alaskan writers charged that dishonest guides were using aircraft openly in illegal operations and that a bootleg traffic in polar bear permits was flourishing. Law-abiding hunters said it was common practice to see sheep and other game herded to the gun with aircraft.

Back of the situation lay two major factors, the size of the state coupled with a short-handed and underfunded game department, and political interference in conservation affairs.

With 590,000 square miles to patrol, most of it roadless, in 1972 Alaskan protection officers numbered only sixty-six, fifty-eight in the field and eight in supervisory positions. In April of that year, too, by Executive Order of the Governor, the law enforcement division of the Fish and Game Department was taken away from that agency and turned over to the State Police. Nobody can say as yet what the consequences of that transfer will finally be. Political interference with the Fish and Game Department has hamstrung conservation programs ever since Alaska achieved statehood.

Under Alaska's constitution, the governor has full power to hire or fire the commissioner who heads the department, the deputy commissioner and division directors. They serve at his pleasure and no cause needs to be shown for dismissing them.

He also can remove at will the ten members of the Board of Fish and Game which in turn plays a role in wildlife affairs that is probably unique in the country. That board has authority only to set hunting and fishing regulations. It cannot make policy for or exercise any control over the department.

It is a system that leaves the Governor completely in the driver's seat. Under it the Fish and Game Department has had five commissioners in the last five years, most of the changes accompanied by major turnover in key jobs down the line. Programs have been interrupted and morale seriously damaged.

Some of the commissioners have been well qualified career conservationists who did a good job. But no matter how good a performance he turns in, any commissioner can be fired at the whim of the Governor. No state can hope to carry out a successful conservation program under a handicap of that kind.

Says Tom Kimball, executive director of the National Wildlife Federation, who made a detailed study of the Alaska Fish and Game Department a few years ago, "As a method of managing fish and game, a political organization which gives the governor complete authority is a total failure."

That should be sufficient warning for the sportsmen of any state whose game department is run by politicians.

6. The Locked Gates

In the mountain states of the West, huge areas of some of the best big-game lands in the nation, publicly owned, are closed to hunters by locked gates that bar access roads leading across private holdings. Millions of acres of Forest Service and Bureau of Land Management lands are barred in this fashion to the public to whom they belong.

There have been angry arguments, fist fights, threats of gunplay, the use of armed guards (Bill Fairhurst, mayor of Three Forks, Montana, and the leader in an unrelenting drive to gain access to all public land, calls them hired guns), and one actual killing. But almost without exception, the locked gates remain locked and local politicians show little inclination to take any legal action.

Much of the blame rests on the influential owners of big corporation ranches, which in many parts of the West are rapidly crowding out and absorbing family-size spreads. In many instances the owners of the big ranches seek to convert their holdings, including even public lands on which they pay grazing fees, into private hunting preserves for their own use.

The top game official of one western state hit the nail on the head when he said: "If I owned a mining claim or had the right to log or graze cattle on federal land, I doubt any private owner would put a locked gate or armed guard in my way. Isn't the use of public land for hunting and other recreation as legitimate as for cutting timber, grazing a cow or taking out minerals? The multiple use concept is talked about. What we need to see is results."

In all likelihood, the hunter-conservationists of the West can do as much as anyone to bring those results about.

Exactly what can the individual sportsman do about this and the other threats to the future of his sport? How can he best protect, for himself and others, the wildlife and wildlife habitat on which tomorrow's hunting depends?

Toward the end of 1970, Earl Guess, an outraged sportsman from Louisiana, wrote *Outdoor Life* a bitter letter to complain about what was taking place in his part of the country.

He described the Ouachita River where he had fished and hunted all his life, spoke movingly of the beauty of its beaches, coves, sloughs, cliffs and the timber that lined its banks. "The Ouachita is a heaven if we can keep it clean," he declared.

Then he went on to describe what was happening. Timber scalped away, sloughs filled, cleared land replacing streams, housing developments in the place of squirrel woods, pollution, beaches strewn with garbage, cans, bottles and paper plates littering the shore and the nearby woods.

Next Guess told what he was doing about all this, describing an almost incredible one-man crusade he was waging to protect the river he loved. He was going up and down with his boat, picking up trash, burning paper, putting up signs that read "Clean It Up." He was preaching that slogan to

every boater, camper and fisherman he met and he was making converts. Some of them pitched in and helped and even gave him coffee at their camps. In three years this clean-outdoors zealot had talked to more than a thousand people along the river. Almost without exception they agreed with him that something ought to be done.

It would be hard to think of a better example of a grass-roots conservation effort, and the sportsmen of the country who follow the example of Earl Guess and do what they can single-handed deserve unlimited credit.

But there are other things they can and should be doing, too. Concerted action has greater effect than individual action. By himself a hunter may not get far in the protection of wildlife and its habitat, but if he will pool his efforts with those of others who share his concern, he can accomplish a great deal.

The most effective way to do that is to become a member of one or more of the excellent conservation organizations that now exist in every community, at local, state and national levels. Among those in the forefront nationwide are the National Wildlife Federation, Izaak Walton League, Trout Unlimited, National Audubon Society and the Wilderness Society. Many of the conservation gains made up to this time have been won by these groups.

Also, letters to congressmen, members of legislatures, and other government officials all the way from local mayors up to the White House can bring surprising results if enough people write them. They must be brief and respectful, specific and to the point. Such letters serve to make the decision-makers aware that the hunter, along with other conservationists, is demanding an end to the things that threaten not only hunting but even human existence on the planet earth.

One other thing the hunter can do. He can police his own ranks, make every possible effort to weed out the vandals and violators when he finds them afield. The sportsman who would not dream of breaking either the letter or spirit of the rules, written or unwritten, that govern his sport can no longer tolerate the game hog and scofflaw. It's high time the minority who bring disrepute on all hunting are compelled by their betters to shape up or ship out.

WILLIAM E. RAE
Orleans, Mass.

PREFACE

The first game I ever carried home was a cottontail rabbit. Nothing much as a trophy, but I was only ten or twelve years old at the time and that was the first thing I had shot bigger than sparrows and blackbirds. No hunter on an elephant safari was ever prouder of ivory that weighed a hundred pounds to a side.

The circumstances of the kill did a great deal to enhance my sense of accomplishment. We had a farm dog named Colonel, a mixture of Collie and something, curly of coat, white with a big brown patch over one eye. Colonel loved to hunt, and he and I were inseparable.

That March morning we had gone back across the farm to the creek that bordered it and I had begun the annual task of giving an old leaky boat a fresh coat of paint. I heard Colonel yip from the edge of a nearby swamp, and when I looked up he was streaking across the field behind a cottontail that was going flat out.

They crossed fifty feet in front of me. By that time I had dropped the paintbrush and grabbed up the Remington rolling-block .22 that was my most prized possession.

When the rabbit was broadside, covering ground in long reaching jumps, I touched off. My lead and swing must have been exactly right, for the cottontail somersaulted like a bowling pin.

It was a once-in-a-lifetime achievement, etched lastingly in memory. That March day is more than sixty years behind me now, and I have never again killed a running rabbit with a rifle.

I was born two years before the new century came in, in the farming country of Oakland County in southeast Michigan, fifty miles from the river front of downtown Detroit. The farm where I grew up lay on a slow-currented creek that came down out of low hills and meandered through a big cattail marsh the last mile or two on its way to join the upper waters of the Shiawassee River.

It was a fine place for a boy to grow up. I learned to swim about the time I first trudged off to country school, started fishing as soon as I could hold a cane pole, began to trap once I could depress the spring of a No. 1 Victor, and to hunt the minute I could persuade my parents that I was old enough to be trusted with a BB gun. From that I graduated to the .22, and next to a cheap and cumbersome 12-gauge double-barrel shotgun that I bought only because the recoil from the cylinder-bored barrels was mild enough that I could endure it.

All through my boyhood, both in country school and high school, I made what spending money I had on a trapline. It's still a source of whimsical pride with me that I was the only kid in the community who could skin a skunk in the morning and go to school in the same clothes, without danger of triggering outraged protests. No one ever suspected that I had been near the skunk.

From boyhood on, hunting has played an important role in my life and given me much pleasure. I have been lucky at it, too, not in the size of the bag but in other more important ways. I have been privileged to hunt big game and small over a fair share of this continent, from Florida to Alaska, from New England to Texas. And I have known and hunted with many men whose skill at it far exceeded my own.

This is as good a time as any to acknowledge my debt to them, to thank them for the secret lore they shared with me and the lessons they taught me.

Some of the game animals I have followed in my sixty-odd years afield I hunted with shotgun or rifle, some with cameras. There is little difference in the craft required, although of the two the camera requires a greater degree of patience, a closer approach, and is in general more difficult to use successfully than the gun. I can recall many times when I came close to getting a wildlife picture of trophy quality but failed by a narrow margin, when it would have been very easy to collect a pelt or a rack of horns.

But that is not to belittle gun hunting and the challenges it holds. I have done my share of it and found every hour pleasurable.

In the pages that follow I have set down the things I have learned in more than half a century about the ways of wild animals, how to find them, stalk them, outwit them and take them in fair chase, for food or trophy. In addition, I have drawn liberally on the lessons other hunters passed on to me.

I am deeply indebted to those other hunters for that opportunity. No one man could have spent enough time on the game trails of North America to accumulate for himself all the information that is included here. That is my reason for making liberal use of borrowed knowledge. I hope and believe the reader will benefit as I have benefitted from the days I have spent with those many companions.

I have one other thing to say. I have .been a hunter since I was old enough. Other men play bridge, sail boats, ski, climb mountains or ride horseback. I make no apology for my choice.

Today, there are many who will fault me angrily for saying that. They abhor the thought of killing, and rate the hunter no better than a red-handed murderer of helpless wild things.

This school of thought is not altogether new. As far back as 1948, in an article "Are Hunters Murderers?" in *Outdoor Life,* the late Grancel Fitz, one of the top sportsmen and trophy hunters of his day, and also a lifelong conservationist, had this to say:

"In the judgment of a good many otherwise sensible and enlightened citizens, I have often committed a form of murder. I am a hunter of big game. Every year I go out and kill beautiful and defenseless creatures. So I am regarded by some people as a sadistic barbarian with no proper place in a civilized world.

"Among the people who see my collection of trophies, every once in a while I encounter a sentimental lover of nature who belongs to what I've come to call the 'Bambi school,' after the inaccurate, bunk-filled movie of a few years ago. This person is usually a lady with a large and tender heart. She is distressed, even horrified. She shakes her head and looks at me reproachfully.

"'I'll never understand how any one could want to harm such a lovely, innocent animal as a deer,' she'll say. 'They have such beautiful big brown eyes.'"

From there Grancel Fitz moved on to talk back to the Bambi school very effectively. If he were alive today, almost certainly he would be saying the same things even more fervently. For if sentimentalists were a threat to hunting in 1948, their ranks have swelled and the threat is far more grave in this decade. The anti-hunting movement mounts and spreads and finds a bigger and bigger following.

Suddenly it's not just the little old ladies with tender hearts who are distressed and horrified that hunters should be allowed to go on hunting.

These shrill and angry critics overlook one or two fundamental points. Grancel Fitz put it very well in that article back in 1948.

"The esthetic and spiritual rewards of hunting can be very great," he wrote. "It helps to make a man strong and healthy, observant, resourceful, and appreciative of the wonders of the world in which we live. These, I believe, are good qualities."

One morning last winter, at his home town of Grayling, Michigan, I had breakfast with Fred Bear, one of the world's foremost bowhunters, and our talk turned to the growing resentment against hunting.

Fred has been subjected to questioning and criticism more times than he can remember. There is a Fred Bear Museum at Grayling that houses his collection of bow trophies, including an African lion and buffalo, an Indian tiger, brown, grizzly and polar bears, and much of the other big game of three continents.

Time and again a visitor asks him why he killed these animals, what satisfaction he derived from it. In short, why has he hunted all his life?

"I've given up trying to answer," Fred told me. "I can't find answers that get through to them. Basically, they want to know why man kills. I content myself with saying that the hunted animal, given a chance to escape the hunter, is hardly more to be pitied than the one that is sledged down in a slaughterhouse. Sometimes I add that a bullet or an arrow is at least as humane as the death that terminates the life of most wild animals and birds. There is no such thing as peaceful death in the wilds."

There is another answer to the question of why man hunts. He hunted before he had fire. If he was brave and skillful his family ate. If not, they starved. He no longer hunts from necessity. He hunts because he is the end product of a thousand generations of hunters. He has inherited the love and enjoyment of it, as the artist has inherited the skills and desires of the primitive man who first drew pictures on the wall of a cave. When he no longer does it he will be a far weaker man than he is today.

I'll say it again. I offer no apology for the fact that I have been a hunter since boyhood. It has brought me rich rewards in addition to the game I have taken.

BEN EAST
Holly, Michigan

xxi

Part I

BIG GAME

1
WHITETAIL DEER

Stand, drive or stillhunt

The first discovery I made when I started hunting deer, fifty years ago, was that the deer had the edge on me in natural equipment. He could see about as well, hear and smell a lot better, read the wind the way you read this page. He knew the woods better, was far more wary and crafty. He'd been hunted for generations, I was starting from scratch. I had him on only one count. I could think better. So if I hoped to outsmart him I'd have to use my head.

I'm talking here about whitetails. Most of my hunting has been confined to them, in the timbered and cutover lands around the Great Lakes. I have hunted mule deer just enough to be convinced they're far easier to take. They will be dealt with in another chapter.

The eyes of deer are just so-so where motionless objects are concerned, but maybe that's not so much because they can't see as because they fail to pay attention. Many times I have had one (always a doe or fawn, never a buck) walk up within ten or fifteen paces while I was sitting mo-

3

tionless on a log or stump. The same thing has happened to every experienced hunter. I recall a couple of instances where does or young deer approached close enough to reach out and sniff a man before they spooked.

On the other hand I have poked my head over the skyline a trifle too fast in an unguarded moment, and sent feeding deer seventy-five yards away into headlong flight almost before my cap brim was in sight. Things that don't move they are likely to overlook or ignore but they take note of motion in a hurry.

I came to the conclusion years ago that color means little to them. Red has long been worn in my part of the country for safety reasons. Yellow is beginning to edge in. I won't go into their relative merits. But I don't think it makes any difference so far as the deer are concerned. They're not likely to notice a hunter whether he wears red, yellow or any other color, so long as he doesn't move.

Many times I have come out to the edge of a clearing, paused for a look and spotted a hunter on a stand at the far side simply by picking up the splash of scarlet made by his hat or coat. And more than once, sitting on a stand of my own, I have watched deer blunder into those waiting hunters, blind to the warning red, and get floored.

Whatever the shortcomings of a

4

Poised in a woodland clearing, a whitetail buck tests the air for a scent of danger and cocks his sensitive ears for an alien sound. Relying for his survival on these superbly developed senses — his vision is just fair — the whitetail poses a formidable challenge to the hunter in any terrain.

deer's vision, his nose and ears more than make up for. On those two counts the hunter who goes after him tackles one of the most superbly equipped game animals in North America. Deer not only hear well, they also know how to interpret what they hear. They know every natural noise of the woods and they're quick to heed one that doesn't belong. Don't ever hope a whitetail will mistake you for a porcupine or squirrel. If he hears you walk or talk, even in the lowest undertone, the sound will shout "Man!" to him.

His nose is his best protection. He relies on smell more than any other sense to keep him alive and healthy, and all the caution in the world won't get you up to him if you give him a whiff. Man's smell is one thing he can't endure. Now and then an exceptional deer may tolerate the sight or sound of humans, but not their scent. Distrust of that seems inborn and no whitetail ever gets entirely over it.

The first step in hunting deer is to decide where and when you are most likely to find them. Over most of the country now, they are abundant and very heavily hunted. Under those conditions by far the bulk of the kill is made the first two or three days of the season. In fact some states, with a modest deer herd and a high human population, offer a season little longer than that and their hunters make out all right. In many cases half the deer shot in a year are hanging on the meat poles by dark of the first day. Even such top deer states as Michigan, which a few years ago was killing around 100,000 in a season sixteen days long, figure that half to two-thirds of the total are downed in the first three days.

That makes it highly important for the hunter to be on location when the shooting starts, and to look things over and make his plans ahead of time. The first day is sure to see the best hunting, unless bad weather interferes, and if he must spend part or all of that day scouting the country and trying to locate deer hangouts he puts himself under a severe handicap. And to make things worse, by the second or third day if the shooting is heavy the hotspots he has found are likely to be as deserted as a swimming beach in January, and he must start his search all over again.

There is a big advantage in hunting close to home, where you know the country like the back of your hand, but if you don't happen to live in good deer range or if you prefer distant pastures for some other reason, then be sure to arrive where you intend to hunt at least a day or so in advance and put in that time sizing things up and getting ready for that first productive morning.

Unhunted and undisturbed, deer do not travel as far as most hunters believe. Except for seasonal movements, such as the long migrations mule deer make from high country to lower range for winter (there's a well-defined trek in the Rio Blanco country of western Colorado that covers more than fifty miles) and the shorter migrations of whitetails into winter yarding areas for food and shelter, their home range is likely to cover not more than a square mile or two, and in that area they follow much the same routine day after day. They feed in the same places so long as the food supply holds out, hole up in about the same bedding grounds, and use the same trails and crossing places in going back and forth. That means the hunter who looks the country over before the shooting starts has a good chance of discovering just where his first-day chances will be best.

Where do you look for sign and how do you recognize it? It's easy to find places where deer have pawed up leaves for acorns or beechnuts. If you discover an old orchard or even a wild apple tree back in the woods, shake down a few apples and be there before daylight on opening morning. Search for openings or meadows with fresh grass, areas of good browse, corn or alfalfa fields or other farm crops that deer like.

Deer beds are easily identified, and so are the broken brush and small rubbed trees where bucks have polished their antlers, but in my book the latter mean very little. They tell you that last night or last week a deer staged a sham battle here. Where he is

Scouting for deer sign, a hunter comes upon tracks along a river bank (left), checks the edges for sharpness to determine their age. Small hollow in a grassy area (below) is a deer bed, a sure sign that a whitetail is in the area.

now is anybody's guess. I've never yet had a rubbing tree point the way to a kill.

Tracks are important. Although it is ordinarily possible to track deer only on snow, prints in mud or sand often yield helpful information. Compare them with your own. Yours are fresh. How do the deer's stack up? If in snow, are they freshly scuffed? Has the track settled in or frozen? Is there frost in it? Has it melted? In mud, are the edges blurred or sharp? In dry sand, is there more dampness in it than in yours, or less? Was the deer walking or running? By noting such small details and taking the weather into account, and by close observation and experience, you can learn to read sign and judge whether the deer is still in the neighborhood. Likely you won't get as good at it as the native African tracker who follows game by crushed grass blades, but you'll master it sufficiently to improve your hunting.

I know no hunter who can distinguish a buck's track from a doe's, although I know quite a few who claim

7

they can. The track of a deer depends on size, not sex, and there are no marks by which doe and buck sign can be told apart. I remember a hunt, for example, on which a buddy of mine followed a really big buster of a track for hours, convinced he was trailing a buck. Finally he found another hunter watching a runway. The tracks led past the stand.

"You see that deer?" my friend blurted.

"Sure did," the stranger nodded. "You been tracking it?"

"Ever since daylight."

"Well, you can quit. She's the biggest doe I ever laid eyes on, but she's still a doe."

Once shooting starts, deer behavior changes fast, and for that reason the runway you watch the first morning may be a poor bet the second. Whitetails wise up in a hurry, especially bucks. It takes only a day or so of heavy gunning to drive them out of their regular haunts into the thickest places they know about. But if there are enough hunters in the woods they can't stay in one place indefinitely. So after opening day pick runways they are likely to use in sneaking from one hideout to another, and remember that a deer pushed out moves whenever he has to.

Except in places where dogs are used, as in the South and some parts of Canada, the deer hunter has his choice of three basic procedures. He can wait on a stand for a deer to come along, either of its own free will and accord or because it's moving to get away from other hunters. He can take part in an organized drive, big or little. Or he can go looking for the deer, tracking if there is snow on the ground, stalking if the country is open enough, or just stillhunting through likely territory.

Which is more likely to put venison liver on the supper table? That's a matter on which the best hunters disagree. Some prefer to pin their faith on standing and watching, others think their chances are better if they move. Actually, most deer hunts are a combination of methods and the wise hunter lets his actions be ruled by circumstance and the kind of country he is in.

Your technique will depend to some extent on where you hunt. The tricks that get you a deer on the Dakota prairies may not work in the cedar swamps of Wisconsin or the mountains of West Virginia, but there's one thing you can count on. A doe or spikehorn is easier to kill than a trophy-rack buck, and there's nothing wrong with settling for a doe if it's legal. They're often better eating.

To find out just how tough whitetail hunting is, some years ago Michigan game men fenced in a square mile of brush and timber stocked with thirty-four deer, then invited in seven experienced hunters. With snow on the ground and hunting under any-deer rules, it took an average of fourteen hours for each man to kill a deer. When they were limited to bucks the average time jumped to fifty-one hours. With seven bucks in the enclosure it took the seven men four days to rout out and kill the first one, and although several drives were made none ever produced a buck. Get the idea?

If your heart is set on a buck or you are hunting where nothing else is legal, keep in mind the fact that it's their habit to follow does. A buck trailing his lady love will let her take all the risks. He'll wait in cover while she moves into the open, sneak around risky places where she crosses. So as long as you have a doe in sight and she doesn't spook there's a good chance the Old Man may show up. And if she keeps looking back the way she has come the odds are even better.

Standing or runway watching is a particularly good bet right after daylight and just before dusk, when deer are going back to cover or moving out to feed. There is hardly a well-used trail in good whitetail country over which deer do not travel at least every day or two, usually more often than that, of their own accord.

At the outset of the season, the hunter most likely to succeed in a hurry, in my opinion, is the one who knows the location of a runway that deer travel regularly, reaches it before the first gray light of dawn has filtered into the timber, and stands or sits quietly in one spot for two or three hours, through the period when deer are moving back from their early-morning feeding grounds to the places where they will bed down for the day.

Two or three mornings or a week later, when gunfire has scared the bejabers out of every deer in the country and most of the population, especially the full grown bucks, has moved into the most inaccessible places they can find, the hunter may do better if he carries the fight to them.

While waiting in one place for a deer to blunder into you can be hard on the patience, and often is, it obviously calls for less skill than going after that same deer. That doesn't mean, however, that you can just go out in the woods, sit down on any stump or rock that takes your fancy, and expect to have deer blood on your hands in an hour.

The first rule of runway watching is to pick a spot where deer are most likely to pass, the second to arrange your location so that you will see them and get a shot before they know you are there.

Study their movements, learn to identify feeding grounds, to tell fresh sign from old, to distinguish between summer trails no longer in use and those that were traveled yesterday.

Don't take your place actually on the runway or too close to it. Get off to one side, and choose sides so the wind will blow from the deer to you. Remember that in early morning he'll

A runway watcher is rewarded for hours of patience as a whitetail saunters into his sights (left). From his post on a tree stand (right), hunter dropped this buck as it came into the open. Trail watching is most productive at start of season, before gunfire has scared the deer into hiding.

be moving from feeding place to hiding place and in late afternoon the pattern will be reversed. But don't overlook the fact that during the day, fleeing from something or somebody that has spooked him, he may be going either way. Wind direction is all-important to the runway watcher. Deer have noses probably as good as any game animal on earth. Select your stand so there is no chance that an approaching buck, no matter which way he comes along the trail, can pick up your scent.

It's important to choose a place where nothing will interfere with your shooting, too. I'll never forget one buck that got the best of me because I forgot that rule. I was sitting with back against a weathered stump, twenty yards from a runway that angled across an old logging road. Concentrating on the runway, I neglected to keep watch behind me. I heard a rustle of noise and when I twisted my head around there was as handsome a whitetail as I've ever looked at, standing broadside in the road about ten steps away. He had seen my head move and was trying to make me out.

Poised in frost-killed ferns higher than his belly, head high and ears pointed, a tall eight-point rack soaring up, every inch of him alert and ready, he was a deer to remember, but there was nothing I could do about it. I couldn't shoot from where I was sit-

11

ting and I knew better than to move. We stared at each other for three or four seconds and I could feel a real hard case of buck fever coming on. Then the spell broke. He cleared a shoulder-high windfall in one soaring leap and the brush swallowed him before I could even wrench my rifle to my shoulder.

Some standers, especially bow-hunters who must do their shooting at close range, like to build blinds in locations near good runways. That has accounted for a lot of successful hunting, but under most circumstances I have never thought it necessary for the rifleman. If you lean against a tree or sit in front of a stump, break your outline by getting behind a clump of juniper or sagebrush or mountain mahogany, there is little likelihood that an approaching deer will notice you.

A deer doesn't rely on its eyesight to any great extent anyway, especially where things that are not moving are concerned, and a hunter on a stand is not likely to be seen if he takes ordinary precautions.

If the cold becomes unbearable light a small fire. Deer pay scant attention to smoke unless they smell it, and if they do that they're going to smell you too and the fire will make no difference. Many successful hunters do all their runway watching in cold weather beside a cozy little blaze. By the same token, I have never thought it important to refrain from smoking. An approaching deer that can smell a cigarette can also smell man. Once that happens he'll no longer be approaching. But if you smoke do it without moving your hands more than you can help, and if you're cold don't stamp your feet or swing your arms.

The safest rule is to avoid anything and everything that can possibly alert an oncoming deer. It's important not to make any motions you can avoid. A deer can materialize out of the brush thirty feet away like a ghost walking and be there in plain sight before you know he is anywhere in the neighborhood. Many a hunter on a stand has been caught flatfooted when one sneaked up behind him in that fashion, and if you happen to be moving at the time he can vanish just as fast as he appeared.

Many hunters fail at standing because they do not stay put long enough. They get cold or restless, make a short circle out into the brush to look for tracks or sign or wander down the logging road a quarter mile to see how Joe is making out, and the deer they are waiting for goes through while they're AWOL. The most important ingredient in runway watching is patience. The more you have of it, the better.

The hunter who undertakes to kill a whitetail deer by still-hunting needs to keep in mind that he is pitting wits, woodcraft and know-how against ears and nose as good as any he will ever go up against, in country better known to the hunted than to the hunter. Stillhunting calls for all the skill and stealth and caution a man can muster. The ones who do it best have a certain native craft that enables them to move with about as little commotion as the deer itself.

I have a theory that the true stillhunter is born, not made. Some men have a natural aptitude for it, others never master it. The best of the breed go pussyfooting along, drifting from one pausing place to the next the way a heron stalks a frog, hardly seeming to move at all.

When I think of the great ones I have known, the one surest to come to my mind is a man I hunted with many times, who died a few years ago. I never tired of studying his technique, but I could never match it.

He did not look where he was putting his feet. He felt. His boot soles were thin and soft enough that he could test the ground at every step. He set his entire foot down flat, not heel first. If he felt something he didn't like, a stone, a stick or even a twig likely to make noise, he lifted the foot and put it down in another place.

Stillhunting came as easy for him as breathing. He moved with the stealth of a cat, circling around thickets, easing over windfalls. I never saw him trip or stumble. His eyes searched this way and that,

taking in everything around him and ahead. He was so intensely alert that, watching him, you found yourself holding your breath, stepping on eggs, carrying your rifle half lifted. His very confidence was catching. If I were a deer I'd hate to have a hunter like that come after me.

The first rule of stillhunting is to watch the wind. Any time you start out to take trouble to the deer it has to be your first concern. Hunt into it or across it at any angle the terrain and cover make necessary, but never with it.

If there is too little to determine its direction, test it by tossing up a handful of crumbled dry leaves or grass, or by lighting a cigaret. And remember that wind is likely to change direction from hour to hour. It's more shifty in mountain country, but it can change quickly and without warning wherever you are. I can recall many days in the deer woods when it blew from every point of the compass at sometime between daylight and dark. So watch it as you go along, never let it out of your mind. If you feel it shift and blow on the back of your neck, you're going the wrong way! Back off, make a circle and take a different tack.

The second rule of stillhunting is to go slow and quiet. "Take one step and stand still two," old hunters warn. I know one who puts it another way. "Half a mile an hour is plenty fast, anything over a mile an hour is breaking the speed limit," he says. Remember it's up to you to see the deer before he knows you're there. Going for a walk in the woods is one thing, stillhunting is another.

Above all, the hunter must stay alert. Unless you are tracking on snow you rarely have an inkling of the exact whereabouts of game, any advance warning that you are getting close. Consequently you must hunt every second as if you expected a deer over the next ridge, behind the next windfall. Maybe he'll be there, maybe he won't, but if you relax your vigilance that's the time you'll bust him out, so you can't afford a careless move. The stillhunter who is always ready is the one most likely to succeed.

Move slowly and make frequent stops. If there's wind take a step or two when it sighs in the trees to cover your movements. When it dies away stand until it breezes up again. Halt at the top of ridges, the rim of ravines, the edge of thickets, the border of clearings. Look over every foot of the country ahead before you move on, wait long enough to give a deer a chance to show himself. When you take your rifle out of the rack in the morning hang a mental sign on the back wall of your mind: "Deer Ahead—Stop, Look, Listen." And remember to watch the wind!

Not every deer will break out under a full head of steam the instant he

Hidden in a thicket, a whitetail watches warily for an approaching enemy. The slightest noise or man scent will send a deer into hiding. Often, he circles back on his own track and observes the hunter from a concealed position in the brush.

hears a hunter approaching. If he thinks his chances are better he may try a sneak getaway instead, and those long stops and careful looks boost your chances of catching him at it. It's never happened to me, but a few times partners of mine have even spotted deer in their beds and walloped them before they got up, as a result of such slow and cautious proceedings.

Weather conditions have much to do with stillhunting success. There is little use to try it on dry still days when dead leaves crackle underfoot like peanut shells. Wet days following rain, when the ground and brush are damp and the hunter can move with no noise, are an ideal time for it. It's also good after a fall of wet snow, but no good on snow that's dry or crusty. A light breeze helps to cover any sound the hunter may make but on days of high wind deer are apt to be spooky.

In the dense cover where whitetails spend most of their time when they are not feeding, there is little

chance of spotting one in advance and making a stalk. I've done it a few times on does or youngsters, never with a mature buck.

A few falls back I watched a hunting partner make a highly unusual stalk on a band of four whitetails. They were in a big field and he worked up to them in the open and without cover, a step at a time when they put their heads down to graze. Whenever and as long as they looked up, he stood still. He was within 150 yards before they spooked, close enough to see that there were three does and a little buck with short spikes in the bunch. Had there been an older buck among them things probably would have been different.

There are many places where driving accounts for more deer than any other method. It has never been quite that popular in the Midwest, maybe because of the big tracts of wild or cutover land in which the hunter must operate and the corresponding difficulties of organizing and carrying out a successful drive.

Personally I have never cared much about it. I have participated in plenty of drives, both as driver and stander, and have gathered in a few deer that way, but I greatly prefer stillhunting or runway watching or a combination. For me the thrill of deer hunting is in pitting myself against the deer in an all-out match of wits, caution and

cunning. If I win that way it's a grand and glorious feeling.

But let me make clear that I am talking only about big organized drives in which ten or a dozen, or maybe three times that many, hunters take part. I have no objection to small drives staged by two or three partners hunting together. In fact I like to hunt that way. Such drives are closely akin to stillhunting, and they account for plenty of deer when conditions are right.

Pick an area of the right size, such as a narrow swamp, an isolated draw, a woodlot, creek bottom or island of cover, and let one man work through while his partners keep pace with him along the edge or move ahead and wait on stands. Somebody is fairly sure to get a shot at any deer that moves.

As for big organized drives, their success depends largely on knowing the country and the habits of local deer. For strangers hunting without guides in unfamiliar territory such drives are not too likely to produce, although it doesn't take an experienced hunter long to size up an area and figure where deer hang out and where they are likely to go if disturbed. But it's the local resident, who knows the swamps, ridges, gaps, runways and crossing places, who is best qualified to put on a successful drive.

In picking your stand for a drive, don't forget to take the wind into account. No matter how badly a deer is spooked he won't come your way if he gets scent of you and you're wasting your time on a stand if the wind is blowing from you into the area being driven.

Although most of the deer taken on drives are killed by the standers, if you are taking part as a driver don't overlook the likelihood that you may have shooting. Gun-wise old bucks often skulk quietly around a driver or slip through a gap in the line, circle back and hole up in the same area where they were just routed. It's inevitable that now and then a deer trying that kind of trickery will expose himself. I killed a good whitetail that way in Minnesota some years ago, by waiting on a ridge in the middle of a swamp after a drive was finished.

Drives often use ten or a dozen men, yelling, baying like dogs, pounding on trees. They move deer, but all too often not in the right direction. A buck big enough to rate as a trophy is likely to keep track of the commotion, circle craftily between or behind the drivers, and still be in hiding, safe from the guns, when the drive ends.

One way to drive a deer out of cover is with a slingshot. Yes, a *slingshot.*

I am indebted for what I know about this method of hunting to my friend Frank Martin. He was for a time Refuge Manager of the Shiawassee National Wildlife Refuge near Saginaw, Michigan, and it was during that period that I got acquainted with him. He now has the same job at the Charles M. Russell National Wildlife Range at Lewistown, Montana. A highly competent all-around outdoorsman, he is as expert a hunter and predator caller as I know.

Basically, using a slingshot is no more than a variation of the old trick of throwing rocks into cover for the same purpose, much like throwing a stick on the far side of a tree to bring a squirrel around to you. But the slingshot lengthens the range of your throwing arm.

Driving deer out of cover with a slingshot is no trick at all. The hard part is in getting them to run where you want them. That calls for craft and patience, and gets the right results only if it is combined with expert hunting skill. Fundamentally it takes advantage of a trait that is universal among deer.

They are most bothered if something alarms them and they are unable to figure out exactly where the danger is. The slingshot hunter alerts them and makes his presence known by the use of the human voice on one side of their cover area, without showing himself. He keeps his voice fairly low, as if talking to someone fifteen to twenty yards away, and makes himself heard at several points fifty yards or more apart, being care-

A blur of brown against snow-laden branches, a whitetail bursts from cover during a deer drive. Hunters rouse deer from hiding by throwing stones, or shooting them into undergrowth with a slingshot; the trick is to get the deer moving out of cover and toward the gun.

ful to stay out of sight. One hunter can do this by himself if necessary, by moving very quietly from place to place, but it's easier for two.

Once the deer have been notified in this way that there are men in the neighborhood, the second step is to move carefully around to a stand on the opposite side of the draw, thicket or coulee, without letting the deer hear the movement or see the hunter. And of course the whole thing has to be planned with wind direction in mind. A hillside stand is ideal, since the hunter can usually pick a spot where he has good visibility.

Once in place on the downwind side, he is ready to go to work with his slingshot. The first stones are sent rattling into the brush along the far side, where the voices were heard. Next the barrage is moved in toward the center of the thicket. Before it reaches that point, nine times out of ten any buck that is present will come busting out, away from the area

18

he considers dangerous, often almost in the lap of the hunter or one of his partners.

Properly done, by skilled hunters, this technique is close to sure-fire. They need two factors in their favor, however, undisturbed cover used by deer for bedding, and quiet walking conditions.

Knowing just where the deer are makes things easier, but not knowing adds to the excitement. It's the unexpected that raises blood pressure, on any deer hunt.

The most critical part of the whole operation is moving from the side where the talking is done around to the place where you hope to get a shot. Any unintentional noise in the wrong place at this point is almost sure to foul up the hunt. If another hunter comes along inadvertently, for example, and starts talking on the near side of the cover area, you may as well write off any deer in it.

Extreme caution is essential, and fifteen minutes isn't too long to spend in getting where you want to be. All that time, if there's a crafty old buck present, he'll be remembering the voices he heard, and watching and listening in the direction they came from. Silence will worry him as much as noise, and when the first stones clatter down along that same side, especially if the noise comes from three or four widely separated points, his nerves are almost sure to give way. He may run or he may sneak, but either way the odds are good he'll come straight into your sights.

For obvious reasons, it's a method that works best in fairly open country with narrow belts of cover. Much of the whitetail and mule deer range of the West is ideally suited to it, since there are draws, coulees and other strips of brush and timber where deer like to hole up for the day.

But with modifications it will pay off under different conditions, too. Even in timbered country the hunter will find patches and islands of thick brush, swales, bogs and other places where deer are likely to be hidden. Approach too close and often the animals will slip away unseen. The slingshot technique will rout them from such spots and send them where you want them to go, as readily as from a Montana draw. The proper procedure is to make small noises on one side, then work around to the quiet side, shoot a few little helpers in the form of pebbles into the right places, and get ready for action.

In hunting farmland whitetails, hunters often fall back on rock throwing to force them out of swales, first surrounding the place with enough men that somebody will get shooting no matter which way the deer run. Properly done, the slingshot method will do that job more easily and more effectively, and for parties of two or three it is far more likely to put venison on the meat pole.

Whitetails nestle into the snow in an area of sparse brush which is already heavily overbrowsed, as indicated by the broomed-out low brush. This is a serious problem in the northern part of the whitetail's range, causing starvation and death for countless deer every winter.

One of its major advantages is that it enables one or two hunters to work out a big block of cover, with better results than any conventional deer drive.

The slingshot Martin uses most is homemade, from a crotch of wild cherry. The rubbers are cut from surgical tubing slit lengthwise with sharp scissors, and it is fitted with a buckskin pouch that has a small hole in the center to keep the stone positioned. Rubbers can also be purchased from slingshot manufacturers. Frank ties them in place with strong, light fishline and covers the line with adhesive tape.

Several commercial slingshots are marketed in the United States, too. They are inexpensive, some selling for as little as $1.50, and that price even includes a small supply of steel balls, a quarter to a half inch in diameter.

Martin uses those steel projectiles in target practice, and he likes to have a few of them along on deer hunts, too. If things get dull he turns his attention to snowshoe hares or grouse, assuming the season is open. The steel balls are very accurate and very potent ammunition. A few sessions of practice will give the shooter all the skill he needs for rabbit-size targets up to twenty-five feet away, and it's noiseless hunting that does not disturb other game. But it's in taking deer, not small stuff, that the slingshot really proves its worth.

Snow is a big help to the deer hunter, whatever method he may use. To begin with it enables him to locate deer, follow them and keep track of their whereabouts. It's far easier to find feeding areas, to tell where they're traveling and what runways they're using, and to pick good stands, when there is tracking snow on the ground. Even driving is more likely to be successful, for to pay off a drive must move through an area that contains shootable deer and snow makes it a simple matter to locate the best places. As for the stillhunter, a fresh fall of snow is the finest break he can get.

I don't advocate trying to take a track and walk the deer down in an endurance contest. I've tried that a few times but it never paid off. I'd see the deer all right, several times if I stayed with him long enough, but getting a shot was another matter.

A whitetail followed in that fashion catches on after he's jumped two or three times. Thereafter he is constantly on the alert, watching for you to show up, and it's hard to surprise him. Usually he stays only a few hundred yards ahead of you. He makes frequent stops but always in places where he can see you first. Or he may circle back and stand where he can watch his track from a safe place off to one side. In either case he sneaks out before you know he is there, or at best you catch a flash of brown or a white flag disappearing in the evergreens, not enough to shoot at.

I remember the time a hunter in our camp followed three deer on fresh snow, hoping to push them through to other members of the party. He hadn't gone far before one of the three peeled off. Deciding it was a buck seeking safety in solitude, Matt took the single track. When it started a circle something warned him and he threw a quick look over his shoulder. The buck was lying under the low branches of an evergreen only sixty feet away. That was one of the few times I've known a whitetail to be killed in its bed, but had Matt walked another dozen steps before he looked, the story would have had an altogether different ending. That's a typical whitetail trick.

So you're not likely to kill deer by walking them down, but there are other ways of tracking that do get results. If you find a fresh track, pussyfoot along on it, use all your stillhunting skill and follow the same rules. Watch the wind. Make frequent halts, especially as you approach windfalls, thickets, swales or other places where he may be lying. When you come to the border of a swamp or the top of a rise look for him walking ahead of you. Try to get your shot before he spooks or, if that fails, the first time you jump him. Your chances will be much poorer the next time.

Two men hunting together can track to good advantage. Once they find fresh deer sign one circles ahead and takes a stand. The other then comes through on the track, moving slowly. He is likely either to get a shot or nudge the deer along to his partner.

Tracking also has its place after a deer has been shot. Not every deer shot drops to the ground and stays where it falls. In fact that is likely to be the exception. Suppose you hit one and it gets away, what then? It would be nice to say that an experienced hunter usually knows, from the location and position of the deer and his point of aim, about where the shot hits. But often that isn't the case, especially when you are shooting at a running animal in thick cover.

The first thing to determine is whether the shot was miss or hit. Many times whitetails are obliging enough to give you a clue. Spooked and running, they carry the flag up. Hit, even nicked, they usually drop it and keep it down. So if your deer goes out of sight with his flag flying you can count it a miss. If the flag goes down figure you connected. There are other ways of telling, too. A deer is likely to flinch, jump, lurch or stumble when hit.

In every case it's a good idea to have a careful look at the place where he was when you fired. Go over the ground for blood, a wad of hair cut away, even fragments of bone. If you find any of these your next move is to figure where and how badly he is hurt. The blood sign and his tracks may tell you a great deal. A broken leg shows up instantly in the track and it's easy to tell whether it's a front or hind leg. If the deer has a flesh wound in a leg blood will trickle down into the track made by that foot. If you are unlucky enough to make a belly shot he may not bleed much, but the blood will spray out and little or none of it will show in the track. A lung-shot deer bleeds heavily and the blood is often pumped out in a crimson spray on weeds, tree trunks or brush alongside the track. You don't have to follow such sign far.

Once you have learned all you can about the injury, proper procedure is hard, especially for beginners. Unless you are hunting in country where you have reason to fear that another hunter may finish your deer off and claim it (and there are such),

Descending a ridge with rifle at the ready, a hunter cautiously approaches a downed buck he trailed by blood spoor and tracks. Trailing a wounded deer is a tricky business, requiring all the skill and patience at a hunter's command.

The end of a hunt brings many rewards, not the least being a handsome buck airing out in camp. But there are others—the fall foliage and crisp, clean air, and the peace that follows the excitement and intense effort of a deer hunt.

sit down for at least half an hour. You may save yourself a lot of time and a long walk.

Somewhere up ahead, probably in the thickest place he knows about, your deer has stopped running and, if he's still able to stay on his feet, is standing in heavy cover watching for you to come along on his track. Give him time to get over the worst of his panic, forget about you, lie down, lose blood and stiffen up. Crowding him and keeping him on the move is the surest way to lose him.

When you do take the track don't walk in it. You may need to come back and recheck, and if you mess up his footprints with your own you make things needlessly tough. So stay off to one side. If two men are trailing a wounded deer one should keep close to the track while the other moves parallel fifty to a hundred feet away. The latter is most likely to get a shot, since the tracker's eyes are too busy for him to keep a sharp watch ahead and the deer isn't looking for two men.

Don't hurry on the track. Catfoot along, try to take him by surprise, and be ready for tricks, for a wounded deer is as cunning and crafty as a fox. He'll circle and cut back to where he can watch his own track. If it hurts him to travel he may lie down, let you go past and then sneak out the other way. I've known a wounded buck to skulk off within ten feet of a hunter in heavy cover without giving himself away.

If the blood sign peters out hang your cap on a branch or bush to mark the last spot of blood you can find, then circle and look for another. That way you can always be sure of coming back to the place where you left the track, for another try at unraveling it.

Finally, once you are sure a deer is wounded stay with him as long as you possibly can. Many are lost because the hunter gives up too soon. I've known seasoned woodsmen to gather in a cripple after tracking it all day. Absence of blood is no reason to quit the chase. Heart-shot deer will sometimes run a hundred yards before they drop, bleeding internally but spilling none where it shows. If you have reason to think you hit, follow until you lose the track and can't find it again. There may be a dead deer or an easy shot waiting at the end of it.

These are the rules, then, as generations of deer hunters have tried and learned them. Oldtimers, men far better at it than I, passed some of them along to me years ago. Others I learned the hard way. You'll do the same. Follow them and they'll better your score, but don't count on anybody really telling you how to hunt deer. There's much about it you have to find out for yourself. That's as it should be, and I can promise you'll have fun learning.

2
FARMLAND DEER
Tactics for the cornfield

Driving a country road a mile from my home in southern Michigan, a month before the November gun season on deer a couple of autumns ago, I saw a buck that would make a hunter's mouth water.

He was feeding with two does at the far side of a field of picked corn, close to the border of a small swamp. I stopped my car for a better look, and instantly his flag went up and he was rocking for the brush.

"Ah, ha," I thought to myself. "A wise guy."

I also thought a few other things. Before he went out of sight I had seen enough to know that he was the kind of deer all hunters hope to meet. I didn't think his rack would make the record book, but he had a big, wide-flaring set of antlers with heavy-looking beams, probably eight points, and he was certainly worth going after.

There was one odd thing about him. He was redder than the average whitetail at that time of the fall, as if a hint of his summer color still remained. I'd know him if I saw him again.

I made up my mind to do some

scouting, try to find where his home hangout was (likely in an area of small but thick swamps a half mile from the road), and discover the runways he used in moving out to feed and going back. Then I'd be on a stand at first light on opening morning.

I didn't kill that buck, and the fault was my own. I got busy and failed to do my homework. When deer season rolled around I had not found time to do the looking I meant to. Wherever he was the first morning, and the second and the third, he was nowhere in my immediate vicinity. A neighboring farmer shot him before the end of the first week.

Actually, the neighbor deserved the deer more than I did. He had kept an eye on it all summer, had even watched it walk down the middle of the road in front of his house in broad daylight, about the same time I saw it in the cornfield.

My neighbor had done the things I didn't do. He had located the places where the buck spent most of its daytime hours and where it fed regularly, and had figured out how it went back and forth. By the time hunting season arrived he knew that deer's habits almost as well as those of the Angus steers that fed in his back pasture. No wonder he outsmarted it.

All this happened no more than a mile from my front door, as I said, and I live only fifty miles via interstate freeways from downtown Detroit. That serves nicely to point up the increasingly important role that farmland deer are playing in whitetail hunting nowadays.

That is true not only in my home state of Michigan, where I have done the bulk of my deer hunting for forty-five years, but also over much of the prime whitetail range in the eastern half of the country.

In such states as Iowa, Illinois, Indiana, Ohio, and even in Minnesota, Wisconsin and New York, all of which have big areas of forested wild land, the deer that feed on a farmer's corn and alfalfa and hide out in a ten-acre brushy swale, supply a big share of the action and the venison.

In Michigan one recent fall, for example, hunters in the wild-land counties of the Upper Peninsula, long considered the state's ace area, killed fewer deer than those who stayed in the farming country.

The day after Thanksgiving in 1970 I saw more than a thousand automobiles parked at two shopping malls in the eastern outskirts of Grand Rapids, Michigan. That same day friends of mine were hunting a very special whitetail buck that had been seen all through the fall within sight of those same malls. Stories had grown up around him, including one that credited him with sixteen points. So far as I know he was still there when the season ended. His presence at the edge of an urban area with more than 300,000 people, within hearing of stores, restaurants, gas stations and motels, tells a great deal about the extent to which white-tail deer are able to adjust to human neighbors.

Game biologists say that 100 per cent of the 11,000 to 14,000 deer harvested annually in Iowa come from a habitat of farmland mixed with timber. The agricultural counties of Missouri contribute about a third of the annual kill there. Ohio puts the figure at 20 per cent. Wisconsin sets it much higher. Of an average yearly take of 100,000 deer there, 60,000 come from counties where farmlands help to maintain the herd. In Illinois John Calhoun, a game biologist, has this to say:

"All deer in Illinois use farm crops. There is no area where such crops are not available within easy travel distance. And another factor in northern and central Illinois, fully as important as food, is the fact that cornfields furnish cover as a substitute for woods. As soon as corn reaches three feet deer move in and stay until harvest time."

But knowing that deer are present in farming country and hunting them successfully are two different matters. Wherever the whitetail lives he is the same wild, crafty, canny creature. But because the surround-ing of the farmland deer are different from those of his forest counterpart, and because all deer learn quickly to fit their habits to the conditions around them, the farming-country whitetail is a somewhat different animal to hunt than the wild-land deer.

He lives, first of all, in a goldfish bowl. His areas of cover are small and often isolated. Brushy woodlots, swales, small swamps, Christmas tree plantations, narrow belts of thickets along streams, even cornfields must serve him as bedding grounds and hiding places in time of danger. His travel routes are likely to be no more than a brush-grown fencerow or ditchbank, a country road, a patch of willows bordering a cultivated field.

As a result, he moves in the open far more than the deer of timbered places. A wise whitetail buck, living in a remote region of forested hills and valleys, may live out his life without stepping into an open place bigger than an average dooryard. If he inhabits farmlands, the same deer must walk fields, cross roads, move out of the brush for his groceries every day of his life.

This does not make him any pushover, however. In fact the opposite is true. For the very reason that he has to do these things, in deer fashion he becomes good at them. If anything he is more wary, more crafty, harder to take than his forest brother.

Two young bucks, having quenched their thirst in a farmland stream (left), cast a wary glance over their shoulders as they retreat to a small patch of woods. Startled by scent or sound, the four deer in a high-grass meadow (below) seem about to bolt. Whitetails in farmland areas, living in the open to a large extent, are even more crafty and elusive than their forest cousins.

Rabbit hunters, pheasant hunters, squirrel hunters and quail hunters comb the places where he lives, fall after fall. He avoids them to stay out of trouble, and in doing that he becomes an expert at dodging, skulking, putting up with human intruders without letting them know he is there.

As in all deer hunting, when you go after him you have two choices. You can let him come to you, or you can try to get within gun range of him. In farming country especially, I prefer the former. But even that way there can be slips between the cup and the lips.

My friend Bill Scifres, outdoor writer on the Indianapolis *Star* and one of the top hunters and fishermen in Indiana, still likes to tell the story of his first deer hunt, back in 1952.

Indiana opened its second season that fall, and twenty-four hours before the shooting started a fellow worker of Bill's proposed a spur-of-the-moment deer hunt. Scifres didn't even have time to go out and test-fire his new 20-gauge shotgun. The two decided to hunt in Jackson County, where Bill's father was living and where he knew the area like the palm of his hand, and had been keeping close track of local deer for years. "He can tell us right where to go," Bill predicted.

They arrived at the father's house before daylight, and Bill's confidence proved well founded. The elder

Scifres directed them to an area laced with runways that showed plenty of fresh deer sign. Bill picked a stand in a dry creek bed where he could watch a runway that ran along the edge of a thicket. He had waited only a half hour when he saw a buster buck coming down the runway. It had probably been moved by other hunters, but was not spooked and was mincing along at a walk.

It was a big deer with a very good rack, and the nearer it got the higher Bill's blood pressure mounted. He waited, gun lifted, heart pounding, until it was hardly more than fifty yards off. Another three or four steps and it would be his, the first deer he had ever killed.

Then to his dismay a hunter whom he had not seen poked his head and the barrel of a shotgun around a tree fifteen feet from the deer and poured in three shots in rapid fire. The buck died in its tracks.

"I just about died, too," Bill recalls.

The next day he found another promising stand, where deer were crossing a small river. He was on it before the first hint of daylight the third morning, and sat down under a leafy pin oak.

The sun was just peeping up when he saw a buck coming, about as good as the one he had lost to the stranger the first day. It was following a runway that led down to the river crossing, but at seventy-five yards it suddenly realized something was wrong.

31

From his post in a blind at the edge of a cornfield, a hunter waits for his companions to drive deer into the open from the surrounding woods. This is an effective method of hunting farmland whitetails; two to four men can drive small islands of cover effectively.

It stopped, threw up its head, walked back and forth a few steps and started to tromp the ground with its front feet. In all likelihood it had picked up a whiff of man smell, but not enough to locate the source.

It would not come closer and finally Bill tried a shot, but his untested shotgun did not put its rifled slug where he held. Astonishingly, he fired three shots at the buck without putting it to flight. Finally, in desperation, he got down on his hands and knees and tried to creep close enough for a kill. He had gone only a few yards when the deer made him out and lammed.

"I didn't have much proof, but I concluded right then that your chances are better if you let a deer come to you than if you try to go to him," Bill says. Most veteran hunters agree.

Driving accounts for plenty of farmland deer, and if it's done right it's an excellent way to hunt. Two to four men, hunting together, can drive small islands of cover very effectively.

Usually the best procedure is for some of the group to move ahead and take stands, leaving one or two to move through the swale, creek bottom or woodlot and push out any deer that may be lurking there. Tracking snow is a big help, since it enables the hunters to know beforehand where there is game to be jumped.

The party resorting to this method needs to keep in mind the fact that driven whitetails do not always go busting out of cover at the first hint of danger. Old bucks in particular are likely to skulk around the drivers, circle back and hole up again in the same place, or leave by a route the hunters least expect.

I recall the time when three partners and I undertook to drive a deer that we had reason to think was a fairly good buck out of a twenty-acre stand of young evergreens on a Christmas tree farm.

The way we had it figured, he'd be almost sure to leave the tree plantation by way of a brushy ravine that ran along one end and led to a swamp on a neighboring farm. There was a runway at the bottom of that ravine, much used, and it seemed very likely this one would follow it once he was jumped.

One man moved ahead to a stand on the side of the ravine, where a windfall gave him a natural blind. Another waited at the border of the swamp. The other two of us proceeded to drive the deer out.

FARMLAND DEER

There was enough snow for tracking, and that made it easy to find out afterward what had happened. To begin with, we didn't jump the deer. He heard us coming, as we intended he should, but he sneaked off ahead of us with no more commotion than a cat going through wet weeds.

He moved almost to the ravine, as we had expected. Then he got cautious, made a wide circle around us, skulked to the far end of the evergreens, safely behind our backs, and took it on the lam across an open field. Many a farmland whitetail reaches old age by such trickery as that.

Now and then, of course, the deer that tries it blunders and exposes himself. In such cases it's the driver, not the standers, that is likely to get a shot. If you are driving, keep a sharp watch on all sides and don't forget to look behind you fairly often, too.

One thing the hunter can do in farming country that is not likely to be successful in big areas of swamp and timber. If there is snow for tracking, he can follow a deer until he or one of his companions catches it in the open and gets a shot.

One of the best non-typical whitetail racks I have ever seen was taken that way in Ohio a few falls ago. The deer had an extra main beam on each side, so long and heavy that when you first looked at the head you thought you were seeing double.

A party of four or five hunters went after that buck, in a hilly area where the ridges were grown up to brush and timber but there were farms in every valley. They knew he was there, and had kept track of him long enough to have a pretty good idea where he spent his time. They picked up his track at the border of a field of unpicked corn and followed him the rest of the day, with one or two men walking the track and the rest going ahead and taking stands.

They didn't overtake him that first day. Shortly before dark, when the track headed into an area of thick brush, they quit, figuring he'd spend the night there. They went back the next morning, took the trail again, and jumped him almost at once.

Early the second afternoon, a little more than twenty-four hours after the chase began, hunter persistence paid off. The trackers pushed the deer over a farm fence in front of one of the standers and the hunt was over.

When it comes to big drives, with ten to fifteen taking part, I have never cared for them and I like them less in farming country. All too often such groups forget about line fences, invade land where they are not wanted and bring down angry complaints of trespass. Many landowners in my part of Michigan are growing increasingly bitter because of deer hunters "running wild all over the place." Most of these incidents arise

*Trail watching is most productive way to hunt farmland deer.
Here a bow hunter levels down on a whitetail trotting along the
border of a field — a typical runway in this type of country.*

in connection with drives that are too big for the area where they are staged.

Stillhunting is probably the least productive of all methods in hunting deer in farming country. In timber, the stillhunter can take advantage of cover, move very slowly and quietly (especially in wet weather when the woods are damp) and make frequent stops. He has a good chance of seeing a deer before it sees him. The odds of that are far poorer in open fields.

Many times I have come on small bands of deer feeding in a corn or alfalfa field or an apple orchard (three of the best places to look for them, incidentally), well away from any cover. But getting up on them in such a place calls for more skill than most hunters possess. In my case, they usually see me first.

The only time I can remember getting the best of a buck under those conditions was on a hunt on Beaver Island, at the north end of Lake

Michigan. I was in an area of mixed woods and brush-bordered farms, some of the latter long unused. In mid-morning I came to the edge of an old hay meadow and stopped to look things over.

The meadow covered maybe ten acres, there was not a bush in it high enough to hide a housecat—and out near the middle a deer was feeding. The binoculars showed a nice six-point buck. There was no natural cover for a stalk but in the center of the clearing stood an old log barn, with the roof fallen in and the walls tumbling down. I decided to make a play for that deer.

I circled around until I was downwind from him and had the barn between us. Then I catfooted straight for it. When I eased one eye around the corner of the old building the buck was only fifty yards off, still feeding, without a worry in the world. He came about as easy as any whitetail I ever shot. He had fattened on beechnuts and clover, and he supplied some of the best venison that has ever come my way, too. But the farm-country stillhunter can't expect always to have a barn in his favor.

Of all the ways of farmland hunting, it's runway watching that is most likely to put deer liver on the supper table.

All deer are creatures of habit to some degree, the farm deer most of all, maybe because he has no alterna-

Crouched behind a tree at the edge of a meadow, a camouflaged hunter "rattles up" a buck from a nearby thicket, a technique popular in the Southwest for bringing a deer into range.

tive. He's likely to hole up in the same block of cover day after day, for the reason that there's no other spot in the neighborhood as good. The runways he can use in moving out to his feeding areas in late afternoon and getting back around daylight the next morning are limited by the nature of the country. Of necessity, he must use the same ones regularly, and it's by taking advantage of that trait that the hunter has the best chance of bringing about his downfall.

The hunter most likely to succeed where farm deer are concerned is the one who locates the deer and the runways they are using ahead of time, picks the right place for a stand, arrives before daybreak the first morning, stays all day if he can and if not is back in ambush by midafternoon.

If he draws a blank the first day, but keeps this up and does enough stillhunting and scouting to make sure that the deer have not changed their location and travel-ways once the shooting started, luck is very

Bowhunters favor tree stands, where legal, when hunting in farmland areas, for they can see a deer approaching in thick cover. Also, the raised platform allows their scent to drift upward rather than toward the deer.

likely to smile on him before the season is too far along.

When the first deer season in modern times opened in our county ten or twelve years ago, a young neighbor of mine was making big plans. All through the summer he had watched four mature bucks at the back of the family farm. He knew where they stayed, fed and traveled, and one of the four was a splendid ten-pointer.

Then the shooting started and the whole situation changed. These were deer in a newly opened area, deer that had never been hunted before. Nevertheless, they wised up in a hurry.

First they stopped feeding in the daytime. They waited until late evening to leave their beds, and by first light they were back in their home swamp and holed up for the day. For three days Spence saw tracks but no deer.

Then he no longer saw tracks, and he was aware that the quartet had moved. He went looking, and on another farm half a mile away he came on what he was looking for. The deer had found a safer neighborhood.

Spence came home that afternoon, got off the school bus, changed into hunting clothes and headed for a runway that ran along the edge of a brushy tamarack swamp. He sat for an hour. The afternoon light started to fade—and then the buck he had wanted all along stepped out of the brush in easy shotgun range.

The rack was disappointing on one score. Sometime in the last few weeks before Spence killed him, the deer had broken off four points on one side. But my young friend still has not killed another trophy as good.

Beginner's luck? Nothing of the kind. Spence had done the right things, both before and after the season opened, and they paid off as they are likely to in all deer hunting, nowhere more surely than in the case of the farm-country whitetails.

In most deer states, no matter how long the season, more than half the kill is downed the first three days, and more than half of that percentage is hanging on the meat poles or in barns at dark the first night. That makes the place you go on opening morning a matter of great importance.

In looking for runways, remember that deer traveling along the borders of fields are likely to follow the edges of thickets rather than going through them. If you are hunting in country that has small rivers, look for runways where deer cross the streams. Bill Scifres tells me that in Indiana most of such crossings are located where the water is deep. Apparently the whitetail prefers swimming to fording.

When it comes to the best location for a stand, a perch in a tree tops all others if the hunter has the patience for it. For thousands of years the enemies of the whitetail deer, whether wolf, coyote, bobcat, man or even a mountain lion, have attacked mainly from the ground. Consequently, it is there the deer has learned to watch and listen for danger. He has never formed the habit of looking up.

Unless a careless movement or noise alarms him, he rarely pays any attention to what is going on ten or fifteen feet above the ground. More than one hunter, perched in a tree, has had a deer, even a buck old enough to know better, walk beneath him so close that he could have reached down and prodded it with the muzzle of his gun, never suspecting the presence of a man.

One other factor is very much in the hunter's favor in such situations as that. Have you ever watched the smoke of a wood fire on a still winter morning? It goes straight up. Even with a wind blowing, it is only under unusual conditions of weather and barometric pressure that smoke or heated air of any kind drifts to the ground. And man smell is heated air. Finally, a tree stand often enables the hunter to see an approaching deer in thick cover, where from the ground it would be impossible to get even a glimpse. It is bowhunters who have perfected this method, and it probably accounts for a majority of the deer they kill. Gun hunters are only beginning to catch onto it.

There is one fly in the ointment where such stands are concerned. They are illegal in a few states. My home state of Michigan, for example, prohibits hunting deer from a tree or any elevated platform.

Some hunters, especially archers, like to do their runway watching from tree blinds. They nail platforms in suitable trees ten to twenty feet off the ground, add twigs and branches for camouflage and crude steps for climbing up and down, and sit or stand in fair comfort. I know bowhunters who put up half a dozen such structures before the season opens, overlooking the runways or feeding areas of their choice, and move from one to another as the habits of the deer change from day to day.

A few use portable platforms that they can carry into the field and hang in any tree they like. Still others (and they are a hardy breed in my opinion) simply climb into a tree that overlooks a promising spot, try to find a comfortable perch, and sit there.

The staunchest believer in the treestand method I know, and also the most patient and persistent, is a young Ohio hunter who uses no platform but simply finds a seat in a convenient fork, takes his lunch with him, and tries to stay in the tree from first light to dark without climbing down. He kills deer regularly, but in my book the rewards are not worth the punishment. However you go about it, however, a tree stand is one of the surest ways to get a farmland deer.

When it comes to guns for this brand of hunting, there is little reason to talk about rifles. For reasons of safety, most states restrict the deer hunter in farming country to shotguns or muzzle-loading rifles. Missouri and Pennsylvania are exceptions. They permit either shotguns or rifles, but in Missouri the shotgunner is prohibited from using buckshot.

Buckshot has been widely outlawed, in fact, as more likely to cripple than kill, but a few states still permit it, Maine for example, and New Jersey lets its hunters use nothing else. Pennsylvania also has an area around Philadelphia where only buckshot is legal.

I don't like a shotgun for deer. To me the whitetail is the rifleman's ideal game, and the rifle is the right firearm for him. But there is nothing wrong with the shotgun so far as effectiveness is concerned. Loaded with rifled slugs, and in the hands of the right man, it's a deadly weapon.

There are shooters (let me say quickly that I'm not one of them) who can shoot four-inch groups with slugs at fifty yards and seven-inchers at half again that far. That's better than many deer hunters can do with their favorite rifle.

There is of course a great difference in the effective range of the rifle and shotgun. The rifled slug will kill at a hundred yards or even farther, but most deer taken with a shotgun are dropped at fifty yards or less, and many hunters will not try a shot beyond seventy-five.

So far as shotgun gauges are concerned, the bigger the gun the more knockdown power, since a 12-gauge slug is heavier than a 20 and has more authority when it arrives where it's going. But a 16- or 20-gauge will do the job nicely if the shooter knows his business. Most states prohibit the use of anything smaller than the 20 on deer.

The shooting performance of any shotgun can be greatly improved by fitting it with a good bead sight in front and a receiver peep sight adjustable for elevation and windage. In the hands of a good shot, a shotgun sighted that way and firing rifled slugs becomes for all practical purposes the equivalent of a short-range rifle delivering a slow, heavy, brush-bucking and deadly missile.

I'll go back to what I said in the beginning about that whitetail in the cornfield. He was a wise guy. Most farmland deer are. However you hunt them and whatever gun you use, they'll give you as good hunting as you will ever find.

Any time you kill a mature buck that has spent most of his days within sight, scent and hearing of houses, barns, tractors and country roads you're entitled to hang a medal on your chest announcing, "I'm a deer hunter."

MULE DEER

The big, bounding westerner

In forty-five years of deer hunting, I have killed very few bucks that came easy. But I can recall one notable exception, the first mule deer I ever shot.

I was the guest of Bill Sweet at Butte, Montana, that fall. Bill was an old hand in the outdoors, a crack horseman, good at deer and elk hunting, an enthusiastic rattlesnake hunter, a member of the Montana Fish and Game Commission, and above all, an excellent host. He has been dead many years, but I'll never forget the trips and hunts I made with him.

Bill was living in Butte, but he maintained a ranch in the foothills above Boulder Valley, forty miles to the east, where he kept fifteen to twenty saddle horses, and he also had a hunting cabin up in the Deerlodge National Forest above the ranch, in what was then one of the best elk and deer areas in that part of Montana.

It was almost the end of October. There were only a few golden leaves left on the cottonwoods along the Boulder River, and elk season was not yet open. Our hunting party was

43

staying at the ranch, loafing, cutting firewood, and looking for a fat young buck that would qualify as camp venison.

I rode out by myself right after breakfast one morning, with my .300 Savage in a saddle boot, a gentle horse suitable for a dude rider under me, telling myself that deer hunting western style had a lot of advantages over the brand I was used to back home in Michigan.

About three miles from the ranch house I pushed the horse around the shoulder of a steep hill. I was riding across a bare, dry area without enough cover to hide a jackrabbit, but two hundred yards ahead there were scattered small pines and clumps of low brush on the hillsides. There was also a ranch fence angling up, and all of a sudden I saw exactly what I was looking for, a sleek three-point buck standing in the open on my side of the fence.

I knew better than to shoot from the saddle. The horse would have jumped out from under me. I swung down and pulled the rifle out of the boot, keeping one eye on the deer. He stayed where I had seen him first, watching horse and rider, until I stepped into the clear at one side. Then he lifted over the barbwire fence in a single effortless bound and headed for the shelter of the nearest pines, bouncing along in the peculiar stiff-legged mule-deer gait.

The range wasn't more than

On the snow-covered slopes of the Rockies, a handsome mule deer pauses to survey the landscape. Forked antlers, black-tipped tail and huge ears distinguish this deer from the whitetail.

seventy-five yards, and I probably could have floored him going at a dead run without any trouble. But before I had a chance to find out, he pulled up short and stood looking back to see what was going on on my side of the fence.

I put a 150-grain bronzepoint angling into his chest just back of the rib cage. He ran again for fifty yards, I threw away a second shot, and then he piled up stone dead beside a clump of pines. He had made the typical mule-deer blunder of stopping to look back after he was spooked, a mistake that in all my years of hunting I can't remember ever seeing a whitetail be guilty of. He was a pushover because of it.

Taken together, these two deer are the most numerous, important and popular trophy game in North America. One or the other is found from Alaska to Florida and from Maine to Mexico, as well as in much of the southern half of Canada. In many places in the West their range overlaps. Occasionally, in areas where the terrain and cover happen to suit

both, they share the same thickets, but that is not a common situation.

In many respects they are alike. Both are fundamentally woodland animals, belonging to the same family and not too greatly different in appearance. Venison from the one tastes about like venison from the other, taking age and condition into account. But in ways that count most with the hunter, in the cover where they are found, their behavior, personality, wariness and cunning, they are as unlike as if they came from different planets.

If a deer can be compared with a rabbit, then the whitetail is a cottontail grown big. He has the same alert, nervous ways, the same stealth, speed and craft. Many veteran hunters have commented that the whitetails of western river bottoms behave more like cottontails than deer. And by that same yardstick the mule deer is an oversized jack rabbit, with the jack's lack of furtiveness and caution, and his simple ways.

Basically the whitetail is an animal of thickets and heavy cover, although he's as much at home in farmlands as in forested regions, provided there are islands of swamp or woodlot for him to hide in. The muley is a mountain deer, fond of arid hills and brushy draws and pockets, preferring semi-open country to dense timber. If he has to, he can make out with very scanty cover indeed. On the sagebrush plains of Colorado I have jumped mule deer out of clumps of brush not as high as a man's belt, where there wasn't a tree within five miles.

In the Boulder Valley of southwestern Montana, where I killed the mule buck I just told about, mule deer are native and whitetails were introduced many years ago. The whitetails thrived, but only in the willow thickets along the Boulder River. They refused to spread back to the dry foothills on either side. Nor will the muleys go down into the willows. You can ride the hills for a week without putting a whitetail out of the timbered washes and you can comb the tangles along the river, only a couple of miles away, for another week and never see a mule deer.

Because of the open places where he hangs out, and also because he's not too foxy, the muley is far more likely to show himself to hunters than the whitetail. It isn't unusual to see as many as twenty to thirty bucks, does and fawns in a morning in good mule deer country, and for me the sight of that much game adds a lot of excitement to the hunt, regardless of whether I get a shot at a worthwhile head. That sort of thing is not likely to happen in hunting whitetails.

The greatest concentration of deer I have ever seen was in the Rio Blanco country of Colorado, on the western slope of the Rockies west of

Meeker. I hunted there one fall in the area around the Game and Fish Department's Little Hills Game Station, on Piceance Creek, and it was an experience I'll never forget.

The night before the hunt started we went out with a spotlight-equipped truck to shine deer, legally and aboveboard. The people in charge of the station were using that as one method of keeping count. In an hour or so, in natural meadows and alfalfa fields, we tallied more than two hundred mule deer. Often, the game men told me, the count ran as high as five hundred in a night. There was a reason for that mind-boggling abundance of deer concentrated in one small area in late October. (Heavy snow fell less than a week later.) The reason was migration.

That Rio Blanco country, in northwestern Colorado, was then the scene of one of the very few great deer treks, if not the last, left in this country. I don't mean the normal seasonal drift of a few miles down from high country into sheltered valleys with the onset of winter. Deer and elk do that all over the west. I mean a true migration, a movement of an entire herd many miles across country to reach the winter range they prefer.

There were many of these big marches in the old days, among both mule deer and whitetails. There was one in the Upper Peninsula of Michigan, for example, south in fall from the big hardwood forests along the shores of Lake Superior, about a hundred miles to the cedar swamps on what is now the Wisconsin-Michigan border. That migration was so heavy and well defined that the Indians built drift fences of brush to funnel the deer to lakes and clubbed them to death from canoes as they swam across, much as the Eskimos once speared caribou at river crossings in the far North.

There were many similar treks in the mule deer country of the West, including three in that same section of Colorado. One of these followed the Yampa River down from the Rabbit Ears Pass country, cut across to the lower White River and wintered in Coyote Basin, a march of about a hundred miles. A second migration moved down the Colorado River from an area north of Glenwood Springs to the desert around Grand Junction. These deer also traveled about a hundred miles. The third migration was from the high country around Trappers Lake, due west down the White River to the arid hills on Piceance Creek, a distance of about fifty miles.

Roads, increased hunting pressure and other factors ended the Yampa migration around 1902. The Colorado River trek petered out a few years later. Only the Trappers Lake herd continued to make the fall and spring march, and it was the migrants of that herd that we encountered that night on Dry Fork.

No one knew exactly how many deer were involved, but Colorado game men said hardly fewer than fifty thousand and some hunters believed the herd might number two or three times that many. It yielded a kill of around thirteen thousand each season for a number of years and showed no signs of shrinking.

The deer began to move out of their summer range early in October, the exact time depending on the arrival of the first heavy snow. By November there was hardly a muley left in the timbered mountains around Trappers Lake but the brushy hills about seventy-five miles down the White were crawling with them.

The return march in spring got under way around May 1 and the

A small herd of mule deer begins its downward trek to a sheltered valley where food will be easier to find. In the old days, before roads and hunting pressure cut into the herds, up to fifty thousand mule deer made an annual winter migration across the Colorado Rockies.

movement was even more spectacular than in autumn. Game men from the Little Hills Station blocked off traffic on a twelve-mile stretch of dirt road which the deer crossed, swept it each day by dragging a tree-top the length of it, and made a daily count of the fresh tracks. They tallied as many as twenty-five thousand in twenty days, all heading east toward the summer range. Once each spring, on an April evening chosen at random, the game technicians took a count by driving the main roads along Piceance Creek with spotlights. That count averaged five to ten thousand muleys. Dick Lyttle, a Colorado game and fish commissioner then living in Meeker, once accounted for five thousand in a single-handed, one-evening count!

By the end of May the Piceance Creek district was virtually empty of deer. The big herd was back in its summer home. But while they were there on their wintering grounds they made the country around Meeker about as good mule-deer range as you could find in Colorado or anywhere else in the West.

Colorado game men tell me that the big migration is a thing of the past now. High-speed roads, fences, heavy hunting and other factors have caused the deer to change their habits, as on other migration routes. The area

49

Lacking the graceful, flowing stride of the whitetail, the mule deer runs with a stiff-legged gait, bounding into the air and landing like a four-legged pogo stick. He can also scale cliffs with remarkable agility.

around the Little Hills Game Station still provides very good hunting, but today no more than a remnant of the herd, maybe five to ten thousand animals, moves back and forth between summer and winter range.

I said the mule deer and whitetail look much alike, but that depends on the view you happen to get of them. Head-on and standing, you can identify the muley about as far as you can see him by the enormous ears that give him his name. On a big buck they'll measure a foot long by close to five inches wide. They actually make him look like a mule. There is even a Colorado yarn about an eastern hunter, making his first trip for mule deer, who knocked over a jughead from a rancher's pack string and had it tagged and dressed before he noticed it was wearing iron shoes and realized he had made a mistake.

On a small two-pointer or three-pointer, as well as on a spike, those big ears all but cover the antlers, and more than one hunter operating under a buck law has passed up a legal muley because he couldn't see horns for ears.

Viewed from the rear, especially in headlong flight, there is considerable difference between the mule and the whitetail, too. The hallmark of the whitetail is his flag. When he is spooked and unless he is hit he carries it erect, waving from side to side, an alarm signal that often looms plainly in the thickets when not another hair on him can be seen.

In contrast, the muley has a spindling little black-tipped tail, so small it's comical, and never lifts it in flight. He wears an identification badge all his own, however, a yellowish-white rump patch not unlike that of an elk, that is lacking in the whitetail, and he may switch his tail back and forth across that patch as he runs.

Even the racks are different. A typical four-point mule deer head will have two forking V's on either side, rather than a main beam with tines branching upward at right angles in whitetail fashion, and if the mule deer has brow tines they are usually short and insignificant.

The sportsman familiar with whitetails, encountering mule deer for the first time, is likely to be both amazed and amused at the gait of the latter. The whitetail runs in long graceful leaps, pushing himself airborne with his hind legs, returning to earth on his front feet. The mule deer flees stiff-legged, bunching all four feet under him for each jump, taking off and landing like a four-legged pogo stick. He can't match the whitetail for grace or speed but in rough, broken country his odd gait gives him a marked advantage, and in addition he has an ability to scale ledges and cliffs that is close to goatlike. If he can get footholds he'll fight his way up an almost vertical face of rock or clay without much trouble.

There is little question that the ground-thumping bounce of a frightened mule deer serves another purpose, too. It's a danger signal to others of his kind. Run a spooked muley within hearing of other muleys and the whole bunch lights out. And if you run him over frozen ground he can be heard a long way.

It's in their behavior when hunted that these two show the greatest differences. The mule deer is easier to get close to, more likely to provide standing shots. Jumped, he picks no certain route, has no definite destination in mind and is in no hurry to get there. He runs helter skelter, uphill, downhill or around the hill, or he may not run at all for several seconds. He

thinks nothing of crossing an opening. In fact he'll run deliberately out in an exposed place and stop to look around. Not so the whitetail. He rarely ventures out of cover in daylight unless cornered and pushed so hard he has no choice.

In the Black Hills, where both deer are found, there are many small parks and meadows scattered through the timber. In some places those grassy, open areas, about three hundred yards across, completely surround a ridge or hill and so make an island out of the timbered slopes. Jump a mule deer in one of those islands and he will break leisurely into the nearest meadow and skip across to the next ridge or valley. But spook a whitetail in the same place and he'll skulk and hide, circle around you or even jump over you rather than break cover and show himself in the open.

I knew oldtimers who had hunted in the hills for years, and had worked out an almost foolproof system. If they wanted a mule deer they relied

As a hunter centers his crosshairs, two desert mule deer placidly return his gaze, seemingly immobilized by their strange trait of curiosity. When jumped by a hunter, the muley will generally pause and look back, as if to identify the intruder on his territory.

chiefly on stillhunting, poking along very quietly and slowly, stopping every few steps for a careful look around. They concentrated on early morning and late afternoon hunting, when the deer were on the move, and they rarely failed to score.

But if they were after whitetails, they hunted in small parties of two to four men and used a drive system that worked like a charm. They picked small pockets and ridges, places they knew well. Their drives were never more than five hundred yards long, and if they chose the right spot and if their teamwork was good, it rarely took more than a two hundred-yard drive to put a buck on the meat pole.

One of the foremost traits of the mule deer, as I hinted earlier, is his fondness for stopping to see what's going on behind him. Put him up from his bed and he's likely to bounce to his feet and stand there, staring straight at you. Or he may run fifty yards and then stop for a look back. He seems reluctant to leave the scene without making sure on two counts—what is it and where is it. And eight times out of ten he looks long enough to give you your chance. If you're wise to mule deer ways, play your cards right and keep your buck fever under control, you can have a standing shot at a muley almost any time you encounter one.

The fall I hunted in the Rio Blanco country, one of my partners, Fran Waugh, then a researcher for the Game and Fish Department, surprised a four-point mule buck in his bed. The deer was lying behind a twisted juniper at the bottom of a draw and there was a tangled belt of sage, a hundred feet wide and taller than a man's head, running up and down the draw for four hundred yards. Once a deer disappears in that stuff you don't even see the brush shake as he sneaks through, and this fellow had about two jumps to go from bed to sage. He made one of 'em — and then pulled up to look back!

Fran had come over the rim of the draw thirty yards above, moving quietly, but the whole country was as dry as a buffalo chip, and the buck heard him and left its bed as if powered with trap springs. It was halfway to the sage before Fran knew it was there and had it kept going my partner would never have gotten his .300 to his shoulder. But the deer wasn't sure what he had heard and he had to stop and find out. He was still looking up in Fran's direction when a 150-grain bronzepoint rammed into his spine just ahead of the shoulders.

If you're a deer hunter I needn't tell you that you'd never catch a whitetail buck making that mistake. Jump him and he knows exactly where he's going and rarely stops until he gets there. Most of the time he makes for a runway that leads across a ridge, over a saddle, through a swamp or to some other place of safety. Surprised at close range, his best chance lies in flight through the thickest cover available. He knows it and wastes no time looking back.

When he's ready to bed down he picks his spot carefully, maybe walks past it and doubles back, and then lies down a few yards off to one side where he can watch his back track. If he sees, smells or hears a man at a distance he's likely to get quietly to his feet and sneak off, in which case the hunter never catches a glimpse of him. Or if he's bedded near a log, thicket or other heavy cover he may even stick where he is, head flat to the ground, doggo as a nesting grouse, and you have to step on him to jump him. If that ruse works, once you have gone by he'll move out behind you, making about as much commotion as a cat walking on a thick rug.

I recall one Black Hills whitetail that lay in a clump of juniper within ten feet of a trail and let nine men in a party of eleven walk by him single file before he finally lost his nerve and spooked. He'd have done better to stay put, for the hunter bringing up the rear snapped a hip shot just as he was disappearing in thick stuff and scored a lucky hit behind an ear.

Dull witted as he seems to be about some things, the mule deer has one shrewd trait. That is his habit of choosing bed grounds on an elevation where he has a clear view of the area around him. Like all deer, he relies on smell and hearing far more than on sight. His nose is at least as good as that of any member of the deer family, and experienced hunters contend that he has the best ears of any game animal in this country. They should be if size means anything. But his eyes are only fair.

Like the whitetail, he sees movement fast enough but takes little notice of things that do not move. Even a hunter attired in the bright flourescent colors so popular in deer country nowadays for safety reasons is not likely to catch his attention so long as he keeps still. But let a heel scuff, a twig break, a pebble roll, or the wind carry the faintest hint of man smell his way, and he takes notice pronto. And since the location of his bed gives him a chance to hear, smell and look at the same time, it's all in his favor. Even so, the still-hunter who watches the wind and takes it slow and easy, moving a little and looking a lot, has a very good chance of catching him off guard.

There is even one time when the mule buck is smarter than the white-tail. That's when he is jumped in the company of a doe. In those circumstances the craftiest whitetail can be counted on to tag along. He'll bring up the rear, letting his lady friend take all the risks, but nine times out of ten he'll come through on the runway behind her sooner or later, and the hunter who knows that and has

the patience to wait him out is almost sure of a shot.

The mule deer has different ideas. Surprised with a doe, he figures the whole neighborhood is unhealthy. Let her go down a draw or up a hillside if she likes. He reasons his chances are better by himself and he doesn't let chivalry stand in his way. While mama bounces off in headlong flight, attracting everybody's attention, he is likely to slip quietly out the back door and sneak away in another direction.

Of course the hunter familiar with that trick can take advantage of it, too. Take the case of the five-point buck that Fran Waugh and his dad surprised in the Black Hills at daylight one November morning. They were driving out from camp when the deer walked across an old fire trail 200 yards ahead. It lammed before they could get out of the car, but wasn't badly spooked and since there was fresh snow on the ground they decided to take the track.

The rut was at its peak, and it turned out the buck was more concerned with finding a receptive lady deer than with what might be coming along on his track. Before he had gone far two other deer, apparently a doe and her fawn, had vacated their beds as he strolled up. The three sets of tracks led down into a brushy pocket on the hill below, hinting at a cozy tryst.

Fran and his dad stopped beside the beds, talking in whispers, trying

With a pair of saddle horses tethered and waiting, a hunter cradles the rack of a mule deer he took on the steep, piney slopes (above). Plains hunter (right) lugs his trophy on foot.

to figure the best way to push the deer out so as to get a crack at the buck. They were still standing there when in some fashion the doe got word of them. They heard a clatter in the brush and she and the fawn broke out on the far side, bouncing downhill, straight away.

If the buck knew what the hubbub was about he hadn't located the cause

of it. He fell back on the basic safety rule of his kind, "If she runs one way I'll run the other!" He pounded out of the pocket broadside, coming uphill not thirty feet away, and piled up like a wet dishrag, with two bullet holes in his shoulder an inch apart.

Despite the fact that the mule deer is easier to outsmart than the whitetail, in my opinion hunting him is far more fun because of the frequency with which you see game.

I recall a Colorado hunt when I walked into the lower end of a brushy draw and started up, making a one-man drive for a partner who was on a stand at the head of the draw. Before I reached him I had spooked out six deer, a doe and fawn, a pair of spike-horns, and two fair bucks that left independently of each other. Because the hills on each side of the draw were about as bare of cover as a sheep pasture, I watched all six of those muleys leave the brush and trot over the ridge, in plain sight all the way. As I said earlier, in good mule deer country it's no rare experience to see a couple of dozen deer that same way in a half day. I recall a three-mile ride on a horse in the course of a Montana elk hunt when we tallied a total of twenty. Some of them let us ride by at two hundred yards with not much more concern than white-face cattle show, too.

We were not interested in deer that day, but I can't remember a morning of hunting I ever enjoyed more.

4

ELK

Ace of mountain game

The most important requirement in elk hunting is that the hunter be in condition for what he intends to do. As with all game, you have to look for elk where they are, and good trophy bulls don't hang out in back yards. First there is altitude to reckon with, and that is hard on a man not used to it. There is climbing involved, steep, hard climbing on foot, up where the air is so thin that a hunter's heart knocks against his ribs with every step. There are brush and rocks and slides to fight, and often enough snow on the ground to make the legs ache from bucking it.

I've never forgotten what Howard Lowry told me. Howard and I were making a hard hike in mountain wilderness at the east end of Quesnel Lake, on an oppressively hot day in August of 1966, and I was witnessing one of the most fantastic feats of portaging I had ever seen.

In summer Howard and his wife Vi operate a fishing camp on Quesnel, out of Horsefly, British Columbia. In the fall he guides big-game hunters in the mountains to the east of his

59

In his lofty habitat in the Rockies the regal elk is a much-coveted trophy. Packtrains take hunters into the mountains (above), but once they arrive at the base camp they face arduous climbing in rugged terrain (right), where stamina and tenacity are vital to success.

place. Winters he does a little cougar hunting, and in the spring he traps beaver.

He and I had beached our boat near the end of Quesnel that day, and headed up a rough trail for a small lake three miles back in the bush. Two years before, on a spring bear hunt, Howard and a partner had sat down on the side of a mountain fifteen hundred feet above that lake to glass for game. He was using ten-power glasses, and somewhat idly he took a look at the lake. He got the surprise of his life. Big rainbow trout, five and six-pound fish, were schooled at the top of the water like cordwood, playing and jumping. He and his partner watched the spectacle for two hours.

So far as Lowry knew, no one had ever wet a line there. He and I were on our way in now, to find out whether the trout in that remote, virgin lake would do business with us. And Howard had volunteered to pack in the canoe that we would need for our fishing.

It was an incredible performance. There was a trail of sorts the first mile. Then the going got about as rough as any I have ever encountered, bare rock, steep ridges, deep ravines, all littered with down timber and roadblocked by brush-grown old burns.

I was carrying a camera and two fishing rods, and having all I could do to keep up with Lowry, striding along with the canoe balanced on his shoulders as if it were a feather pillow.

We didn't make it to the lake. On a high ridge within sight of the water, a quarter mile away, we encountered a tangle of blowdown timber so thick that it was impossible to take the canoe through without cutting a trail. We had no ax, and anyway it was too late in the day for that.

At one point Howard stopped in an open place, leaned the bow against a stub and stepped out from under his burden for a rest. I looked at the high mountains rearing into the sky to the east, and said something about the hard climbing that must be involved in hunting there.

Howard gave me a dry, unsympathetic grin. "If you want to hunt mountain game you have to be willing to climb mountains," he said bluntly.

He wasn't talking about elk, but I have never heard elk hunting more eloquently described. The elk is a mountain animal, and if you hope to hang his splendid rack on the wall of your den you must be willing and also able to climb where he lives.

A couple of falls ago a young friend of mine drove to Montana from Michigan for his first elk hunt, with a partner with whom he had hunted deer a few times at home. My friend spends enough of his time in the woods to stay in first-class condition. The partner was as soft as a tub of lard.

The packer took them into the Bob

Cleaning his rifle at day's end, an elk hunter relaxes beside his tent with one superb rack to his credit.

Marshall Wilderness. Unused to the saddle, they rode the thirty miles to camp in one day, and after that the hunter who hadn't conditioned himself hardly stirred out of camp. He didn't get far enough from his tent to see an elk track. The other member of the team hunted hard and came home with a pretty fair elk. The moral of the little story is self-evident: The most common error the inexperienced nonresident makes is failure to toughen himself physically in advance. Then, new to the West, new to the mountains, new to the saddle, he's likely to overestimate what he can do.

I know a Western guide who does a lot of elk hunting, whose home is at an elevation of three thousand feet. That's quite a bit more altitude than the places where most Eastern hunters live.

On an average of once a week all summer this man hikes back to a remote mountain lake, often six or seven miles from the road, walking in and out in one day. You'd think he'd be in top trim the year around, but his way of life does not put him in condition for elk season and he knows it.

For ten days before he leaves on an elk trip he takes a daily hike over a steep hill, a walk that requires about an hour, carrying a load roughly as heavy as his rifle to accustom his arms to the weight they'll be carrying.

His earnest advice to beginners planning an elk hunt is to do the same or its equivalent. If they don't have a hill handy they can walk up and down stairs for an hour at a time.

A horse can take you up where the elk are, but actual hunting from the saddle is rarely a paying proposition. You seldom take a trophy head that way. For one thing, in timber a horse puts the hunter up among the low branches where his view of the country ahead is limited. For another, a man can walk more quietly than a horse. Finally, elk often go where a horse can't follow, either in cover too thick or up a slope too steep, and the hunter needs to be able to follow them no matter where they go.

Although elk hunting can involve spotting a good animal and making a stalk to get within range, that method does not account for any great share of the kill. Far more elk are shot by a combination of stillhunting, standing and driving, done much as in deer hunting.

It's not uncommon for a hunter to blunder into a whole band of elk and be able to take his pick of the bulls, and under those conditions they are hardly as spooky and crafty as whitetail deer.

I remember riding over the rim of a gulch with Bill Sweet of the Montana Game Commission, on a hunt for elk and mule deer above the Boulder Valley east of Butte. Deer season was open, elk season would get under way the next morning. We broke over the rim of the gulch with our horses making very little noise in soft snow, and before we knew they were there we were literally on top of a band of nineteen elk, less than fifty yards ahead. They threw up their heads and stared at us for three or four seconds, then lit out at a pounding run. There were two heads in the lot that I'd have walked from Michigan to Montana for.

Tracking snow is a great asset to the elk hunter. Three bulls (above), making their way to low-country feeding grounds, nuzzle the snow for forage. Hunter (right), coming upon a pair of grazing bulls after a long stalk, raises his rifle for the long-awaited shot.

"Always happens a day too early," Bill told me with a grin.

That is a fairly common experience in elk hunting, especially if the hunter is on foot and moving slowly and carefully.

Weather has much to do with success, and hunting methods vary somewhat as the season goes along and conditions change. For a pleasant hunt, late September and early October are likely to be best, provided the regulations allow. The weather is at its finest then, and for the most part the elk stay high until snow comes, above the thick timber of the lower slopes, where they are easier to find and approach. With the arrival of the first hard snow storm they move down to lower elevations.

Tracking snow is then the greatest boon the elk hunter can ask for, just as it is for the deer hunter. Trailing on new snow and matching wits with a wise old bull that has lived long enough to know all the tricks, and is far more familiar with his surroundings than the hunter, is hunting at its best. I know no better illustration of that than the trophy bull that Fred Mercer killed in southwestern Montana in 1958. At the time it was taken it stood in No. 2 place on the Boone and Crocket record list.

Mercer and his partner were camped high, at ninety-two hundred feet. They got a good fall of tracking snow in the night, and more was coming down. They left camp right after breakfast. Mercer was looking for a trophy and vowed, half kiddingly, that if he found the track of a big bull he'd stay on it until he killed, even if it took a week.

He found one, in open timber where a bull and his harem of nine or ten cows had left a broad ribbon of tracks. Mercer knew he was in for a hard hunt. The elk were at least an hour ahead of him, and by now had probably holed up for the day in thick timber. The snow was dry and noisy and he'd have to move very carefully. But it was the kind of elk hunting he liked.

He had been on the track an hour when he spooked the band out of thick cover. The bull had led his cows around in a circle to a place where the wind would give away anybody coming along on their track. They had caught only a whiff of the man, however, and were not badly spooked. They ran a short distance and then settled into a walk, making a big circle into some of the roughest country in the area, a place of creeks, canyons, passes, steep hills and gulches.

By late afternoon Mercer had trailed them twelve to fifteen miles, through hard going every step, but he figured they were no more than five minutes ahead. He labored up a mountain for another forty-five minutes, pulling himself up the steepest places by hanging onto trees, close to exhaustion. When he reached the top and poked his head over the rim the biggest bull elk he had ever laid eyes on was standing broadside, less than fifty yards away.

That's a hard way to gather in a trophy elk, but it's also one of the surest if the hunter has the skill and stamina to do it.

Some elk hunting is done with the help of a call but that method does not account for a lot of kills. In the rutting season, when the bulls are bugling, it is not too difficult to bring a bull within range if the guide is a skilled caller. Hunting that way is not greatly different from calling moose, except that moose usually show at the edge of water and in plain sight, while a bull elk responding to a phony invitation from a cow is likely to keep to timber.

One thing the hunter needs to remember. A full-grown bull elk can be quarrelsome under any circumstances, and a wounded one with a spark of life left in him is dangerous in the extreme.

When we were hunting out of Bill Sweet's camp on Bull Mountain in the Deer Lodge National Forest in 1954, Bill's wife and mine rode out just after daylight, and in a big open park they saw something walk out of the timber ahead, coming toward them. For a minute, in the poor light they mistook it for a man dragging a deer. Then they made it out as a bull elk with a very heavy rack, walking slowly with its nose to the ground. The bull paid no attention to them until he was fifty yards away. Then he stopped, shook his head, pawed the ground and took a couple of threatening steps closer.

Lou Sweet was looking for a young elk for eating, not for a trophy, and my wife was not hunting. This old bull was the last thing Lou wanted, but she piled off her horse and cut loose a shot over his back. He didn't even flinch. Lou levered in another shell and waited, ready to kill him if he made one more threatening move. He stood watching, insolent and surly, for a lagging minute or two. Then he turned away and went back into the timber at an unhurried trot.

It was hard to account for his behavior, since the rut was about over with. Maybe he had had an argument with another bull and was still looking for a fight. Whatever his reasons, the encounter was one to remind any hunter that a bull elk is nothing to fool around with, even if not wounded. And once he is hurt he's likely to be pure poison.

I know a Colorado hunter who knocked a big bull down at close quarters, hitting him high in the shoulder so hard that he turned a somersault. But before the hunter could lever a second shell into his rifle the elk was back on its feet, shaking its head and glaring at him.

"I've killed mountain lions that

When the rut is in full swing, and the bulls are bugling their challenges (left), hunters imitate the mating call to bring a bull into range (right). Below, elk bugles and high-powered rifle with scope.

A packtrain heads home after a successful hunt.

were pretty snarly looking characters and I've seen range bulls that a man wouldn't walk up to," George told me, "but I've never laid eyes on an animal that looked as mean as that elk."

His hunting partner came along just then, walked face to face with the bull at fifteen yards, and was put up a scrub pine so fast he dropped his rifle on the way. The hunter who had wounded the bull ended the affair with a second shot in the neck. That will give the general idea of what they are capable of.

Partly because they are not easy to kill, partly because they are dangerous if the hunter fails to do a complete job, many guides advocate a rifle with knockdown power not less than that of the .30/06 or the .300 Magnum.

"You need to put an elk down for keeps to be sure of him, especially when there is no snow on the ground," one Western guide told me. "The next best thing is to bust him so he'll leave a blood trail a floorwalker could follow. Either way, it calls for a rifle with a knockout punch."

There is another good reason for using enough gun. Much elk hunting is done in grizzly country, and there is always the likelihood of an encounter with a bear that has a chip on its shoulder. The elk hunter may go for years without seeing a grizzly, but if it happens, the meeting is likely to be unexpected, in brush, and at short range.

That once-in-a-lifetime encounter may come at a turn in the trail, or the hunter may find the bear standing over the elk he killed, dressed and left in the woods late the previous afternoon. The grizzly is far more likely to act than to argue, and the man needs an adequate rifle.

"I want a gun that will put a soft-nose all the way through the biggest bear in the mountains, endways if necessary, whether I hit him in the head, the shoulder, the chest or the tail," one guide says.

One final thing must be said about elk hunting. Without exception, the men who have taken this majestic, beautiful and big member of the deer family agree that he is a magnificent trophy, one of the greatest this country has to offer. There is a challenge hard to match in tracking a regal bull elk through the rough going of his high-altitude home country, and any hunter who hangs a royal rack (seven points on each beam) on his wall has just cause for pride.

As for the hunt itself, the wild places where elk are found is half the pleasure. There is frost on the grass in the autumn mornings, fall colors like a rainbow on the lower slopes of the mountains, snow peaks shining in the distance, and tamaracks on the slopes turning the dull yellow of the elk's own coat. It's hard country to beat at any season, and the elk hunter sees it at its best.

5

MOOSE

The majestic lummox

On one of the best hunting days I ever had, I didn't fire a shot. But I did trip a camera shutter on more than thirty moose between noon and supper time.

The place was Lake Richie, in the roadless wilderness of Isle Royale, the big island in upper Lake Superior that is now a national park. The time was in the early 1930's, when the Isle Royale moose herd had built up to an estimated three thousand animals. It crashed disastrously from winter starvation a few years later.

I was carrying two cameras that day, a standard Graflex and a big and cumbersome Naturalist Graflex that had a focal length of twenty-four inches, for telephoto purposes. I brought home some fine trophies, including two pictures that I still prize as among the rarest I have ever made. They show two cow moose in pitched battle at the water's edge, along the swampy shore of the lake. We watched those two cows feed slowly toward each other, not expecting anything out of the ordinary. But when they were only three or four times their

73

own length apart the tempers of both suddenly flared.

They rushed at one another with the hair on their necks standing up, their ears laid back like those of an angry horse. They reared up on their hind legs and pummeled each other with their forehoofs, with water flying in all directions. The fight lasted long enough for me to level the big camera and record both their approach and the battle on film. Then one got enough. She dropped down, wheeled and ran. The other pursued for a hundred feet or so, flailing at her opponent's rump with those merciless front feet.

Battles between bull moose are common in the rutting season, as every outdoorsman knows, but that is the only time I have ever heard of cows fighting, and I know no one else who has witnessed it.

The moose of Isle Royale taught me a great deal of what I know about the big ungainly animals. There was never an open hunting season on the island, but I stalked them with cameras often in the thirties, and when Michigan live-trapped almost two hundred and moved them to the mainland of the Upper Peninsula for release (in the face of a critical starvation threat), I took part in an advance survey of the herd and in the hard job of loading the captured animals aboard a boat for the trip across Lake Superior.

I had some lively and exciting encounters on the Isle Royale moose trails. There was, for example, the bull I met on the Chickenbone Lake trail one afternoon in July. The rut was still months away, and there was no reason apart from inborn moose cussedness for him to behave as he did. He walked over a low rise fifty feet ahead, coming down the trail to meet me, and we were face to face before either knew the other was there. He stopped short and so did I. The coarse hair of his mane stood up, he shook his head truculently, and I could see that he had no intention of yielding the trail.

I was carrying a .38 caliber handgun on my belt. That seemed a sensible precaution when hiking on Isle Royale. I unholstered the gun now and uncorked two quick shots over his head.

I don't suppose he had ever heard a firearm up to that minute. It didn't faze him. He shook his head again and took a couple of steps my way. I shot a third time, then decided to save the rest of the cylinder in case I needed them.

There was no tree within reach suitable for climbing, but I slipped out of the pack I was carrying and backed slowly into a thick stand of small aspens. Maybe I could outdodge him there. We eyed each other for several minutes. I talked to him, telling him what a fool he was to pick a quarrel when he didn't need to. In the end I must have stared him down, for

Stalking through the thick northern bush, his huge antlers polished for the rutting season battles, this bull moose may look ungainly but he's one of the most unpredictable and dangerous animals on the continent. Wounded, a bull moose is as deadly an antagonist as a hunter is likely to encounter.

he walked slowly off the trail, angled down the ridge twenty feet from me, and went out of sight in the brush.

Then there was the young bull that treed two good friends of mine, Dick Lahti and Chips Larson, while they were fishing a small brushy trout stream inland from Todd Harbor. Dick was the Isle Royale game warden at the time, Chips the fire warden. They maintained a headquarters on an outlying island, but spent most

of their time cruising the shoreline in a small patrol boat.

This little punk of a moose came out of the willows, splashed across the creek and rushed them without even pausing. They evaded him by scrambling up two cedar sweepers, trees that leaned out over the stream at an angle that made them very easy to climb.

The moose pawed the ground, grunted and grumbled, and kept the two men treed for the better part of an hour. Then he went back across the creek and disappeared. Dick and Chips waited a short time, and when he did not reappear they slipped very quietly out of the trees and started down the trail to the harbor where they had left their boat. They had gone less than three hundred yards when they heard the moose coming pell mell behind them.

Larson shinnied up a wild cherry out of reach. Lahti grabbed a low branch on the first tree he came to, a big birch, and swung himself off the ground. The branch was dead and dry. It snapped like a matchstick and dumped Dick in a heap.

"That was the first tree I ever slid up," he told me. "When I got ten feet off the ground I looked down, and the birchbark was smoking behind me."

They waited out the moose for an hour or so that time, and made it back to the boat without any more trouble.

Those two encounters serve as well as any I know about to illustrate something that every moose hunter learns sooner or later. There is no animal in the woods, not even the black bear, more unpredictable than the bull moose. He is at his dangerous worst in rutting season, but he is never to be trusted at any time of year. And wounded, he can be as deadly as anything a hunter is likely to confront.

A solitary moose leaves a wandering trail in deep snow on Isle Royal. Moose find the going hard at such times, and fall ready prey to their chief natural enemy, the wolf.

I have known a number of woodsmen who have hunted moose all their lives, either for sport or for food while living in remote country. On a few points all of them agree.

The moose has ears as good as those of any big-game animal on this continent, deer and bears included. His nose is also as keen as a whitetail buck's, and he makes even better use of it. Often if he hears a hunter approaching in thick cover he will make a deliberate circle to bring him downwind from whatever has disturbed him, relying on scent to tell him what it is. That is something deer rarely if ever do.

As for eyesight, as with elk and deer, a moose is not too likely to take note of a man unless movement catches his attention, and he doesn't do too well at making out an approaching canoe. Often he will stand and watch, plainly not identifying it for what it is, until it drifts within easy shooting range.

When it comes to wariness and craft, he is no match for a deer. He is less likely to take alarm at the first hint of danger, easier to stalk, more apt to offer a shot in thick cover where a deer, especially a whitetail, would skulk away unseen. But he is far from a pushover.

There are three basic ways to go about getting a moose. You can stillhunt in brush and timber, much as deer hunters do; you can scout carefully and quietly in a canoe along marshy streams and lake shores where moose come to feed in early morning and late afternoon; or you can bring a bull to you during the rutting season by calling.

The last two methods probably account for the greater share of the animals taken by nonresident sport hunters hunting with a competent guide. Bush trappers and woodsmen living in moose country are more likely to pick up their rifle, head for a place where they know moose are plentiful, and bushwhack a winter's meat supply about as they would a whitetail or muley.

The hunter's first problem, of course, is to find a shootable moose. The best place to look for one is in a feeding area or on worn moose trails. The latter often lead from one swampy lake to another, or converge like the spokes of a wheel at a feeding place, coming down off higher land. Once the hunter locates a promising spot he can stillhunt or watch from a stand, exactly as a deer hunter does.

That method is well illustrated by the experience of four men from Michigan who went to northern Manitoba on their first moose hunt a couple of years ago. They arrived in late September, in the middle of a spell of rainy weather, to find the bush dripping wet and the foliage still so heavy that a man couldn't see much more than three times his own length in the willows and alders. Even the Indians laughed at them when they

proposed to go into the bush and find themselves a bull. "Too much leaves," the Crees jeered.

But the Michigan men knew that the woods are quietest in wet weather. They made use of all the know-how they had acquired in years of hunting deer back home. They went into the thickets, looked for tracks and other sign, sneaked through with as little commotion as possible, stillhunted hour after hour, found places where lovesick bulls had trampled the mud and torn the brush — and left for home with three good bulls, butchered and quartered, in their two pickup trucks.

Ted Updike, a retired trapper living at the hamlet of Love, on the edge of the bush in northern Saskatchewan, who has hunted moose for food for almost fifty years, has a few words of advice for the hunter who goes after them that way. "Walk slowly," he urges. "If it takes an hour to cover a quarter mile, so much the better. Move as quietly as a ghost and be ready for a quick shot if you catch sight of game."

It was Ted who passed along to me

Moose hunters paddle silently along the shore of a bog-bordered lake. The sternman uses a birchbark call to imitate the grunting sound made by a cow or bull during the rut, hoping to bring a bull out of the bush and into rifle range.

a very interesting trick for the still-hunter, one that was taught to him by an old Cree many years ago. You carry a dry twig about the size of a pencil, and if you see a moose within fifty yards but can't get a clear look for a shot, break the stick. The moose will hear it crack, and almost certainly he will lift his head to locate the sound. He won't wait long, but if the hunter is alert there is likely to be time for a shot.

Hunting from a canoe is an easier method. It takes advantage of the fact that moose do much of their feeding along swampy creeks and in the shallow water of bog-bordered lakes, and that it is not difficult to sneak within range in a canoe paddled slowly and quietly, hugging the shore for cover. I can recall half a dozen times when I have turned a bend or rounded a point of swamp under those circumstances and surprised one of the animals up to its belly in the stream or lake, no more than fifty to a hundred feet ahead. Almost always it stood and looked long enough to permit a hunter a shot before it splashed ashore and crashed into the brush. Paddling and looking for moose sign and for the moose that left it is a very productive way of hunting.

As for calling, although it seems that less of it is done today than a generation or two ago — maybe because of a shortage of guides who have mastered it — so long as the bulls are rutting and fighting other bulls it

A moose hunter, with an enormous rack strapped to his pack-board, pauses along a waterway on his way back to base camp. The palmated antlers may have a spread of five to six feet.

80

remains one of the surest methods of all.

It calls for skill and the ability to mimic the grunting of either a cow or a bull, and few hunters learn it on their own. The most skilled calling I have heard was done by north-country Indians who had lived all their lives in moose country, hunted for meat, and called since they were kids.

The caller has one final trick in his bag. If grunting alone does not bring the moose into the open for a shot, he dips his birchbark megaphone full of water and trickles it slowly back into the lake. It sounds like a cow urinating, and the result is likely to be a red-eyed bull smashing out of the brush in headlong haste, full of fire and insane with lust.

One thing that few hunters killing their first moose — or their first elk, for that matter — are aware of until it happens to them is the fact that dressing one of these animals is roughly equivalent to dressing a horse. Unless he has a guide to do the job for him, or if he is the kind of hunter who insists on doing his share of the hard work, he is in for a very hard chore. One of the most useful tools for it is a light ax for getting through the pelvic ring and the breastbone. It's worth carrying such an ax whenever the hunter is working from a canoe, and some stillhunters even like to slip one, properly sheathed, into their pack.

I have always liked the description the late Ray Voss, a fellow outdoor writer and good friend, tacked onto the moose:

"There's something about a bull moose that makes him a lummox," Ray wrote after his first moose hunt. "He's ungainly, with neither the grace of an antelope, the dignity of an elk nor the alert intelligence of a deer.

"With his flat antlers rampant, his overhanging snout, bell and the hump on his back, he looks to me as if he had been built in sections by subcommittees with separate blueprints for a buffalo, a cow and a camel, and then assembled by the general chairman after dark." Then Ray added, "But he's imposingly big, not much afraid of anything, and for all his looks there is something sort of stately about him, just as there is about an elephant. He lives in country I admire, and he's enough of a trophy to satisfy any man."

Nobody has said it better. Although admittedly awkward looking, with anything but handsome features, nevertheless a big bull moose is a majestic animal. There is a certain imposing wildness about him. He breathes the incarnate spirit of the northern wilderness, he hints of bogs and lonely lakes where man seldom goes, he wears his huge rack — wide enough for a grown man to lie across — with lordly grace. He is as splendid a trophy as any hunter can ask to take.

6

BLACK BEAR

With dogs or without

The black bear is among the greatest game animals and most coveted trophies in the United States. Many hunters rate him second only to the grizzly. And the way to get the most out of him is with a pack of dogs. Until you have heard hounds go insane on a hot bear track you have missed the most hair-raising dog music a hunter will ever listen to.

Before bear dogs came into use in my home state of Michigan, in the late 1940's, the bears killed each fall (and we accounted for fifteen hundred and more a year) were shot mostly by deer hunters, who blundered across them by accident and collected them as a bonus. It was an exciting experience and yielded a fine trophy, but there is more action and excitement in one bear shot ahead of dogs than in a dozen taken that way.

The dogs are after something capable of killing them if they get reckless, a tough and crafty animal, long-winded, given to running in tangled laurel hells, dense swamps and through beaver ponds, fond of the hardest going he can find. It takes a

83

good man to follow a bear chase on foot, and even intercepting one rarely comes easy. About ninety-nine times out of a hundred the hunter who kills a bear ahead of hounds earns his trophy. That happens to be the way I have always liked my hunting, and I suppose that is one reason why I rate this bear chasing so highly.

In the fall of 1945 I went to Tennessee for my first bear hunt, in the mountains near Tellico Plains. I didn't kill a bear, but I was not disappointed. As a matter of fact, that was not my real reason for making the trip.

There had been much talk in Michigan of hunting bears with dogs. I knew two or three hunters who had shot bears ahead of their coon hounds, almost by accident, but at that time there was not a real bear hound in the state. More and more sportsmen were coming to believe, however, that such bear hunting, as it was done in the West and in the mountains of the South, had the potential to become a major sport. Others argued that the swamps of the North were too big, that bears could not be driven to the hunters, that the dogs would run deer out of the hunted area, that it just wouldn't pan out. Even some state game authorities agreed with this belief.

I went to Tennessee for a firsthand look, to see how the hunts were arranged and carried out, how the bear and the dogs behaved. I wanted to decide for myself whether the method that worked in the mountain coves of Tennessee would work as well in the cedar swamps of northern Michigan. I came home convinced that it would.

A year later, in October of 1946, at my urging Michigan United Conservation Clubs, the state's leading federation of sportsmen, arranged the first bear hunt with dogs ever undertaken in our part of the country. At MUCC's invitation, Hack Smithdeal of Johnson City, Tennessee, brought his hound pack and a group of handlers north for a test. Smithdeal owned one of the most famous bear packs in the southern mountains and was one of that region's top bear hunters.

The hunt was a smashing success. If there had been any question as to the interest of Michigan sportsmen in this kind of hunting, it was laid to rest when upward of a thousand applicants asked to register for the hunt, far more than could take part.

The hunt was staged in the Dead Stream Swamp northwest of Houghton Lake. Ten or a dozen bears were started and chased, but several of them made it into a neighboring county where the season was closed. Two were killed, and we had the answer we sought. Apart from the danger of the dogs encountering porcupines, this sport was every bit as good where we tested it as in the states where it had been time-honored for a century or more.

Among the dog men who took part

Yelping noisily but keeping their distance, a pack of Plott hounds holds a black bear at bay until hunters arrive for the kill. Reckless dogs often get mauled or killed when a bear tries to fight its way through the pack, but cautious ones can't hold a bruin at bay.

in that hunt and came down with a hard case of bear fever was my good friend Carl Johnson, a Grand Rapids insurance man. Before Smithdeal went home, Carl bought one of his hounds and started to build and train a pack of his own. In the next dozen years he killed more than 125 bears ahead of his dogs, and became the sparkplug and ringleader of bear hunting in Michigan, organizing and heading the Michigan Bear Hunters Association, which grew into one of the most active conservation groups in the state.

The sport took firm hold. Within fifteen years Michigan hunters owned more than a hundred top-notch bear dogs, and more were being trained and used each season. Next this method of hunting spread to Wisconsin, and today it is firmly established there. It's also of major importance in Maine and New Hampshire now, and both states supply excellent hunting.

Somewhat paradoxically, a few states with a substantial bear population (New York among them, with a plentiful supply in the Adirondacks) continue to prohibit the use of dogs in hunting bears. Repeated attempts to legalize that method have failed, blocked by worried deer hunters who argue, honestly but mistakenly, that bear hounds would run all the deer out of the country. Actually, bear dogs are no different from those used in hunting coon, bobcats, foxes and coyotes, save that they are even less likely to molest deer. If a hound will mess around with a deer track, no matter what the provocation, he can't qualify as a bear dog and no bear hunter wants him.

Successful hunting calls for good bear country, of course. The hunter going into unfamiliar country should scout it carefully ahead of time, seeking the advice of state game men, conservation officers and local woodsmen. Farmers, sheep ranchers, bee keepers and apple orchardists also have good reason to know where bears are hanging out, and will do all they can to help the hunter. Blackie's predilection for mischief knows no limits.

In looking for bears, however, it is necessary to remember that they are great travelers, covering a big territory, often twenty miles across, and moving many miles in a few days as food conditions change. Sign seen in August may mean nothing by October.

Once you find a good area, the next step is to look for feeding grounds and fresh sign, and your chances are best where bear groceries are most plentiful.

The black bear's foremost interest is food, and if he finds a good supply he stays near it as long as it lasts. He is as completely omnivorous as an animal can be, eating almost anything edible. His food list includes grass, clover, alfalfa, ants, grubs, hornet larvae, wild honey, all kinds of wild berries and fruit (chokecherries excepted), apples, mushrooms, acorns and beechnuts, turtle eggs, and any meat he can find, fresh or otherwise. He's even capable of cannibalism. Art Jackson, an oldtime bear trapper in the Dead Stream Swamp country of northern Michigan, once came on and shot a huge black that had killed and was feeding on a smaller one caught in one of his sets. Bear meat is as effective in bear baiting as any other kind.

When the black comes out of hibernation in early spring, in the northern states, he is likely to head for deer yards. There are almost unfailingly winter-killed deer carcasses to be found in such places, and bears stay in the vicinity until this food supply is cleaned up.

By June they are falling back on ants and grubs, digging them out of stumps and old logs, and you find them anywhere in thick cover. In July

Bear tracks show up well on dirt logging roads that wind through wilderness areas, and dogs can tell if they're fresh. Hunters drag dirt roads after dark, towing a brushy tree behind a car or jeep, then check next morning for fresh tracks.

the berry crop ripens and they go berrying. Wild cherries and acorns are the preferred autumn foods. Beechnuts are good wherever they are plentiful enough, and apple orchards or wild apple trees around old logging-camp clearings are always worth a look. If there is dew on the grass it's easy to tell whether the tracks are fresh. Broken branches in apple or cherry trees not only testify to bear work but often reveal how recently it was done, and dung scattered in such places can tell you much about the size of the bear and when he was there.

Blueberries and blackberries are likely to be gone by the time hunting season arrives, and in years when the cherry or acorn crop fails you must look elsewhere. Dead cattle or sheep, or deer killed in early hunting seasons, are likely to attract hungry bears, as are anthills, hornet nests and stumps and logs that harbor grubs or ants.

In heavily populated bear country padded trails run for miles through the swamps and thickets, and it's often easy to hit a fresh track on one of these beaten paths. One of the best places to look for tracks is where bears have crossed dirt roads. By driving such roads you can cover miles of territory in a short time, and your dogs will quickly tell you whether the trail is fresh.

An excellent way of striking a fresh track, and one that many hunters rely on, is to drag sandy roads after dark in the evening. A brushy tree towed by a car or jeep will do nicely for the dragging, or so will a farm implement if one is handy. Any track found crossing the road the next morning will be less than twelve hours old. If a bear hound can't handle such a track under normal weather conditions, best replace him with a better dog.

There are likely to be fresh bear tracks around garbage dumps, too, but no real bear hunter will run those bears unless they are doing real mischief or scaring people to death. The dump setup is too much of a pushover to be rated a sporting proposition.

In general, the best months for this hunting are September, October and November, although bear hunters almost without exception stay out of the woods with their dogs while deer seasons are open.

Success is all a matter of having good fast dogs, bred for the business. More than one bear hunter starts out thinking he can make a bear dog out of any hound, but he soon learns better. It's as natural for a bear dog to run bear as it is for a setter to hunt birds. It's bred in him, and you don't want any other kind in your pack.

An effective bear pack must have one or two good strike dogs that are dead true. If they'll take coon or monkey around on an old cat track they waste time and cause trouble, and if they will run a deer under any circumstances they are worthless. The pack must all be tireless at the tree, at least one or more must have good voices, and also one or two must be close, fearless fighters that will stay to the death. Dogs that stand back in a fight have little chance of either treeing or holding.

As for breeds, a real bear dog is where you find him, whether a blue-blooded aristocrat or a crossbred mongrel. Looks, pedigree or breed mean little. Among the good ones I have known have been blueticks, Walkers, black and tans, redbones, Plotts, airedales, airedale and hound crosses, and mixed hound breeds including some that were half bloodhound.

Regardless of blood or appearance, the bear dog must be big enough to stand up to the rough work required of him and have unlimited endurance and courage that never falters. It also helps if he has enough sense and judgment not to crowd his luck too hard. Above all, unless he'd rather run bear than eat and has the guts to keep at it no matter how many times he gets licked out or how badly he is hurt, he doesn't belong in the pack.

Hunters pick their dogs by trial and error and it takes many trials, plus the prompt rejection of those that fail to qualify, to develop a pack that satisfies. As Carl Johnson once told me, "I've gotten rid of dogs because their noses were not good enough, because they were poor performers at the tree, because they were too fast or too slow, because they wouldn't fight a bear hard enough, and because they just went along for the ride but didn't really have their hearts in bear hunting. You must select and cull, and whether you buy your dogs or breed 'em keep only those that prove themselves."

Probably the best way to develop a pack from scratch is to acquire a proven dog, preferably one getting along in years, use him as a strike dog and build around him. Really good bear dogs are not often for sale, and no matter how much you are willing to pay you can't count on stepping out and buying an entire pack. Top dogs, if sold at all, bring $1,000 and up, and few bear hunters ever sell their best ones at any price.

It does happen sometimes, however, that a reputable owner will part with a great dog that is getting along in years and approaching the end of his usefulness, at a reasonable price, and such a buy is ideal for the beginner who wants to build a pack. But don't try to build too fast. You're far better off with three dogs that know their job than with six that don't. Take your time and keep at it until you have what you want.

The most troublesome problem confronting the owner of bear dogs is deerproofing. In states where the dogging of deer is prohibited by law (and that takes in about everything except the South) any hound that takes a deer track brings down the angry wrath of sportsmen, stirs up opposition to all bear hunting and is likely to get himself shot. In most places a dog that is not deerproof is worse than useless.

It's the same problem the coon hunter faces. He wants nothing but straight cooners in his pack, and the bear hunter wants dogs that will run nothing but bear. You develop them in the same way. Some hunters even start young dogs on coon and deerproof them thoroughly before they are broken in on bear.

Deerproofing is difficult at best, but it isn't quite so hard in the West, where the hunter is on horseback in fairly open country and can overtake promptly and punish any dog that breaks on a deer track. It's a different story where the hunting is done on foot, often in cover so dense that the hunter can neither see nor hear the dog, and where catching him is almost an impossibility. Probably the best way of breaking a deer chaser is with an electric shocking collar, the method described elsewhere in this book, in the chapter on coon hunting.

Don't try to deerproof more than one dog at a time. Above all, never turn a youngster loose on a cold bear

A black bear pads through a snowy woodland. Blackie does little prowling after the ground becomes snow-covered, but sometimes leaves his winter den for a short hike. He sleeps lightly, and now and then hunters stumble across the den and prod him out.

track. Leave the cold trailing to old dogs that can be trusted no matter what the provocation. Follow as close as you can with your young hounds on leash until the bear is up and running, then let only one of them go at once. A bear chase is strong medicine. Dogs become hysterical when a black is jumped. Deer are almost sure to be plentiful wherever bears are found, and if a deer happens to take off at the same time you can ruin two or three young dogs by turning them all in at once.

The most successful bear hunters I know follow the hot-track-only and one-at-a-time rule with every dog under three years old, no matter how promising he is. By that time they can tell how he is going to develop, but they still don't expect him to turn in a trustworthy performance under the stress of great excitement. He's not likely to do that before he is five.

Don't forget that it's as important for your pack to have confidence in you as for you to have faith in them. There are owners who nag and punish their dogs until they cringe when they see the boss coming. You can't build a first-class pack that way.

Finally, never permit a known deer

90

Stand hunter posted by a stream gets set as a black bear emerges from the woods. This is the toughest way to hunt.

runner or a dog you are not absolutely sure of to run with yours under any circumstances. One wrong performance can ruin every youngster in your pack.

The condition of the dog is almost as important as his qualifications. You're pitting him against the fastest and toughest of game animals. He has to be able to go the whole distance and fight like blazes when he catches up. The better shape your dogs are in, the shorter the run and the greater the likelihood that even a mean bear will tree.

Some of the best bear hunters I know road their dogs ten to fifteen miles a day for at least three weeks in advance of a hunt, and also hunt bobcats and coons to keep the dogs in top shape. Hunting beats roadwork by a wide margin.

But no matter how the dogs are conditioned, if they have a tough hunt today you can't expect to use them on another tomorrow. For that reason, if you intend to do much hunting you need extra dogs just as a football coach needs a squad. (Most hunters like a pack of four or five.) No bear dog can be run three or four days in succession, and it's not unusual to lose an entire pack for a day or two when a tough bear leads 'em on a chase that winds up twenty-five miles from the starting point. When this happens the hunter needs a second pack. But of course he must take time out to locate the lost dogs. No man has any

business bear hunting unless he is willing to stay out in the woods overnight if necessary, waiting for his hounds to come in. Above all, he never abandons them if he can help it, although now and then he has no choice.

I know no one who has summed up bear behavior better than El Harger, a biologist with the Michigan Department of Natural Resources who has specialized in field studies of predators, chiefly bears, bobcats and coyotes. He has livetrapped, drugged, weighed, measured and tagged more than 300 blacks, handling as many as 140 in a single year.

"If I have learned anything in dealing with that many, it's that they are totally unpredictable," El says. "I have one firm rule even in talking about them. I never say never. No matter how much contact a hunter has had with them, let him lay down a firm rule of bear behavior, let him say that they are sure to run under one set of circumstances and attack under another, and along will come a bear to prove him a liar."

In our part of the country they are for the most part reluctant to tree, maybe because our swamp timber isn't big enough to suit them. Hunters in the mountains of Tennessee and North Carolina say the same thing is true there. In the West it's different. I know guides and bear hunters there who look down their noses at the idea of killing a black on the ground, but in Michigan we have to kill three out of four that way or not at all. And with the exception of cubs, most of those that are treed climb only if they are driven by fast, hard-fighting dogs.

Even if they tree they don't all behave the same way. One will climb high and stay as long as the dogs are there. Walk in, and he'll lick his paws, settle himself comfortably and look down with neither fear nor resentment. He's so good natured you hate to kill him. If the hounds didn't need the experience and the reward you'd walk away and leave him up there.

The next one is so mean he deserves to be killed. If he trees at all he climbs only beyond reach of the dogs and if he hears or smells a man coming (his eyes are not the best but his nose and ears are terrific) he drops, fights his way through the pack and runs again. More often he refuses to tree and if the dogs crowd him he picks one and goes for it with blood in his eye. Those are the bears that will kill any dog that gets close enough. I do not know a bear hunter who has not lost a prized dog or two in such fights, and it's a rare hunt when at least one dog doesn't get mauled and hurt. Carl Johnson once told me that he had never owned a really good one that did not get badly torn up at one time or another. In all, Johnson has lost almost a dozen to vicious bears, and they were among his best. It's the dog with more courage than judgment that gets clobbered.

A bear pack must be able to do a great deal more than just trail and overtake the bear. In fact, unless he's a small one, it's when they catch him that their real job begins. Whether he stands and fights or keeps going and fights, a full-grown black bear is a tough customer to handle. If he comes to bay in a thicket or windfall he has a good chance of licking out the entire pack, no matter how good they are, unless help arrives promptly. And the more often he does that the bolder and more dangerous he becomes. In other words, the hunter with an inferior pack is inviting trouble.

It's important that all of the dogs run a track at the same speed and reach the bear together. The one that catches up ahead of the rest is almost sure to get thrashed or killed. The one that arrives late is no help to the others. Once they close in they must work as a team, and the more expert at harassing the better. Good dogs seem to sense just how much pressure to put on. They can fight one bear unmercifully, the next will be a rough character that calls for caution. The dog that is too reckless doesn't live long, the one that's too careful can't hold the bear at bay. It's the job of the hounds to fight him to a standstill, unless he trees, and then keep him occupied until hunters can get there. With a big, mean black, it takes close, savage infighting to do it.

The most dangerous bear of all is one wounded by careless or inexperienced hunters, either in a tree or at bay. A big black, crippled but not killed, can wipe out an entire pack, and the first rule is not to shoot until you are sure you can make good. You have to move in carefully and quietly to get close enough for that. A treed bear spooked by approaching hunters will often let go and fall to the ground, especially if the tree is not a tall one, dropping among the dogs, scattering them and starting a fresh run.

Good hunters are almost as necessary as good dogs, and by that I mean hunters with the endurance and determination to stay with their pack. The old saying that a dog is only as good as the man behind him is never truer than in bear chasing. Somebody has to keep up with the dogs if possible, to give them backing when the bear is treed or bayed, and most of the time it falls to the owner or handler to do it. To let dogs overtake and fight a bear with nobody behind them is not only discouraging to them but dangerous.

At bay on the ground, the toughest bear is afraid of the hunters, and any noise or even a whiff of man smell often causes them to break away from the dogs and hightail off. Consequently, getting close enough to wind things up calls for extreme caution, plus having the wind in your favor.

For the hunter unable to follow dogs, because of age or poor physical condition, the best bet is to take a stand. It's not an infallible method,

for although bears have regular trails and crossing places, when pushed by dogs they are likely to change routes. But a stand in a good spot often pays off, especially if there are enough hunters in the party to cover all the best places. Picking the right locations should be left to someone thoroughly familiar with the country, of course.

When it comes to guns, most bear hunters carry a rifle. Any standard deer caliber is adequate, but the gun should be short, light and easy to handle in the thick brush where bears run and come to bay, and it should also be sufficiently rugged to take hard use. In spite of all you can do, it will get wet, dirty, muddy, sandy and marred up. And forget a scope. It will only be in your way. When the dogs overtake a bear you have to hurry, and the shooting is likely to be done at no more than twenty to thirty feet.

For ease in getting through thickets, walking logs over streams, and for the sake of having both hands free for brush-busting, some hunters prefer a handgun in one of the Magnum calibers. In the hands of a competent marksman, and at the extremely short ranges involved, it will do the job nicely.

To prevent the dogs from being torn up by a wounded bear, a killing shot is essential, but it isn't always easy when there's a fight going on, with dogs and bear all over the place.

A head shot is best if you can be absolutely sure of it. But too often that is impossible, and if the bear looks to be of record-book size the head shot has the added disadvantage that it is likely to damage the skull and leave the trophy ineligible for Boone and Crockett measuring. A neck shot is probably the best second choice, a shoulder shot next. Whatever happens, the bear should be killed as cleanly and quickly as possible, for the sake of the dogs as well as for humane considerations.

That kind of almost hand-to-hand finish furnishes the excitement you can expect if you go after bears with dogs. As Bill Mason, a dedicated bear hunter from south-central New York, said to me once, "It's the greatest hunting there is. As long as there are bears to run and I have hounds to run 'em, I wouldn't ask to live in a better world."

Next to hunting with hounds, the most productive way to hunt the black bear is to bring him to the gun by baiting. In my home state of Michigan, this method of bear hunting did not catch on for half a century. Almost without exception, the bears killed were gathered in by deer hunters who happened to run across them, most often by accident, when a bear was farthest from their thoughts. Within the last twenty-five years or so, however, the situation has changed. Today baiting is recognized as one of the surest ways of collecting a bearskin, and many hunters are practicing it.

It remained for bowhunters to pioneer and perfect it, at least in the midwestern states. It is ideally suited to their needs, luring the bear in at very close range where an arrow can be placed surely and effectively. Today most of the blacks taken in bow season in our part of the country are killed over bait. And once bowhunters had demonstrated the effectiveness of that method, gun hunters were quick to take it up.

The most skilled and successful practitioner of baiting I know is Art LaHa, a dedicated bowhunter living at the hamlet of Winchester in Vilas County, Wisconsin. In the first twenty-five years he hunted bears over bait he hung up the remarkable score of thirty-one, all killed with bow, most of them at ranges of twenty feet or less.

In addition to his own kills, he has set things up for a good many other bowhunters and helped them to collect a bear. He operates a bowhunting lodge and guides hunters during deer and bear season. Not a fall goes by that his clients do not take at least two or three bears. And because stillhunting and driving are very unlikely to produce a kill, when LaHa wants a black he baits it in. Something like nine out of ten of all he has killed or helped to kill have been taken that way.

Western guide ties baits to a pine tree and douses them with syrup to lure a bear into range. Baiting is a favorite technique of bowhunters, who want to get close to their target.

Although the hunters Art has guided have killed quite a few bears on deer drives, he does not consider that a satisfactory method of bear hunting, either for the bowman or rifleman. For one reason, the bear is too likely not to go where you expect him to. You may see or hear him coming but before he walks into the open the odds are good he'll change direction and take off for some other place.

As for walking up on a bear by stillhunting, save in cases where the hunter has exceptional luck and blunders onto one by accident, that is close to impossible, LaHa warns.

"It's bait that turns Blackie into a sucker," Art says. "Once you have him coming regularly, killing him

is hardly more difficult than shooting fish in a barrel. It's a lot more exciting, however. Now and then somebody asks me whether I don't think baiting is taking unfair advantage. My answer to that is that killing a black bear over bait in northern Wisconsin is no more unsportsmanlike than killing a leopard that same way in Africa, or shooting mallards in an Iowa cornfield where they come to feed."

The first step in baiting is to locate a place where bears are traveling regularly. Look for tracks, dung, and for hair rubbed off on the underside of fallen trees. In the fall old orchards are likely to be hotspots.

For bait LaHa uses almost any kind of garbage. Meat scraps are good in early autumn, and the higher the meat the better. A few weeks before bears are ready to hibernate, however, their food habits undergo a change. They turn to a vegetable diet, including a lot of mushrooms, and their droppings become white. When you see that, switch over to apples, acorns, lettuce, and bread with honey or syrup.

LaHa puts his trash in cartons or boxes and hangs them in the low fork of a tree, to keep skunks, coons, ravens and stray dogs from getting a free lunch. When he is ready to sit up over a bait he puts it in a stout box, usually one bound with wire, so it will be harder for the bear to tear open. That gives the hunter more time.

A wild bear, one that has not been feeding at a garbage dump until he has lost all fear of humans, approaches a bait as spooky as a cat at a dog show. He has no intention of being surprised if he can help it. He comes padding in, sniffing and listening, very alert and very cautious.

When he arrives at the bait he usually reaches up and pulls the box down. It hits the ground with a thump and almost unfailingly he turns and runs like a streak. But he doesn't go far. Within fifty to a hundred feet he'll stop, look back, often lie down and watch, turning his head first one way and then the other. You can almost hear him saying to himself, "I wonder if that thing is really safe to fool around with." After a minute or two he'll get up, shuffle in, rip the box apart and start to feed.

That interval of waiting gives the rookie hunter a chance to settle down and get ready, and nine times out of ten he needs it, for bear fever is worse than buck fever any day.

For all his wariness, a bear will often approach a hunter astonishingly close if the wind is right and he hears no noise. Using a bow, LaHa likes his shots at twenty feet or less. He points out that a rifleman has no need to get that close, but he wants his arrows to kill in the shortest possible time and that means shooting at a range where he can be absolutely sure they'll go into the lung area. He builds a natural blind, just enough to screen him, within five to seven yards downwind of where the bear will feed. The hunter does not need to be too well hidden, provided he stays absolutely motionless until he is ready for the shot. A camouflage suit helps and the bow should be dull finish or taped, so there is no possibility of sun flash. Art's blind is often no more than a small evergreen dropped where he can hide behind the top. A conspicuous blind is worse than none. Unless it matches the surroundings a bear is not likely to come near it.

The best shot for the bowhunter is just back of the shoulder from the side, so the arrow goes into the lungs. It can't break heavy bone, so you have to slide it in behind the shoulder. With a rifle it's better to dump a bear by a shoulder shot. Most of the bears LaHa has killed have been lung shot and have gone down within fifty yards. Above all, the bowhunter needs to be careful not to put his arrow back of the diaphragm, Art warns. A gut-shot bear is a dead bear you won't find. The wound plugs

This record black bear scored 19-15/16 points in the 1964 Boone & Crockett book. The hide measured 8½ by 8½ feet. Trophy was taken by Erwin Bauer on a hunt with hounds in the Tavaputs Cliffs area of Utah.

up quickly because of heavy fat and leaves little if any blood trail. That same rule of avoiding a shot in the belly applies to the rifleman, too, for the same reason.

LaHa has never heard a bear, hit with an arrow, snarl or growl, but they do what he calls hollering. It's a wild sound, pain and anger mixed, a combination of bawl, scream and the gobble of a turkey. When he hears it he knows he has made a good hit.

He believes there is little excuse

for losing a wounded bear if your shot has been right, although they are harder to trail than a deer. Blackie is a log walker by nature, and once he's hurt he takes to every fallen tree he comes to, including small ones only a few inches through. He'll even jump from one log to another to keep off the ground. That makes the blood trail difficult to follow.

A wounded bear will run uphill or down, through the thickest tangles or over the worst blowdowns, swim rivers, cross beaver ponds, and go where he pleases. Nothing stops him. LaHa's rule is to wait an hour after he makes a hit. An arrow kills by bleeding and is not likely to be as fast as a bullet. He gives the bear time to die if it's going to. Then he takes the trail and stays on it till he finds the bear.

LaHa uses a sixty-five to seventy-five-pound bow and three-bladed arrows in his bear hunting, but says readily that a lighter bow will do the work in the hands of a good shot.

Once in a while a beginning hunter, whose hair stands up at the idea of slamming an arrow into a bear at fifteen or twenty feet, asks LaHa how much danger is involved. That's hard for him to answer, since he is not much afraid of black bears. But at the same time he knows they can be dangerous on occasion, and nobody can predict their actions thirty seconds ahead. They have hair-trigger tempers and if anything hurts or even displeases them they're likely to see red.

Black bears have attacked humans totally unprovoked on more than one occasion, and there are numerous instances of attack by wounded ones, and even a few cases of actual man-eating. But of all the bears he has killed, Art has seen only one or two show fight.

"I'm fully aware, however, that the next one I shoot may change that," he told me.

The only time he has had a wounded bear come near him, and it came very near indeed, it didn't know he was there. That was a big black that dressed 594 pounds, killed by one of his hunting partners, Dick Cooley. He and Dick were sitting on runways on opposite sides of a bait, about twenty yards apart. The bear walked in at exactly the right angle and Cooley's broadhead sliced through its heart.

It screamed and came barreling downhill, straight for LaHa. He had to roll aside to get out of its way. But it was badly hurt and running to get away, not charging. It ran only thirty-five yards and was as good as dead when the hunters reached it. Even if it had fallen on top of Art, he does not believe it would have done much damage. But he'll tell you that it's encounters of that kind that make a bow and a bait station an unbeatable combination for any hunter who covets a bear rug.

7
BROWN and GRIZZLY BEARS

The dangerous bruins

Frank Dufresne spelled out the No. 1 rule for me many years ago. It was May of 1941, and we were cruising up the Inside Passage from Seattle to Juneau, aboard the motorship *Brown Bear,* patrol vessel for the Aleutian Island Wildlife Refuge. Frank was executive officer of the Alaska Game Commission at the time, and he and his wife Klondy had been outside on business connected with Alaska's wildlife affairs. They were gcing home.

I was on my first trip to the Territory, to spend the summer in the Aleutians and on the Pribilofs. The *Brown Bear,* lost not long after that while on duty in World War II, was a fine little ship, manned by a great crew. That was one of the best summers I ever had.

"Never surprise a brown bear," Frank told me as we leaned on the rail, watching the green mountains of the Inside Passage slip by. "Above all, never let a brown bear surprise you!"

He was speaking of the bear that most sportsmen call the Kodiak, the

On the banks of an Alaskan river, a brown bear rips into a salmon it caught in the rushing water (left). Despite its great size, the brownie is agile and quick on its feet, and extremely dangerous. Enormous tracks of male and female bears (below) were found along bank.

biggest bear on earth and also the biggest land carnivore, renowned for its short-fused temper, and I listened with both ears. Frank Dufresne had mushed over most of Alaska with a dog team, traveled far and wide by canoe and on foot, and he knew the ways of the Territory's game animals about as well as any man alive. When he laid down a rule, I figured it paid to pay attention. He went on to tell me of what he considered the closest call he had ever had with brownie, one that he surprised and that also surprised him. The encounter was unavoidable on both sides.

Frank had left his small boat on the beach that day and hiked inland two or three miles, following a worn bear trail that ran along the bank of a stream bordered with very thick brush. Coming back down the trail, he was still a mile from the boat when he rounded a bend and saw the silvery shape of a fresh-caught salmon lying in the trail only a short distance ahead.

Dufresne's blood turned to ice water. He knew that a brown bear had dropped the salmon there, probably when it heard him coming. It was an almost certain bet that the bear was watching now, hidden in the tangles of alder and devil's club, maybe less than fifty feet away. And it was equally certain that it would not give up its fish or let him pass without a fight.

103

Frank stood stock still for a long minute, wishing there were some way to know how long the salmon had lain there. If the bear had dropped it for some other reason, an hour or two earlier, he might not be in danger, after all. Then, while he held his breath and stared at it, the fish flopped. Frank Dufresne's heart came up in his throat. But he knew he had to make the first move, so very carefully he inched one foot behind the other and started to back slowly away, up the trail in the direction from which he had come. He sidled around the bend, wheeled and ran for his life.

Half a mile from the spot, he sat down to think things over. There was only one way to get back to the beach, down the bear trail where that salmon waited like a land mine. The brush was too thick for him to detour around, and with the bear in the neighborhood he had no relish for going into the brush anyway. He waited an hour. Then, with the afternoon beginning to run out, he walked carefully back and peered around the bend where he had seen the fish. It was gone.

Frank crept past the place with his skin crawling. Once a safe distance beyond it, he raced for the beach as hard as he could run. He never saw the bear or heard it make a sound, but there was no doubt in his mind that he was very close to death that day.

A month after he related that story to me, on the steep slope of a high-walled canyon that angled down from the snowfields of Frosty Peak, far out on the Alaska Peninsula, I broke Frank's first rule and the bear involved broke the second one. The result was that Jack Benson, the wildlife agent from Kodiak Island who was guiding me and carrying our only rifle, came within a very few feet of having to shoot a brownie that we didn't want to kill—or we came within a very few feet of getting mauled. We were hunting with cameras.

Jack and I, with two other wildlife men off the *Brown Bear* and Malcolm Greany, a photographer from Dufresne's staff in Juneau, had hunted bears along the coast west of Kodiak for two weeks, going ashore from the ship day after day, with no success.

Then we landed at the head of Morzhovoi Bay, under the glistening white cone of Frosty Peak, climbed to the snowfields, and hit the jackpot. Between noon and the time when the afternoon light failed, we spotted, overtook and photographed twelve brown bears, six grownups and six young cubs.

The first sign we found was the track of a medium-sized bear, leading up the snow beside a tumbling stream in a deep canyon. We followed, and on the bare rock where he left the snow we spotted him, made a steep but uneventful stalk, and got within about a hundred feet of him before he discovered us.

He was a young male, traveling by himself and not the least quarrelsome. He didn't run, but neither did he give us any argument. He walked off slowly, stopping every few yards to look back, his fat rear end waddling in a fashion that led us to give him the name of Droopy Drawers. He became a favorite character with lecture audiences, in the movie film I made that day.

The next bear we spotted, after he got away by climbing a snowfield too steep for us to hope to overtake him, was a beautiful red-brown sow with three cubs at her heels, coming slowly up along the stream in the bottom of the canyon.

Three cubs are not too common in the bear world, and this was a very attractive family. They were out of winter quarters hardly more than a month or six weeks, and the youngsters still wore the pale yellow rings around their necks that mark the infant brown bear. We really wanted pictures.

We dropped back over a ridge to wait for them to work up to us, and when we looked again they had disappeared. We started very carefully down into the canyon. The slope was so steep that every step started a small rock slide, but the brawling, snow-fed stream below covered the noise.

We came over a low ridge with Benson in the lead, and he looked down an almost vertical slope. There, just seventy-five feet (not yards) below him, the sow brownie was sitting on a shelf of rock with her back to us, giving her youngsters their lunch. But there were three of them and only room for two at the table, and the third one was running around her in circles, hungry and begging. About the second time around he looked up and saw us at the top of the cliff. I don't know what he said to his mother, but she lunged to her feet, spun around, and her bawl of rage carried loud and clear above the racket of tumbling water. We had surprised her, and in that instant I knew exactly why Frank Dufresne had warned me.

She led the cubs, not in flight but around the shoulder of the canyon wall, closing toward us in a tight half circle. The three of them went out of sight behind a rock as big as an average house, and then the old bear poked just her head up over the back of it, swinging from side to side, growling and raging.

I was carrying a 16mm movie camera, loaded with color film and equipped with a six-inch telephoto lens. She gave me time to level it on its tripod, focus it, and run through fifteen feet of film that I rate the most exciting wildlife footage I have ever made.

I heard Jack Benson say quietly,

105

"She'll come for us when she climbs down." Her head vanished from view, and seconds later she rounded the end of the rock, barreling uphill at us like a lumbering brown tank.

Jack had his .30/06 on her, and I was waiting for the blast of the gun, when the three cubs broke out from behind the rock, running pell mell for the bottom of the canyon. Not more than forty feet away she checked her charge, looked over her shoulder at them, swiveled and followed them. The last we saw of that family she was leading them over a snow-covered ridge, traveling at a slow walk and waiting every few yards for the cubs to catch up, so high that they all went out of sight repeatedly in drifting patches of cloud.

That encounter sums up, as well as any I know, what a hunter can expect if he goes after the world's mightiest bear. I'll say it simply. He can expect almost anything. Above all, if he gets close he can expect the bear to fight back.

Even then, however, there are exceptions to the rule. On a Kodiak Island beach, my friend Fred Bear, one of the most skilled bowhunters I have ever known, once drove a hunting arrow to the feathers between the ribs of a brown bear at sixty feet. It hadn't seen the hunter and didn't know what had hurt it, but it came for him full tilt simply because he was in its path, rolling like a giant brown bulldog. At fifteen feet it sighted him, veered off the the trail and ran head-long into the alders.

Then, on the other hand, consider what happened to Dr. Russell Smith, an expert rifleman whom I hunted with when he lived in northern Wisconsin.

Russ moved to Alaska, lured by the hunting opportunities, and became a close friend of Hosea Sarber, a wild-life agent in southeastern Alaska and one of the greatest brown-bear hunters that ever lived. By the time Russ and Hosea went bear hunting on Admiralty Island in the spring of 1950, Smith had killed seven Alaskan bears, three browns and four blacks, with seven shots, and he had come to the conclusion that given enough gun for the job and a chance to place his shots where he wanted at reasonable range, a good rifleman could be almost certain of an instantaneous kill, even on a brownie. It took his eighth bear to teach him that that wasn't true.

He got a good hit in the chest at a hundred yards and knocked it down like a steer in a slaughter pen. But it leaped to its feet and went into the alders before he could shoot again.

Sarber and Russ waited an hour and then took the blood trail into thick brush, not relishing the job. At the edge of a little open place the doctor saw two big brown ears over the top of an alder clump. The bear ripped out a blood-thinning bawl and, despite its wound, came for him.

When the shooting was over the bear had been hit seven times with softpoints from two .375 Magnums, all well placed. It fell dead exactly four paces from Smith.

"I wish every sportsman who plans to hunt Alaska browns could have seen the inside of that one when we finished skinning him and cut him open," Russ told me afterward. "It was a very convincing object lesson in the destruction a bear of that size can endure. I didn't wonder any longer why careless hunters are mauled or killed almost every season somewhere in Alaska."

As with all mountain game, including grizzlies and even elk, most of the time brown-bear hunting is a matter of spotting a shootable animal and then stalking within range. And because the brownie is an animal of Alaska's coastal country and the big islands offshore, much of the spotting can be done from the deck of a hunting boat. That makes that part of the hunt easy. The hard part is the stalk, often up steep mountain slopes or through thickets of alder and other brush where a man has to stay on bear trails to get through.

The thing the brown-bear hunter cannot forget for a second is that he is after a quick-tempered animal, one of the most dangerous on earth. Probably fortunately, most sportsmen hunt the brownie only under the direction of an experienced and competent guide, who knows better than to let the client take chances.

When it comes to grizzlies, the brownie's first cousin that reaches its greatest abundance in the interior of Alaska, the situation is much the same and the rules are identical. The hunter who gets too close to a grizzly is in danger. He may not even know the bear is there, but it will know exactly where he is and be ready for him on its own terms.

Jack Turner, who lives with his wife and young daughter on a homestead on the Atnarko River just above Lonesome Lake, in the mountains of southwestern British Columbia, knows grizzlies and their ways as well as any man I have ever talked with. The Turner place is twenty-five miles from the nearest gravel road, and Jack hikes out once a month for mail. In that isolated, beautiful valley along the Atnarko grizzlies are as common in autumn, when salmon are running in the river, as black bears around a Midwest garbage dump. Jack has counted as many as ten adults and five young ones on a seven-mile stretch of the Atnarko in one day, and he figures that from September on there are never fewer than ten or a dozen within a few miles of his home.

Several times he has had to kill a quarrelsome bear in his front yard, when it refused to let him get into

Feasting on fall fruit before winter sets in, a huge grizzly roams the berry patches of Alaskan interior (below). Meat is the grizzly's preference, however, and it pulls down weakened elk and deer when possible. The bear in the water (right) is standing on an elk it killed at streamside, while bruin in meadow (left) devours the remains of a deer carcass.

the house, and on two or three occasions a trouble-hunter has given him a close call for no very good reason.

The one that came the closest to clobbering him was an exceptionally big male that he met on a trail along the river one morning in May. He rounded a bend and the bear was waiting for him forty feet away. It rushed him savagely the instant he came in sight.

Jack was carrying an ax, intending to mend fence. But he also had a battered old .30/30 Winchester hung over his shoulder by a length of cord. That rifle goes with him whenever he leaves his clearing. He never knows when he will need it, where he lives. He whipped it off his shoulder and fired one shot. It hit the bear in the forehead between the eyes, and blew its brains out. It fell dead three feet from the muzzle of the gun. Turner had given it not the slightest reason to attack, except that he had walked in within forty feet of it, and in the mind of the average grizzly that is too close.

That encounter will give you the general idea of grizzly behavior. Authentic instances of unprovoked attack by the humpbacked bear are too numerous to leave the slightest doubt as to his dangerous nature.

In the fall of 1967, for example, a California hunter and two companions were following an old brush-grown skidding road along the North Fork of the Flathead River, near the border of Glacier National Park. Without the slightest warning a grizzly smashed out of the brush, knocked the California man sprawling and attacked his face and head with its teeth.

It took his two partners less than a minute to blast the bear off its victim with their shots, but in that minute it had mauled his face to a bloody pulp. The bear dropped twelve feet from the men, dead from half a dozen .30/06 rifle bullets plus two from a .41 Magnum pistol that were fired into its head to make sure.

In the winter of 1970, with almost a foot of snow on the ground, a grizzly that had not gone into hibernation jumped an Indian trapper and guide fifty miles north of Fort St. John, in British Columbia, killed him probably before the man knew the bear was there, and partly devoured the body. The man had been tracking the bear, and apparently was attacked for no better reason than that he walked within a few yards of where it lay, watching its own backtrack, perhaps hidden behind a log or windfall.

Two years before that, in the early spring of 1968, a British Columbia rancher, checking feed on his range, inadvertently walked within 150 feet of a sow grizzly with a cub. She hit him like lightning, before he could climb the nearest tree. He kicked her in the face and she ripped off his boot. She went for his head but he

A pair of large male grizzly tracks compared with a hunting knife. Hind-foot track, at bottom, is about twelve inches long. Forefoot track looks larger than usual since heel print shows in soft snow.

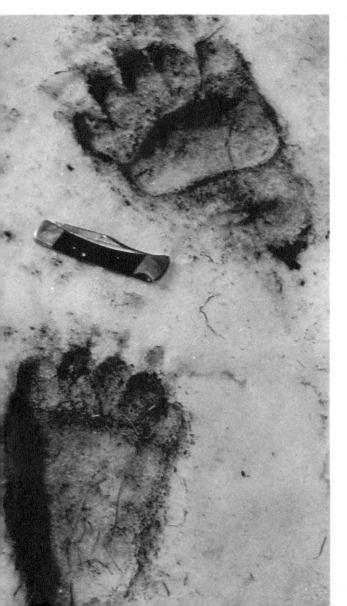

shoved his arm between her jaws. When she finally left him he was still on his feet, but badly chewed up and minus one eye.

In the Tum Tum Lake district of British Columbia north of Kamloops in 1963 a moose hunter had the misfortune to walk close to the carcass of a cow moose that a grizzly had been feeding on for a week or more, either its own kill or one it had found. The bear attacked like a thunderbolt, raging at the man from only a few feet away. When his hunting partners drove it off by shooting over the top of the brush he was left with a broken jaw, three skull punctures, and wounds that took more than 200 sutures to close. By a miracle he lived.

Much the same thing happened to three fishermen hiking in remote wilderness in Alberta's Jasper National Park in the spring of 1968. In keeping with park regulations, Steve Rose, Dave Slutker and Leonard Jeck had no gun with them. In a thick stand of spruce Jeck came face to face, at five feet, with a sow grizzly running through the timber with two cubs in tow. She grabbed him by a leg as she went by, knocked him to the ground and pressed a savage attack.

When Rose scrambled up a scrubby spruce he attracted her attention and she turned on him. She clawed her way into the tree with no difficulty (the belief that grizzlies can't

This grizzly was killed by Bill McRae on the edge of Montana's Bob Marshall Wilderness Area with a .30/06 Model 70 Winchester. The bear had stolen a deer killed by the hunter's fourteen-year-old son.

climb does not always hold), sank her teeth in his leg, dropped to the ground and took him along. She mauled him severely, and when Slutker came to the rescue with a club it was his turn. She knocked him down, tore his face open with her teeth and crushed his eye socket.

The whole murderous attack lasted not more than six or seven minutes.

The bear ran off then, leaving three men torn, bitten and smashed, close to death.

So goes the grizzly record. Any hunter who seeks this bear as a trophy will do well to keep it in mind.

I said earlier that hunting browns and grizzlies usually involves spotting and stalking. There is one exception to that rule. Many grizzlies taken today by sports hunters are killed over bait. It's close to standard practice with outfitters and guides in some areas to shoot a decrepit horse and leave the carcass to lure a bear in.

Admittedly that's an easy way to collect a grizzly rug. The suspense and excitement of watching the bait are about like those involved in baiting a black bear. But any grizzly is capable of fighting back, and although the blind is usually in an open place and farther from the bait, shooting such a bear on a dead horse, even at a hundred yards, is anything but a tame experience. As with the brownie, the first rule is not to let the bear take the hunter by surprise. And if the hunter and his guide have the misfortune to confront the job of following a wounded grizzly, the danger of attack is very great.

8

COUGAR

Houndsman's dream cat

For many years I believed that the cougar, or mountain lion, was one of the most long-winded and difficult animals to hunt on the North American continent. Everything I knew about him was second-hand, but it all pictured him as having great speed ahead of dogs and almost unlimited staying power. Without exception, the cougar hunts I had read about had lasted for hours or days, usually on horseback, with the hunters riding through the roughest of rimrock country. Such a hunt was always a grueling test of hounds, horses and men, or so I thought.

It came as quite a surprise when I made a trip to Montana to hunt with Howard and Wendell Copenhaver, then operating a dude ranch for hunters and fishermen at Ovando, and learned the truth about the big mountain cat.

The facts are that he has very small lungs, and if he is run at top speed he is probably the shortest-winded critter ever chased by dogs. And if he happens to be full of venison or some other meat at the time, he gives out

Backed against a thicket after a grueling chase, a cougar snarls defiance as a dog pack moves in. A good cougar hound can follow a two-day-old track on bare ground, sometimes cold-trailing for miles before jumping the cat.

even more quickly. A young one or a gaunt female will run farther than an old tom, but if even they are pushed, a mile is about as far as most of them will go; and if they are full fed, they are likely to tree within three hundred yards.

Don't get the mistaken notion that he is any pushover, however. It's only when he is driven hard that a cougar's lungs let him down. Taking his own time, he can travel steadily for nights on end and cover a huge block of the roughest kind of country. In an average night of hunting, a lion will make six or eight miles. Often he covers more than that, and if he has some special reason, as when a tom goes in search of a receptive female, he may walk twenty-five to thirty miles between dusk and daylight.

Don Ellis, a retired British Columbia game warden who has kept good cougar dogs and hunted the big cats for some thirty-five years, once told me, "No two of 'em are alike and there is no such thing as an average

cougar chase, but I figure I've walked something like six or eight miles for each one I have taken. That may not sound like much, until you try it in the country where they hang out."

Every hunter I have ever talked to, men who have run lions in Washington, Oregon, Idaho, California, Montana, Nevada, New Mexico, Arizona, Wyoming, Colorado, Utah, and in the mountains of northwest Canada—in short over the entire range of the cats —has agreed that very rarely do they come easy.

The longest cougar hunt I know about lasted seven days. The shortest ended just seventy-five yards from the place where it began.

My old friend Roy Murray of Boulder, Colorado, made the seven-day hunt, on horseback. He had a phone call one cold February evening, reporting that hunters had found the track of an unusually big mountain lion about fourteen miles west of his ranch.

Roy hated lions, both for their deer killing and their raids on livestock. At sunup the next morning he saddled a tough little horse and rode away from the ranch, carrying a .30/30 and four sandwiches, with his cougar dog, an Airedale-Collie cross, trotting behind him.

He found the cougar track and followed it through six or eight inches of snow. He rode twenty-five miles the first day and made a cheerless camp under a shelf of rimrock, with no shelter, no blankets and no horse feed. He was to fare about the same for another night, with the horse making out on green browse, the dog eating well on the carcasses of deer killed by the lion, and Roy rationing his four sandwiches.

The third night he took shelter in a forest ranger's cabin, where he cooked a good meal of cougar-killed deer for himself. The next night he made it to a cabin of his own that he used when he was herding cattle in summer, and the horse got its first feed of hay and oats in four days. The night after that Murray spent at a well-stocked hunting camp, and the sixth night he left the track, rode down to a ranch for a warm supper, a bed and plenty of horse feed.

When he finally cornered the lion in a thick stand of evergreens, late on the seventh afternoon of the hunt, he had tracked it more than 150 miles, through seven bitterly cold days of steady riding. In that time the cat had killed four deer, four elk and a steer. Roy told me it was the toughest hunt of his life.

The Copenhaver brothers, Wendell and Howard, had a hunt that lasted almost as long. They hunted five days from daylight to dark on foot, in the rough Blackfoot Canyon country west of their ranch. Their lion also proved to be the most murderous they had ever killed. For a week he pulled down deer at the rate of almost two a day.

The story of the seventy-five yard

Cougar on a hunting foray lopes silently down a mountain trail. Though short-winded, the cat's stealth and blinding speed make him a lethal predator capable of breaking a deer's neck in a single bound. His attacks on sheep, cattle and colts have earned him the hatred of stockmen.

chase was related to me by the Copenhavers. They surprised the lion at his kill. He had pulled down a deer and the torn belly was still steaming and oozing blood when the hunters got there. The lion had then killed a second deer within sight of the first one, torn it open and eaten about half of it. Full fed, he had bedded down close by. The dogs drove him from his bed and pushed him up the side of a mountain at top speed. He could have killed either of the two hounds with a swipe of a paw, but had no stomach for a stand. A big tom, he went up on the first tree he came to, and didn't even do a good job of climbing.

Hunters who have seen them do it tell me that a mountain lion rarely climbs into a tree. He can jump with the grace and power of a gigantic squirrel, and when he comes to a tree that suits him he sails into it in a long running bound. This one was carrying too much venison for that. He scratched and hauled himself up to a

point a little higher than a man's head, and clung there with his forelegs around the trunk, yards short of the first branches. His long, black-tipped tail hung down within reach of the dogs.

The dogs went insane, growling, bawling and jumping for that tantalizing tail. One would leap high enough to get a grip, slide down until her teeth pulled out, fall back and roll away. Then the second hound would take its turn. By the time Howard and Wendell got to the tree the tip of the lion's tail was shredded to a bloody broom. He was snarling like a buzzsaw, but wouldn't drop off the tree and face the dogs on the ground. Wendell ended the affair with a .38 sidearm while Howard held the two hounds back out of harm's way.

On one point every cougar hunter I know agrees: They rate the big furtive cat among the top trophies this continent has to offer. Don Ellis calls him the finest game animal that prowls the woods of Canada or the United States, giving a hunter the last word in action and fun. "He's a houndman's dream," Ellis says. The respect and admiration the men who hunt him feel for his strength, his inborn cat stealth, his wildness and toughness know no limits.

Most of the cougar hunters I have known do their hunting on foot. The Copenhavers, for example, have taken most of their lions in winter, and in their country at that season of year the cats go where no horse can follow. They drive as close as they can to the cougar or his track, and then take out on foot. They go light, no grub except a sandwich or two, an empty pack-board for carrying out the pelt, and sidearms instead of rifles.

Hunters in British Columbia follow that same method. For the most part, except in the case of a cougar that must be destroyed for one reason or another, they do not hunt in summer or on bare ground. For one reason, scent fades out very quickly in hot weather. For another, the country is too rough for horses and summer hunting on foot is a very rugged business. On Vancouver Island, where cougars are numerous, however, a great deal of bare-ground hunting is done successfully, using packs of cold-trailing dogs.

Farther south, in Colorado for instance, the bulk of the hunting is done on horseback. Cap Atwood of Craig is one of the most successful cougar hunters I have known. Originally a rancher, Cap worked for a few years as a government hunter, and for the last twenty years has operated a hunting camp and guided deer, elk, bear and lion hunters. So far as possible, his lion hunting is all done in the saddle.

"In my book, if a man has to have snow he's not a lion hunter," Cap told me one day when we sat talking about mountain lions in the living-room of his home, with a magnificent life-size mount of a big tom looking down at us from the wall.

"Almost anybody can go out on new snow, drive roads until he cuts a track, lead a hound or two on leash until the cat is jumped, then turn loose. If a dog is worth his salt he'll catch that cougar in a hurry."

Atwood's favorite method is to camp in good lion country, ride out on a horse early in the morning with four or five hounds, including a couple of good strike dogs. He lets that pair hunt for a track while the others follow the horses, necked together. If he has to lead a lion dog he gets rid of it.

An experienced hound will run a two-day-old track on bare ground without difficulty. Once Cap's strike dogs make a find and the going gets good he turns the other hounds loose. The pack is likely to cold trail for miles before they jump the cat. One lion will move out as soon as he hears them coming. That gives him a start and is likely to mean a long chase. The next one will stay where he is, maybe on a rock or under a pine or an overhanging cliff, until the dogs are almost on top of him. That kind trees in a hurry.

Although Colorado lions do their running chiefly in broken rimrock areas where horses can't go, a good horse lets the hunter stay closer to his dogs. "Usually you can keep near enough to hear them," Atwood says. "But don't expect to ride to the tree.

Once the cat is up, you do the rest on foot."

Most cougar hunters prefer not to turn their dogs loose until a cat is jumped and they can be sure they have a hot track for the hounds to run. Cold trailing with dogs is likely to mean a long chase, with the hunters left hours behind. Walking a lion up on foot, without letting the dogs go, can be a tough job, especially if the cat has not killed and lain up nearby. But it's likely to be easier than following hounds on the same cold track.

Here and there a few unscrupulous guides and outfitters follow a shameful practice. They book a client for a hunt, go out ahead of time and capture a lion alive, using a tranquilizer in a dart gun. They cage the cat until the client arrives, take it out and turn it loose secretly and put their dogs on the track. The unsuspecting hunter, who has probably paid in advance for a week's hunt, kills his trophy after a short and easy chase and goes home. It's a shabby business, and it means that an outsider booking a lion hunt should check his outfitter carefully ahead of time for honesty and ethical hunting methods.

The key to success in lion hunting is good dogs, combined with hard work on the part of the hunter. The dogs must be deerproof, rabbitproof and lynxproof if there are lynxes in the country, of course.

After a long chase, a hunter leads his horse homeward with a cougar strapped to the saddle. Sometimes a hunter will spend up to six days finding and trailing a cougar; it's tough hunting for an elusive quarry.

They, and the hunter as well, must be in top condition, able to stay as long as necessary and willing to put up with whatever hardship may be involved.

"On the average, it takes about six days of hunting to get a good lion where I hunt," Cap Atwood once told me. "That's likely to include a day or two without eating because I'm too far from a side camp to ride back, and often a night or two of lying out under a tree as well, with a fire but no blanket and no food. You can figure to earn any lion you kill."

When Don Ellis starts out after a cougar there is always a billy-can in his pack sack to boil tea in. He makes 'em by punching two holes near the top of a tobacco tin and fitting a piece of wire for a bail, for hanging over the fire. In the can he keeps a small container of matches, some bouillon cubes, tea bags, sugar and raisins. He uses nothing out of the billy-can unless he has to. With those few emergency provisions he can live out in the hills for a week, bolstering his food supply with a grouse or two if he gets the chance.

122

"More than once I've had to do just that," he says.

He also carries a ten-by-ten piece of very light canvas. If night overtakes him he rigs a lean-to, cuts fir branches for a bed and enough more for his dogs, and builds a small fire where the lean-to will reflect the heat.

Although the big cat shows little fondness for water, he does not hesitate to cross any stream he comes to and he doesn't bother to pick a shallow place. He likes to cross on a log if he can find one, but if not he swims. Wendell and Howard Copenhaver once cold-trailed an old tom down to the Blackfoot in the dead of winter, at a point where the river was deep, swift and rock-broken, with a shelf of ice along each shore. The track showed that the lion had walked along the bank for a short distance, turned out across the ice shelf and slid into the icy black water. On the far side he had climbed out, given himself a good shake, and walked into

These hounds have been trained for hunting cougars, having been broken of any tendency to pick up the trail of a deer, rabbit or lynx. Most hunters send out a couple of strike dogs to pick up the trail, keep the others necked together or leashed until the chase begins.

the timber as if nothing had happened.

That kind of behavior poses tough problems for both dogs and men.

The cougar hound must have a good nose, intelligence, endurance and a limitless love of the job. Regardless of breed, whether Walker, bluetick or Plott, not every hound develops into a top-grade dog for lion hunting. Cap Atwood once gave away eleven in a single day, by way of culling the failures out of his pack. Those that qualify are seldom for sale at any price.

It's at the tree that the hound's enthusiasm for his work faces its harshest test. Atwood has had dogs stay at the tree for as long as thirty-six hours when he was unable to find them. He has also seen one of his hounds climb sixty feet into a scrubby pine after a lion, but that is something he doesn't favor.

Most hunters use a pack of four to six dogs. Don Ellis is an exception. He lets only one hound go at a time, and that one is always belled. He often takes two dogs out, but never turns them loose together.

"It's like the old saying that a boy is a boy, two boys are half a boy, and three boys are no boy at all," Ellis explains. "Often it works out that same way with dogs.

"I've seen three or four hounds run a good track until it went up a bare hillside or deer walked in it or fresh snow interfered, and in the confusion one dog found an old track instead, took off on it, and the rest followed. I've also seen four dogs take off in four different directions on old tracks around a kill. Using a single hound eliminates the risk of a dog fight at the tree, too.

"I want my cougar dog to know his business, I want him to stay at the tree until I get there, and I want just one of him at a time. That's all it takes."

Ellis is also a strong believer in belling the hound. He lost the greatest hound he ever owned when he forgot to bell it. The cougar, a female with two kits, ambushed it and laid its chest open with one rake of a paw. Cougars have little fear of a dog that runs silently, Don explains, and that happens sometimes when a track is hard to follow.

"A lap dog could tree the biggest cougar that ever lived and keep him treed, if he'd bark loud enough," Don says. "But let either the lap dog or your best hound run head-on into a cat without giving tongue and you're almost sure to have a dead dog." The bell eliminates all chance that the hound will surprise the cougar and get killed on the spot.

The cougar population of British Columbia is almost certainly the most dense north of Mexico at the present time. That province has plenty of rough country, mountains, canyons and rock bluffs, in big chunks that are still roadless and wild. That is what the big tawny cat requires.

He also requires deer. He does not live on venison alone, by any means, but it's one of his mainstays and he rarely remains long in country where he can't get it, even if moose or elk are available instead. All the same, he may go for months without killing a deer, settling for rabbits and porcupines instead. It's common to find porky quills in a cougar stomach, and they seem to cause no trouble. If the cat gets his face, neck and feet stuck full, however, that's another matter.

In reality, the lion eats just about anything he comes upon, from grasshoppers to moose. His diet list includes squirrels, rabbits, skunks, beavers, grouse and turkeys, and now and then fish. He also kills and eats coyotes, lynxes, bobcats and even smaller lions. He is a proven cannibal on occasion. And he's fond of domestic stock where it's available. One thing is certain, any time he wants a feed of deer meat he's going to have it if there are deer around.

Although he is short-winded, over a short distance he is one of the fastest animals on four legs. He seems to do his stalking by sight, and the procedure is always the same. He creeps up within three or four jumps, as silent as a drifting shadow. His final rush is as fast as a lightning bolt, and he strikes like a tawny projectile. A full grown female cougar will weigh from 75 to 140 pounds, a tom between 135 and 175. Now and then one reaches a weight of 200 pounds or better.

Cougars belt a deer down as if it had been shot, often knocking it fifteen to twenty feet to one side. The terrible momentum of the attack breaks its neck and it dies in its tracks. It's not unusual to find a lion-killed deer without a claw or tooth mark on it. Even a medium-sized elk that goes down when a cougar strikes it is not likely to get up again, and they can kill a full grown wild horse without too much trouble. If they need to finish the job they bite into the neck behind the head. All told, it's a good thing for man that they let him alone the way they do.

If the quarry escapes the cat's first rush, however, he does not chase it far. Unless he catches it within a hundred yards or so, he gives up, rests, and tries for another kill.

Often the cougar moves his kill to a preferred spot, usually under a tree or rock, before he feeds. Normally he drags it, but a full grown one is capable of throwing a deer, a small elk or a moose calf across his back and carrying it, even in deep snow.

When he is ready to feed he rakes leaves and litter down to bare ground at the spot and claws all the hair off the deer on the side where he is going to start. He eats, and if he intends to return to the kill he covers it with sticks, litter and the deer's own hair.

When you find leavings cached and covered that way it's a good bet that the cougar has found himself a dry place under a tree or rock, not far off, where he can sleep, watch his kill and keep ravens and other predators away. Often he lies up in that fashion for three or four days, and that's a very good place to put dogs down. On the other hand, if the kill is not covered the odds are that the cat is traveling. He may be thirty miles away, and it will be ten days or two weeks before he comes back. In such cases, unless the track is very fresh it's hardly worth following.

The mountain lion has long had a bad reputation among sportsmen because of the inroads he makes on deer and elk, and with almost no exception stockmen hate him for the sheep, cattle and colts he kills. Only in the last few years has he won a place as a protected game animal in almost every place where he is found. Before that he was regarded as a destructive predator, to be hunted or trapped the year around without restriction, and many states continued to pay bounties on the big cats until they were all but wiped out.

There is no room for argument about their predatory habits. How much killing they do depends, apparently, on the individual cat and the abundance of prey.

The Copenhaver brothers believe that in the area where they hunt a grown lion takes an average of a deer a week, or about fifty a year. Some kill more, and they once kept track of a big tom that killed twelve deer in seven days. Cap Atwood says the lions he has followed killed a deer or elk every three or four days, an average of two a week.

If hunting is lean, the lion covers his kill and comes back and feeds until it is gone. But if game is plentiful he is likely to eat only the choice parts, move on and kill again. One thing he rarely does is to feed on a carcass unless he has killed it himself.

"For all their deer killing, cougars and deer have lived together in the British Columbia mountains for a long time," Don Ellis points out. "I have never found any evidence that a normal cougar population does much damage to a healthy deer herd." Don adds, however, that there is no truth in the contention, often heard, that the cats kill only the weaker deer, those that would die in a hard winter anyway. They do take fawns and weak deer, but only because that kind are easiest to get. They also attack the biggest buck without hesitation if that happens to be the first one they come across.

As for livestock raids, once a lion starts killing stock he keeps it up until he is done away with. He may move out and strike in another place, but in a night or two he'll be back, and he doesn't quit. He takes cattle only now and then, and in a cage shows little liking for beef. Colts and sheep are his preferred prey. Atwood killed one Colorado lion that had slaughtered eighty-five sheep in a single night and another that had accounted for seventy woolies in two nights. They can brain a sheep with a single blow. Luckily sheep do not graze regularly in lion country and not all lions become sheep killers. They have been known to walk through a herd without turning aside.

When it comes to guns for cougar hunting, most experienced hunters prefer a handgun to a rifle. For one thing it is far easier to carry, especially in windfalls and thick brush. The sidearm can be carried in a pack, where it is no bother, and as one cougar hunter told me, "If you can hit a milk can at thirty yards with your gun you can hit a treed cougar."

Somewhat surprisingly, many hunters want the handgun in no more than .22 caliber, too. They load the gun with long rifle hollow-points, and kill the cat with a shot in the lungs.

"Never shoot a cougar in the head," Don Ellis warns. "You can spoil a record skull, and worse, the cat will come out of the tree with enough life left in him to kill any dog he can reach. You tie your hounds before you shoot, of course, but now and then one will get loose, and a wounded cougar can do a dog in with one swipe.

"Put a .22 hollow-point into his lungs and he'll either hang in the tree until he wilts and falls, stone dead, or he'll jump and run. If he runs his lungs fill with blood and he's dead before a dog can overtake him."

Even where cougars are numerous, it's rare for a man to get sight of one unless he runs them with dogs. They do most of their traveling and hunting by night, seldom in open country, and no animal alive is more stealthy.

In all likelihood the cougar sees man far more often than man sees him. He is crafty enough to stay out of sight. For all his furtiveness, however, he is not greatly afraid of humans and one of his habits is to follow a man on foot, sometimes for miles, keeping only a few yards behind. If the person trailed in that fashion discovers what is going on, it's likely to be a hair-raising experience.

On a deer hunt in cougar country, a friend of mine sat down on a log to eat lunch, and because he was tired and the day was mild he loafed there for an hour. When he was ready to leave he decided, for no particular reason, to take a look at his own back track. He hadn't walked fifty yards when he found where a big cougar had lain and watched him the whole time, twitching its tail from side to side in the snow. Probably it had drooled while he ate his sandwiches, wishing it had the guts to knock over a meal of its own. The tracks showed it had followed the hunter a mile before he stopped for lunch.

This big cat of the western mountains tugs at a hunter's imagination in a unique fashion. He is one of the most mysterious animals on this continent, padding his wilderness trails in the darkness on feet as noiseless as a housecat's, leaving a track big enough to scare any man. Few humans ever see him, but those who follow dogs to the end of his track are rewarded with one of the most exciting sights the eyes of a hunter will ever look upon.

RIFLES FOR BIG GAME

Savage Model 99 is a fast-handling lever-action rifle with a 20-inch barrel and 6 round rotary magazine. The 99 is available in .250/3000, .300 Savage, .243 and .308.

Winchester Model 94 is no newcomer to the deer woods. Chambered for the traditionally popular .30/30 Win., the lever-action 94 has a 20-inch barrel and weighs 6½ pounds.

Browning Lever Action Rifle (BLR), chambered for the .243 or .308 Win., takes a 4-round detachable magazine and features a lever-housed trigger that travels with lever to avoid finger pinch on return.

Remington Model 700 BDL bolt-action rifle features detachable sights for scope mounting, drilled and tapped receiver, Monte Carlo stock and cheekpiece. It comes in 17 calibers.

Winchester Model 70 bolt-action rifle comes in 16 calibers. Monte Carlo stock, undercut cheekpiece and detachable sling swivels are standard equipment.

Weatherby Vanguard, a bolt-action rifle chambered for the .30/06, is shown here equipped with the maker's Imperial variable scope on a Buehler mount, complemented by a Monte Carlo stock and cheekpiece.

Savage Model 110 bolt-action rifle comes in .30/06, .243, .270 Mag., 7mm Rem. Mag. and .300 Win. Mag. Available with ejector clip magazine or hinged floorplate, depending on model. Monte Carlo stock and cheekpiece.

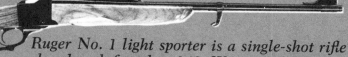

Ruger No. 1 light sporter is a single-shot rifle chambered for the .243 Win., .30/06, .270 Win. Barrel is 22 inches; weight, 7¼ pounds.

Remington Model 760 carbine is only pump-action rifle chambered for the .30/06. (It also comes in .308 Win.) Takes a 4-round clip magazine; barrel is a short 18 inches.

Savage Model 170 pump-action rifle is designed especially for deer hunting. It comes only in .30/30 caliber, has a Monte Carlo stock, drilled and tapped receiver for scope.

Remington Model 742 automatic fires 5 rounds, comes in 6mm Rem., .280 Rem., .30/06, .308 Win. and .243 Win. Receiver is drilled and tapped for scope mount.

Browning Automatic rifle is chambered for the 7mm Rem. Mag., .300 and .308 Weatherby Mag., .30/06, .270 Win., .308 Win., and .243 Win. Fires 4 or 5 rounds, depending on caliber. This is the Grade IV model, with gold-plated trigger, engraved receiver sides and hand-checkered stock.

Part II

SMALL GAME

9

COTTON-TAIL

Four-footed rocket

The favorite game of shotgunners over most of the United States is a four-footed commoner that takes off like a rocket, runs like a streak, dodges like a boxer, and winds up on the platter crisp and brown and about as good as anything you'll ever eat—the cottontail rabbit.

More shotgun shells are expended on him fall after fall than on any other target, feathered or furred. In many places the number of his kind gathered in by hunters each year adds up to as many as the total harvest of all other small game put together. To cite a few examples, not many years ago Kentucky shotgunners were knocking off two to three million cottontails annually; the average kill in Indiana was 2.5 million or better; the Ohio count ran one million higher than that; and in Missouri, which may well have been the cottontail capital of the country then, hunters were racking up a score as high as six million in a good year.

The cottontail population has declined in most states in recent years, for reasons which game managers are

135

not sure of, and the kill today is well below the figures I have just cited. But over the country it still adds up to a lot of rabbits. The cottontail ranges from Maine to California and from Florida to Washington, and in most of the places where he is found he is appreciated.

The best rabbit hunting, and the only kind most sportsmen are interested in, is with dogs, and the dog best suited for it is a hound with a good nose, the ability to find rabbits, the know-how to run them, and sense enough to take his time. He should also have persistence and staying power.

A good jump dog is highly important. You can't chase or kill rabbits until you locate them and get them up and going. Dogs do that in two ways, either by cold tracking or by knowing where the cottontail is apt to be and probing into every likely spot, such as thickets, tall grass and brushpiles. Some hounds combine the two methods. A cold trailer is not necessarily the best at this job. He may putter along on a stale track, wasting time, where a smarter dog, discovering cold tracks, would dive headlong through the thickets and have the rabbit on the run in a matter of minutes.

Some of the best jump dogs I have hunted behind have not even been hounds. Some were springers or cockers, some plain feists, and some cross-breeds, but they all had one thing in common: They knew where a rabbit was likely to be sitting and they looked for him in the right places.

My friend Pete Petoskey, who in addition to being chief of the Wildlife Division of the Michigan Department of Natural Resources also happens to be one of the most knowledgeable rabbit hunters I know, says he has seen reasonably good rabbit dogs of almost every breed except the Mexican hairless.

I'd have to agree. As a boy I had a farm dog that loved rabbit hunting, and years later a springer, the best pheasant dog I ever owned, developed unbounded enthusiasm for it, along with considerable skill at finding what he was looking for. But once the rabbit was beyond his sight that ended the hunt; he had no interest in trying to trail it.

For that very reason, if you use a jump dog that is not a hound you need a sure-nosed hound or two along, to take over the tracking that is a major part of good rabbit hunts.

Once under way, rabbits are not as tricky as a coon or fox, but if hard-pressed they do have a few proven devices for throwing a dog off their track. They'll make abrupt turns, back track and leave the trail with a long jump to one side, run in their own tracks or a man's, circle around or in and out of a thicket, dodge through it and go out where they went in. A hound needs to know something of their ways to stay with them at such times.

Slow dogs make the best cottontail dogs, for the reason that they do not crowd the rabbit too hard. Given his time, the cottontail hops along in no hurry, commonly not more than fifty yards in front of the dog, often less than that, stopping now and then to sit up and see what's going on.

But if he is pushed by a fast dog he lights out and is likely to hole up in the first woodchuck den, stonepile, brushheap or culvert he can find. The faster the dog behind him the faster he runs, too, and the more difficult target he offers. A slowpoke hound will give you better shooting and far more of it than one that trails like greased lightning.

Most hunters prefer the short-legged breeds. Beagles and cottontails go together like ham and eggs, and basset hounds also make fine rabbit dogs. I have had some lively cottontail shooting ahead of the bigger foxhound breeds, but in general they run the rabbit too fast and too far.

As Erwin Bauer, the sportsman and outdoor writer who is so well known to readers of *Outdoor Life,* puts it, "Rabbit hunting isn't really rabbit hunting without hounds, specifically beagles, and the best beagle is one that never, or almost never, loses the track."

Bauer's own rabbit hound, incidentally, comes closer to talking than any dog I have ever known.

I got acquainted with Hungry Homer one day a few years ago, when I had driven to the Bauer home in Columbus, Ohio, to spend a week with Erwin in the field, taking a look at the ravages of strip mining. He introduced me to Homer, who was polite but bored. Then Erwin turned to him. "Rabbits, Homer, rabbits," he said softly.

The beagle pointed his nose to the ceiling and sang as mournful a lament as ever poured from the throat of dog or man. The time was June, but he was pleading for the frost-browned fields of autumn, the mellow warmth of the October sun, and a cottontail to run.

He fell silent and sat staring hopefully at his boss with melancholy eyes.

"Rabbits, Homer, rabbits," Bauer prodded him again, and at that magic word Hungry Homer lifted his muzzle and wailed again. I'll always think of him as a beagle that almost spoke English.

One headache plagues rabbit hunters over much of the country today, and it grows worse with each passing year. That is the problem of dogs forgetting the business at hand to run deer. In the East, all through the Midwest, and in many places in the West and South, whitetail deer are spreading out and becoming more numerous in the farmlands, where their range overlaps that of the cottontail. They hang out in the same thick-

As a hunter tromps into a thicket, a cottontail bursts out. For an instant the beagle is caught flat-footed, but seconds later he will be bawling happily in pursuit, unless his boss ends the episode first. The small hound and the cottontail go together like ham and eggs.

A cottontail streaks away in front of two hunters and their surprised dog, almost underfoot. There are few things that happen in small-game hunting more heart-stopping than the sudden, explosive takeoff of one of these small rabbits leaving his hiding place in thick cover.

139

A beagle picks up a fallen cottontail. He'll mouth it, but unless he is a rare exception he will not bring it back to the hunter. Hounds are not normally retrievers.

ets, and because deer leave strong scent a hot whitetail track presents an almost irresistible temptation to a hound. The end result is usually a long, illegal chase (running deer with dogs is outlawed everywhere except in the South), often a lost dog, since deer are likely to lead them far out of the area, and a ruined rabbit hunt.

More than one sportsman of my acquaintance has reluctantly given up rabbit hunting because of the growing numbers of deer in cottontail or snowshoe territory, and the frequency with which they lead a hound into trouble.

Deerproof rabbit dogs are lamentably rare, but they can be trained as coon hounds, bear hounds, bobcat hounds and fox hounds can. One sure-fire method of deerproofing is described elsewhere in this book, in the chapter on coon hunting.

All rabbits have an inborn trait that's a big help in hunting them. Driven by dogs, they circle back to their starting point unless they are crowded into a hole first. Cottontails make fairly short circles, bigger rabbits travel farther. But sooner or later the desire to get back home overwhelms them all, and they come hopping or streaking toward the place where they were jumped, no matter what the consequences.

I've never seen that habit better illustrated than when hunting the big European hares that became so abundant as to constitute a serious pest in the farmlands of Ontario north of Lake Erie some forty years ago. They were rabbits of the open fields, much like the jacks of our western states, avoiding woods and heavy cover, and the favorite method of hunting them was by organizing big drives in which fifty or more men took part, forming an open U-shaped line and moving slowly across the fields, usually covering a square mile at a time.

Jumped from their daytime forms along fences and behind clumps of grass, the hares would go bounding away from the drivers, running like the wind. It wasn't unusual to see a dozen or more racing across the fields in all directions at one time. But they could be driven just so far. Unfailingly, once a rabbit had been pushed a half mile or so from his starting place he'd make up his mind to circle back, come headlong at the line of hunters, and the shooting would start.

Those European hares weigh up to twelve pounds or better, and because of their size it was hard for a hunter used to cottontails to judge the range. They looked deceptively close when they were actually far out of shotgun reach, and as a result the marksmanship often was more funny than deadly. The first shooting was likely to turn the rabbit parallel to the line of drivers and send him streaking broadside in front of maybe ten or fifteen men, every one of them pouring coal at him as he went by. But time after time, in spite of that rolling barrage, he would wheel suddenly at right angles and make his try to break through the line, the determination to get back where he came from overriding all other considerations. Now and then, if two drivers were far enough apart, a rabbit made it. Most of the time they died trying. But that didn't keep the next one from repeating the performance, and that was how we got our liveliest shooting.

Cottontails, varying hares and all the rest of the tribe behave the same way. They cling to their home territory like leeches. Once your dogs have a rabbit up and running, if you

The camera caught this cottontail hunched up in mid-jump. Actually he was covering ground in long, soaring leaps, leaving the danger zone at his best speed, seeking the shelter of the thicket ahead.

don't get a shot at him on the getaway pick yourself a stand not far from the place where he was jumped. Give him time enough and he'll come back that way, and if you choose a spot with a clear view on all sides you are almost sure to get your chance on his return trip. It's not unusual for a rabbit to circle a swale, small swamp or other patch of cover several times if the hounds give him time enough.

I recall a hunt one October when a partner and I jumped rabbits three times in one morning out in weed-grown, uncultivated fields. Each time the cottontail went lipperty-lip for the heavy cover of the nearest willow-grown swamp, and each time we divided our forces, one staying back in the field while the other moved to the swamp in case he decided he liked it there. And each time Mr. Rabbit took one turn through the thickets, went kiting back for the field, and got himself shot within a hundred feet of the place where our dogs had opened on him. That's typical rabbit behavior.

Like all game animals, the cottontail's habits are governed by two factors, food and cover, and he is lucky enough to be able to eat most of his environment and thrive on it. One wildlife authority commented years ago that the list of plants he feeds on is far too long to set down, but summed it up by saying it takes in about 99 per cent of everything that grows in the area where the rabbit lives. Anybody who has tried to grow a young orchard, a garden, flowers or shrubbery in prime cottontail country will agree.

This ability to find food wherever he happens to be is a big help to the rabbit in meeting seasonal weather changes. Through the summer and early fall, when every fencerow, hay-field, briar patch and weedy corner provides a hiding place, the cottontail population scatters widely over the countryside, and at the beginning of hunting season the gunner must plan accordingly.

In October in a good rabbit area you can find them almost anywhere, in alfalfa and clover fields, along ditch-banks and brush-grown fences, in grain stubble, in dry marshes, small swales and at the borders of brushy ponds. One place is about as good as another for cottontails then, so long as it has enough cover to shelter them.

Some years ago I had forty acres of young evergreens growing into Christmas trees on my farm. The plantation also grew rank with grass and weeds, and I rarely walked through it, up to

On deep snow, a cottontail races for thick cover. On bare ground the little brown rabbit is willing to endure a long chase ahead of a hound that does not hurry him. But once the snow gets deep he hurries quickly into a thicket or holes up in a groundhog burrow.

the end of October, without sending a rabbit or two into unhurried flight. An experienced beagle with ability as a cold trailer, put down there on a damp October morning, could have gotten himself a whole day's quota of exercise in a couple of hours.

But with the onset of cold weather and snow in the north, the cottontails change their ways in a hurry. They head for the best shelter available, congregating in grass-grown brushy swamps, big swales, willow thickets, dense growth in creek or river bottoms, and other areas of heavy cover. Many of them take up residence under abandoned buildings, in brushpiles, or underground in woodchuck dens.

Cottontail hunting becomes more difficult then, but it's still productive if you seek out the right places. In my part of the country brushy swamps are the best areas, once cold weather comes. They provide ample cover and are sure to harbor a rabbit population. It's easy for dogs to nose a rabbit out of his hiding place in the tall snow-covered grass, and because he does not have to expose himself in the open he is likely to make two or three circuits of the swamp before holing up. If the hunter knows his business that's all the running he needs.

There are two such swamps within a mile of my home, thickly grown with willow, osier, alder and other brush. Either of them is good for a couple of hours of lively action and two or three rabbits most any crisp November or December day.

The best example I know of cottontails gathering in big concentrations in dense cover in winter takes place in the willow batts on the Missouri River bottoms along the Iowa-Nebraska border. I haven't hunted there, but my friend Frank Heidelbauer, formerly a pilot and protection officer for the Iowa Conservation Commission, once told me that in making aerial game surveys he had counted as many as sixty cottontails in a half-acre patch of willows, after snow came. But he added that the brush was about as tall as a man, and a hunter would need two things to hunt successfully, a good rabbit dog and a stepladder.

Snow adds greatly to the fun of rabbit hunting, since it enables the hunter to locate game more easily and keep track of what is going on as the hunt develops. And for the hunter working without a dog (not a productive method in most places, and you miss the hound music that is the best

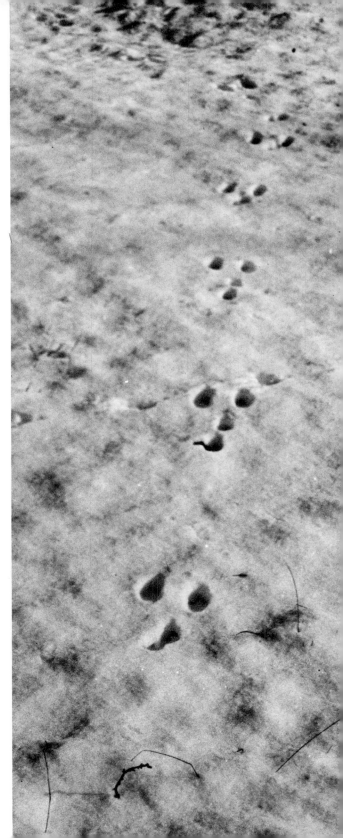

The tracks of a cottontail can be told at a glance from those of any other wild thing. When bounding at high speed, the rabbit places its hind feet side by side in front of its forefeet.

part of the hunt, but you can collect rabbits that way) snow is a big help. In mild weather, when cottontails are prone to "sit out" at the edges of swamps, in weedy fields and along ditches and roadsides, the dogless hunter can pick up a fresh track and follow it to the rabbit without much trouble. The cottontail's habit of feeding and frolicking all night long makes him easy to locate and trail the next morning. But with a good dog, while tracking snow is no handicap, neither is it a help, and you'll kill about as many rabbits on bare ground.

As winter goes along and snow gets deep in the north, rabbit hunting becomes harder and harder. By January much of the cottontail population in my part of the country is holed up in woodchuck burrows, muskrat tunnels or any snug spot they can find away from storms, snow and bitter weather. Here in southern Michigan the woodchuck is considered so beneficial to the cottontail supply, by providing holes for winter shelter, that he enjoys the benefit of protection as a game animal himself.

When it comes to a choice of weapons, the cottontail is the shotgunner's meat, first, last and all the time. What size shot? Fives, 6's or 7½, as you prefer. There is no need for heavy shot or magnum loads on rabbits. They carry little lead and fold easily.

There are other methods of hunting cottontails that provide good fun, too. Where they are plentiful they make lively and interesting targets for the bowhunter. It's often possible to get sitting shots, especially in fall and early winter, by moving slowly and carefully along ditchbanks, roadsides, fencerows, the edges of swales and other areas of good cover, and keeping a sharp watch in brush, grass and weeds. And it's also possible to hunt cottontails ahead of dogs with a bow with fair success if there are enough rabbits. The shooting is difficult but the sport is Grade A.

The liveliest carnival of that kind I know about was held annually in December for many years near the town of Perry, about forty miles from my home in southeastern Michigan. An organized and carefully planned affair, sponsored by Stylie Ferris, an enthusiastic bowman and all-around sportsman who owned the land on which the hunt was staged, it lured up to fifteen hundred archers and resulted in a kill of close to two hundred rabbits in a day. You earn any cottontail you knock off, hunting them that way, but the action and excite-ment more than make up for the small kill.

If you are looking for something off the beaten track, the same combination of conditions that makes stalking sitting cottontails with a bow an interesting proposition also offers good possibilities for the hunter who wants to take 'em with a handgun or a .22. He won't gather in a great many rabbits, but he'll have fun with those he collects.

One other way of hunting cottontails, by moonlight (in states where after-sundown hunting is legal), deserves more attention than it gets. Pick a clear night of full winter moon and hunt at the edges of swamps, in old orchards, along hedgerows, any place the rabbits are likely to hang out on such nights. Walk slowly and without commotion. Now and then you'll spot a cottontail before he moves, but if you try to bust him sitting you're likely to confuse a clump of grass or a swaying weed stalk with a rabbit. It does no harm to try, but you'll shoot more mistakes than rabbits that way. If you wait for him to move you can be sure your target is what you think it is.

Skipping along on the snow in bright moonlight, he's a dim gray ghost, and you will see his blue-black shadow drifting beside him more clearly than you see the rabbit. It makes no difference. Shoot at the shadow, and your pattern will take care of things. The odds are with the

rabbit, but it packs plenty of laughs and action, and once you get the hang of it you can rack up a respectable score, too.

If you want your rabbits big, the swamper or cane cutter of the south is your dish. An overgrown cousin of the cottontail, found in the southern half of the Mississippi Valley, he is known to only a few sportsmen, but those who hunt him become addicts.

Weighing six pounds or even more, as compared with the cottontail's two to three, he has many of the same habits but lives in much thicker cover and for that reason supplies more difficult shooting.

No grassy pastures, weedy fields or briar patches for the swamp cane cutter. Instead he wants the densest thickets of willow and cottonwood, cane brakes, honeysuckle tangles, piles of driftwood and rank grass along the edge of water. He's found only on low land, in the swamps and river bottoms and on the brushy

Although not as well served by natural camouflage as his cousin, the snowshoe hare, the cottontail is no slouch in staying unseen in the frost-killed weeds, dry grass and leafless brush where he hangs out in autumn.

islands of the Mississippi and its tributaries from the Ohio south. He swims as readily as a muskrat, seldom holes up, runs like a small deer, makes bigger circles than the cottontail, and is close to tireless ahead of hounds. Hunting him calls for big, tough dogs. As a friend of mine in Tennessee puts it, "That ol' cane cutter will run a little beagle plumb to death." You can expect a chase to last for hours unless the rabbit is killed.

There's not much use trying to kill the swamper in the thickets. Look instead for levees, logging roads, or open ridges and wait for the dogs to drive him across. In many ways hunting him is like hunting the varying hare farther north.

The western jack, in many areas the most plentiful of all rabbits, is of little interest to shotgunners but does offer good possibilities for the bowman and is close to ideal as a varminter target. Walloping him with a scoped, high-velocity, light caliber is a rifleman's pastime hard to beat, and there is no better way to sharpen your eye in readiness for deer or other big game.

Even a beginner can do well hunting jacks on the open sagebrush plains where they reach their greatest abundance. Jumped, they usually run like small antelope for a short distance, but most of the time they pull up within two hundred yards and squat for a look back. That's when the varmint hunter gets his chance, unless he's hot enough to take them running. The rifle must be flat-shooting and shove its bullet along at a fast clip. The .220 Swift, .243 and .244 will do the job neatly, as will any good wildcat caliber.

I've shot 'em with a .22/.250, for example, that moved its dose of poison out of the muzzle at just under 4,000 foot-seconds. At such extreme speed the light bullet is deadly on jacks— even a graze will kill—and has the further advantage of disintegrating on contact with a tumbleweed, sage twig or clump of grass, which makes for safe shooting.

Many hunters like to gut their rabbits as soon as they are shot, to save weight in the game pocket. Some carry a thong and loop the dressed rabbits at their belt. It's a good way of carrying them, but dangerous in deer country during deer season. Accidents have happened when another hunter mistook a swinging rabbit, seen briefly through brush, for the legs of a walking deer.

Fear of tularemia has discouraged rabbit hunting in some parts of the country in recent years. How real is the danger? Slight if you take a few simple precautions. To begin with, the disease seems to be on the wane. At least I have seen fewer reports of it in humans recently than when it first began to attract attention some thirty years or more ago. Second, there are easy ways to protect yourself from the danger of infection.

150

The cottontail is hunted to a limited extent by bowmen, but once he is off and running, as here, he is far from an easy target.

Avoid rabbits that act sick, that refuse to run or lack normal pep and stamina, to begin with. If you want to be perfectly safe carry a pair of ordinary household rubber gloves and slip them on before you dress your game. Then discard any rabbit whose insides look abnormal or diseased.

Finally, how do you cook what you have shot? I've never found a better recipe than the one my mother used when I was a kid on the farm. She cut the rabbit up, soaked it overnight in salt water, parboiled it for a few minutes with a little soda added to the water, drained it, started with fresh water and stewed it until it was tender. Then she rolled the pieces in flour and fried them in butter. The leftover stock made wonderful gravy.

Pete Petoskey is the author of another recipe that's worth passing along. Cut two or three rabbits into pieces, soak a few hours in salt water, dry the pieces thoroughly on paper towels and shake them in a sack with flour or cracker crumbs that have been salted and peppered. Braise until golden brown. Add a quarter cup each of wine and water, two cans of mushroom soup, a couple of sliced onions, a dash of tabasco, two or three strips of bacon and a teaspoon of salt, and continue braising until the onions and bacon are done.

The fact is, you can cook yourself a great dish with rabbits, either in the field or the kitchen.

10

SNOWSHOE RABBIT

Artful dodger of the north woods

A great many years ago I went on a rabbit hunt I'll never forget. It was my first try for snowshoes, the long-legged, light-footed northern hares that turn white in winter, and I remember it not for its success but for its failure. There were three of us in the party, plus one hound, and we got skunked. It was the first and only time in my life that ever happened to me on a rabbit hunt, and I suppose that's why the whole thing sticks in my memory.

I was teaching country school in southern Michigan at the time, more than a hundred miles south of the nearest snowshoe rabbit country, and in those days that was quite a trip to make for hunting of any kind. But I'd heard a lot about those north-woods bunnies from deer hunters who made an annual November pilgrimage to their haunts, and all I had heard fascinated me. A cottontail fan from early boyhood, I finally concluded that snowshoes would be even more fun to hunt. I was right, too, although I failed to demonstrate it on the first attempt. Anyway, a couple

153

of friends and I decided to go north for a week-end in late October. We'd put in half the time hunting rabbits, the other half driving a Model T Ford up and back.

None of us owned a rabbit dog but that proved easy to remedy. The butcher in our little town possessed a lady beagle, or at least part beagle, by the name of Pokey, and he gladly agreed to loan her for the occasion. He mentioned casually, when we approached him, that Pokey was an expectant mother but neglected to tell us just when the blessed event was due. Pokey turned out to have the general outlines of a ripe pumpkin.

We made the long ride north without mishap. We camped out, sleeping on piles of dry fern that we heaped up in the stalls of a tumbledown logging-camp stable, long unused. The night was clear and frosty, we yarned for hours around the fire, and the whole thing was pure adventure.

But the weather didn't stay frosty. By the time we finished breakfast the next morning the temperature was climbing, the sun shining in a cloudless blue sky, and long before noon the day had turned hot and dry enough for August.

We knew nothing of the habits or habitat of snowshoe rabbits but we did know cottontails and their ways, and so we went looking for their northern cousins where we'd have looked for them, in briar patches, fern thickets and other areas of cover on the high, dry plains of that cutover pine country — where no snowshoe would be caught dead.

An hour of that kind of going, combined with the heat and a pronounced lack of water, was enough for Pokey. Somewhere in that dry country she must have found a cool nook, maybe beside a small stream or bog, and lay down. We missed her by midmorning and spent the rest of the day hunting the lost dog. The fact that she was borrowed only made matters worse. But in the cool of late afternoon we met her, trudging along an old logging road toward camp, grinning serenely, rested and unconcerned, entirely satisfied with the way she had spent the day. I don't think she even realized we were supposed to be on a rabbit hunt, for neither she nor the rest of us had seen so much as a rabbit track.

We got one break. We made it home in time. The pups, a mixture of beagle and something else, arrived a couple of days later.

It wouldn't be accurate to say that that was my introduction to snowshoe rabbits, for nothing remotely resembling an introduction took place. If there were any snowshoes in that township, they certainly were totally unaware of my presence. But that trip did represent my first attempt to find and outsmart a rabbit that I still regard, almost fifty years later, as one of the greatest small-game animals on this continent. It has led to more days of exciting and pleasurable hunting than I can count. And it also serves nicely to point up a first rule of all hunting, that it's useless to look for game in places where it doesn't live. In the case of the snowshoe, he doesn't live on high, dry uplands with open cover.

I'm aware, of course, that this big light-footed hare ranks far behind the cottontail in popularity among hunters. But I contend that is only because he is far less widely distributed. His main range is in Canada and Alaska, all the way from Newfoundland to the mouth of the Yukon, and north as far as timber grows and there are willow or evergreen thickets to shelter him. That is country where not much rabbit hunting is done. South of the Canadian border he is limited chiefly to the northern states, New England, New York, Michigan, Wisconsin, Minnesota, parts of North Dakota and Montana, and Idaho, Washington and Oregon. Only in the mountains of the East and West is his range greater than that. In the Appalachians he extends as far south as West Virginia, in the Rockies at least to Colorado.

If he were found in every brush-bordered field, briar patch, swale and creek bottom from Florida to Oregon and from Arizona to Massachusetts, as the cottontail is, and known to as many shotgunners, Lightfoot would win any popularity contest in a walk, for he's a better game animal than the cottontail on almost every count. Many sportsmen may disagree, but I'll stick to my guns. I love the cottontail as much as any hunter can and I'm indebted to him for a lot of top-flight sport, but in my book he's just not the rabbit the snowshoe is.

I can think of a dozen reasons why the swamp hare is entitled to top billing with any hunter who enjoys hound music. There is his inborn caution, his speed, his artful dodging, and the natural camouflage that changes with the seasons and makes him hard to see and harder to shoot; his tendency to travel the instant he hears a hound and his great abundance in good rabbit years; his endurance ahead of dogs, his big padded feet that hold him up on the deepest snow, and the fact that while he runs in circles as all rabbits do, the circles may be a mile across; his liking for dense cover, his distaste for open places, the tricks he can play and, above all, his refusal to hole.

To win a high place on my game list any animal or bird, large or small, from rabbits to mountain lions or woodcock to turkeys, must provide hard hunting. I have little use for pushovers. I don't care especially what makes a species hard to hunt. It can be because he is hard to find, hard to follow, hard to hit or big enough and mean enough to fight back. So long as there is an element of difficulty and excitement in gunning for him, he gets my vote. And on that

The snowshoe hare is the champion turncoat of the hunter's world. Brown in summer (below), he changes to mottled brown and white about the time the first snow comes in October, and to all-white, save for the tips of his ears, by December. If snow falls later than normal, and catches him wearing white too soon, he is the most conspicuous thing in the woods (left). It's then he supplies unusual hunting on a moonlight night.

Tracks left by a snowshoe on light and fluffy snow. In winter this rabbit grows pads of thick fur on his over-size feet, equipment that holds him up and makes travel easy.

score the snowshoe rabbit qualifies very nicely.

Admittedly he's not hard to find, especially with a good rabbit dog. When he's plentiful he's very plentiful and his tracks are everywhere. It's not unusual to find the snow under evergreen thickets packed down as in a sheep pasture, where the hares have frolicked during the winter nights, with little trails as hard packed and much used as runways in a deer yard, leading from one place of shelter to another. It rarely takes a hound, put down in good cover, more than three or four minutes to get a rabbit up and going and even a hunter who is not using a dog has no difficulty jumping rabbits in the right kind of place.

On any snowshoe hunt the excitement at the outset is likely to be made greater by the fact that every hare in the neighborhood is almost sure to start moving as soon as the dogs open, too. They rarely wait to see whether it's their track or some other rabbit's that is being run. Once they hear a hound on the loose they take no chances. I've known half a dozen to take off in as many different directions within a minute after the music struck up, and it often happens that hunters get good shooting at strays while the dogs are running their particular rabbit plumb out of the area.

By a curious contrast, until he hears a dog the snowshoe is often so unwary that hunters are misled into rating him the biggest dunce in the whole rabbit family, about on a par with the fool hen among grouse. It's no trick at all for a hunter without a dog to pussyfoot up within twenty feet of one of these hares, hunched in his form under a branch or beside a log, and pick him off with rifle or sidearm. Many a snowshoe winds up in deer-camp stew because of that kind of behavior.

Back in 1927, when bowhunting was just beginning to get a toe in the door around the country, Frank Mosher, a bow maker at Grand Rapids, Michigan, where I lived then, and I went north to the deer woods together. Frank was to hunt with a bow, I with a rifle. I was outdoor editor of a chain of eight daily papers at that time. If he succeeded in killing a deer with an arrow it would be the first taken by that method in Michigan in modern times, and would provide the makings of a great story.

Neither of us killed a deer but we did make the discovery that the snowshoe rabbit is the perfect all-round small game for bowhunting, something about which I have not changed my mind down to the present day.

We found an alder and cedar swamp where there was an abundant rabbit population. Every few rods we'd come on a hare sitting trustfully beside a stump or in the shelter of a clump of brush, and Frank would slam an arrow. Now and then he'd hit. More often he'd miss. Even then some of the targets stayed put and gave him a second chance.

It was tough shooting, in thick cover, and the score was low. I think we went back to camp the first afternoon with only three rabbits. But the action and excitement were everything an archer could ask.

Lightfoot's habit of sitting quiet until he is sure the neighborhood is unhealthy — and sometimes he takes considerable convincing — makes him an ideal target for either the bowman or the sportsman who wants to collect a few rabbits with a .22.

Once a dog starts to beller in his vicinity, however, he's a different rabbit altogether. There's nothing stupid or trustful about him then. He lights out jet propelled and keeps going until he loses the hound or bad luck overtakes him in the form of a charge of chilled 6's.

He can be gathered in with a small-caliber rifle, or even with a handgun, as I have said, and a few hunters go after him that way, but he is basically a shotgunner's rabbit and must be hunted with hounds to get the most out of him. The choice of shotgun and loads is up to the individual hunter. A 20-gauge will kill as many hares as a 12, if it's pointed right. Like all rabbits, the snowshoe isn't good at carrying lead, and you don't need magnum loads, heavy shot or full choked barrels, since most of the shooting is in thick cover at short range. My own preference is for 6 or even 7½ shot in a good brush load, and I carry a 20-gauge because it's light and easy to handle.

Traveling ahead of dogs, no rabbit offers a more difficult target. His summer color is brown, darker and less grayish than the cottontail's. With the approach of cold weather in October he starts to shed this brown coat and replace it with white. By the time snow patches the ground he is mottled brown-and-white, and shortly after that he turns pure white all over except for the tips of his ears, which stay black the year around. His ears and his big dark eyes are the only giveaway spots on him in winter.

At the same time he grows thick pads of coarse fur on his hind feet, which are enormous to begin with. Fully furred, they cover about three times as much area as a jackrabbit's. By the time deep snow arrives he's ready for it. In the spring he sheds again, going from white back to brown.

His protective coloration is as good as any in the woods, and it enables him to slip through the undergrowth like a brown shadow in the fall and a white ghost in winter. In the kind of cover where he attempts his getaway it's not unusual for him to cross in front of a hunter unseen, at a dozen paces. More than once I have stood on an old brush-grown logging road in a north-country swamp and waited for a shot while an elusive hare dodged and twisted through the thickets for thirty yards without giving me more than one or two glimpses, and those too brief to do me any good.

I've had some very unusual hunting for snowshoes a few times when they turned white on schedule in the fall but the snow was late in coming. One of those white hares on bare ground, with black brush all around him, is about as conspicuous as anything I know of.

Hunting them the usual way is too easy under those conditions, but if the hunter will find a place where there are plenty of rabbits, and pick a moonlight night or on a moonless evening wait until dusk has fallen and he can no longer see the barrel of his gun against the undergrowth, he's in for lively fun.

The technique is simple. You spot a rabbit, get within thirty or forty feet of him, aim as best you can and cut loose. If there is no moonlight to glint on the gun barrel you point it up against the sky, tuck your cheek down in place, lower the gun and shoot by

160

guess. It sounds easy, but misses are far more common than hits.

The snowshoe can run like furred lightning, and when it comes to twisting, turning, getting through tight places, and doubling back he has no peer. Wherever I have hunted him, the thicker the cover the better he likes it. In our country he's a rabbit of cedar and tamarack swamps, of willow and alder thickets along streams, of ground hemlock tangles mixed with balsam fir. He's also fond of young evergreen plantations if they're thick enough, and of dense stands of pine, balsam or spruce that have grown up after fire. In the eastern mountains he keeps to the dense laurels and evergreens, rarely much below four thousand feet, in the west to the thick growth at the bottom of canyons and similar hideouts. Some of the most tempting snowshoe habitat I have ever seen was along the Columbia in Oregon, in thickets of yew, other evergreens and brush where a hunter could hardly get through. In such places the odds are all in favor of the rabbit.

Bigfoot distrusts open places and stays out of them if he can. Some of the finest rabbit hunting I have ever had was in the dense evergreen swamps along the back of Sleeping Bear Dune, on the east shore of Lake Michigan west of Traverse City. Back in the days before deer moved into that area, making it necessary to use deerproof rabbit dogs (which are few

and far between), that was the best place I knew about for a snowshoe hunt.

Shintangle, young cedar, balsam and brush grew so thick you couldn't see a rabbit twenty feet off, but old logging roads snaked through the swamp, winding in every direction, and that was where we waited for the dogs to drive game across. How the hares hated to cross those roads! They'd come out almost to the edge, turn and dodge back, run parallel to the danger zone for another one hundred yards, and when the hounds finally pushed them so hard they had no choice they didn't run across, they flew! They rarely took more than two jumps to make it from the thickets on one side to the thickets on the other, and sometimes only one. The shooting was slim but it was great hunting. Many days a partner and I listened to dog music from breakfast until noon, almost without a letup, and came in with no more than two or three rabbits.

I know no rabbit that can outdo the snowshoe for endurance. He has the ability and willingness to run ahead of hounds as long as they choose to follow. I've often known them to keep going for two or three hours, turning the chase into something closely akin to a fox hunt. Like all the members of the rabbit clan, they run in circles and no matter how far the dogs drive them sooner or later they are almost sure to return to the starting point and begin over again. That can be a big help to the hunter familiar with the crossing places in a swamp.

The snowshoe's circles are far bigger than those of the cottontail, however. (The rabbits themselves weigh about the same, around 3 to 3½ pounds on the average, but the snowshoe is more rangy and has longer legs.) I have known a freshly jumped one to run a mile in a straight line, and then make two or three short circles in the hope of shaking off the dogs, before starting back. It's a common experience to have the hare lead the hounds out of hearing, not once but two or three times. In a swamp with a small lake in the center I've seen them run entirely around the lake half a dozen times, never exposing themselves in the open. As they tire, however, their circles usually become shorter.

No rabbit is more clever at thinking up tricks to fool the dogs. Any time a critter with the wits of a hare does something that's too much for a seasoned old hound to figure out it's a credit to the whole rabbit tribe, and I've seen a snowshoe do just that more times than I can remember.

Bigfoot knows exactly how to leave a dead-end trail by backtracking, hopping in his own footprints and finally making a long jump off to one side. He can easily cover a dozen feet at a bound if he needs to. Often he'll make a big hop to left or right in full flight, reverse directions and go back the way he came without even slowing down.

Once he has completed a circle and started around the second time, he's not only likely to run in his own tracks or those of another rabbit; he'll even run in the dog's tracks or the hunter's if he thinks it will do any good. By the time he has made two or three circles he has things so messed up that it takes a wise and sure-nosed hound indeed to solve the riddle. I can remember snowshoes that in the course of a long chase sought out a thicket of some kind, maybe a big clump of dense, low-spreading juniper, ran around it three or four times, then dodged through the center, left with a jump that would have done credit to a small deer, and took off in a fresh direction. It doesn't take too many shenanigans of that kind to drive the best rabbit dog to drink.

Hunters new to the swamp hare's ways often make the mistake of trying to follow the dogs. That's an unproductive method of hunting. It's far better to get ahead of the chase and try to intercept it. About as good a procedure as any is to go to the place where the rabbit was jumped, pick a stand and wait there, even though the hounds go out of hearing at the far side of the swamp. Sooner or later they usually come back, and about the time you head for them the odds are good the rabbit will be heading back to you. It's better to stay put and keep still, and wait for him to show.

Above all, don't talk, move around or make commotion while you're waiting. If you're in the right place and do nothing to spook him the swamp hare will all but hop into your lap. More than once I've had them come up within two or three paces, stop and sit and look around, without knowing I was there. But when that happens take your shot in a hurry. The big-footed spook is nervous ahead of dogs and nothing in the woods knows more about vanishing in one quick jump.

Snowshoe hunting is good from the time the season opens until it ends, whenever that may be. Some states have no closed season on the swamp hares. I have had excellent hunting around the middle of October, but tracking snow helps in finding rabbits and adds greatly to the fun, and the time I like best of all is midwinter, when the snow is three or four feet deep in the north-country swamps, powder dry and light as feathers. Under those conditions the hunter has to wear snowshoes, the rabbit has grown his own many weeks before, and only the dogs are left at a disadvantage.

Winter hunting calls for big dogs, something taller than the standard beagle, with plenty of staying power. Most hunters prefer a dog with fox-hound blood or a large beagle with long legs.

The rabbit skips along over the snow as light as milkweed silk, sinking no more than a few inches. The hunter gets through brush and over logs as best he can on his webs, and he's an expert if he doesn't take a header every now and then. The dogs wallow along with only their backs and heads showing, literally swimming in snow and plowing a deep furrow as they go. It's a game the rabbit plays with ease, and often wins.

On a hunt of that kind a few winters ago three of our dogs started a big, long-winded hare and drove him (ran is hardly the right word) for more than an hour. Two young hounds finally played out and quit. The third, a determined oldtimer, wouldn't give up. The rabbit got down to small circles, and I made my way along a logging road to a place where I thought he'd cross. After a few minutes I saw him coming. He was in no hurry. He'd hop behind a log, sit for a few seconds, duck under a low-hanging snow-loaded evergreen, wait some more, make two or three lazy jumps to the shelter of a big stump.

Then I saw the dog coming, too. He was less than a hundred feet behind the rabbit, but he had slowed to a walk and was floundering along, one weary step at a time. About every third or fourth step he'd lift his head clear of the snow and blast out a defiant bawl to let his boss know he was still on the job. The rabbit came close enough at last and showed himself in the open, and I wrapped things up.

A hunter on snowshoes crosses an open ridge and heads into thick cover, with his hound ranging ahead to bounce out a white hare. When the snow gets deep in the swamps and woods of the north country, the hunter needs snowshoes, the dog wallows—and the rabbit bounds along the top as light as thistledown.

That old hound had no further interest in bunny tracks that day.

Another factor that handicaps the dogs and gives the rabbit a break in midwinter hunting is dry, loose snow falling into the track, apparently deadening the scent and making it hard to follow. A good dog can handle that pretty well, however. I've seen experienced hounds run snowshoes when I thought they were relying on sight more than on smell.

The trait that does most to win my admiration for the swamp hare is his determination to stay on top of the ground, and I think most hunters who know him agree. No matter how far he is driven or how hard the dogs crowd him, he takes his chances without holing. Even when wounded he seldom does more than crawl into a windfall or thicket. Other hunters tell me that once in a while they have driven a snowshoe into a hole, but in a

lifetime of hunting 'em it has never happened to me.

It's on that score that Lightfoot avoids the worst fault of the cottontail. As soon as cold weather arrives, at least in the northern states, the little gray rabbit is likely to bolt for the nearest stonepile or woodchuck den the minute he is jumped, and if he is crippled by shot he is almost certain to seek haven in a hole. I have known a snowshoe, on the other hand, to stay ahead of a dog for half a day on bare ground in a very thick swamp. Apparently it never occurred to him that he could get out of danger by going underground.

All told, about the only flaw in this turncoat rabbit's makeup, so far as the hunter is concerned, is the fact that his population soars and plunges in periodic cycles, swinging from almost incredible abundance to almost total disappearance.

The mysterious die-off of the north-country hares every few years, reaching unbelievable proportions in times past, has long puzzled hunters and game researchers alike. Nowhere has it shown up more clearly than in the fur records of the Hudson's Bay Company in the far north of Canada, where the snowshoe rabbit is the bread and butter of the lynx.

Years of rabbit abundance coincide roughly with years of lynx abundance. When the rabbit supply falls off the lynxes likewise go down in numbers, and these recurring times of plentitude and scarcity beat like a slow pulse through the fur records for more than a century, at about ten-year intervals, five of feast and five of famine.

In his *Life Histories of Game Animals,* Ernest Thompson Seton, the ace wildlife writer of a generation or more ago, quotes figures on the lynx harvest that tell the story graphically. In 1896, he relates, the Hudson's Bay Company took in 56,000 lynx pelts. By 1900 the take was down to 4,400, but by 1906 it had climbed back to 61,000. A few years later it fell again to less than 10,000, and each rise and fall in the lynx take reflected a time of boom or bust among the snowshoes.

Seton also relates the story of a dramatic die-off, to show what was happening. He tells of seeing as many as 10,000 rabbits to a square mile (that's a tremendous population, more than fifteen to the acre) in the MacKenzie River valley one year, and of camping for seven months in that same region three or four years later without sighting a rabbit.

If Seton's estimate was correct, the snowshoes apparently reach vastly greater numbers in the far north than along the southern border of their range. I have never heard of an example anywhere in the northern United States to compare with the one cited by him. In northern Michigan, where I have done most of my hunting, a population of a few hundred to the square mile is high.

Wherever they are found, however, they rise and fall in cycles and it is not unusual for them to all but disappear from places where they have been extremely plentiful only a year or two before. I recall one fall when I hunted deer in a remote area on Drummond Island, at the north end of Lake Huron, when the hares were so abundant that we could pick off the makings of a camp hassenpfeffer in a few minutes by walking along the edge of a swamp and beheading three or four with our deer rifles. A year later we returned to that same spot and camped a week, but did not see a rabbit. No hunting had been done in the meantime, either, for the place was too inaccessible for rabbit hunters to bother with.

The cause of the ups and downs is still unknown. Various theories, including disease, predators and starvation, have been advanced but have failed to stand up, and the reason for the cycles is as much a mystery today as before modern game research got under way. "They appear as if by magic and disappear just as mysteriously," says Dave Jenkins, a mammalogist in the Michigan Department of Natural Resources.

About the only good thing about the cycles is the fact that just as surely as Bigfoot vanishes he will come back. He's been doing it for centuries and there's little danger he'll change his ways. When his numbers are low hunting is lean. But when his numbers are high they are very high, and you'll never get better shotgunning behind hounds than he supplies then.

11

SQUIRRELS

The fun of hunting bushytails

Some of the best squirrel shooting I have had was from a corner of an old-fashioned rail fence where a cornfield bordered squirrel woods. The bushytails moved in and out of the field, harvesting corn, and a fair share of them used the top rail of the fence for a runway. On a sunny, windless October afternoon it made for lively action. It also hints at one of the secrets of successful autumn squirrel hunting—waiting patiently for the squirrels to show themselves.

More than once I have walked through a farm woodlot where there was plenty of squirrel sign, moving slowly and quietly, without catching sight of so much as a flirting tail vanishing around a tree trunk. But if I found a log or stump in a promising location and sat quietly for half an hour or so, I was almost sure to score.

The smartest squirrels are found in open country, and in general the fox squirrel is more wary than the gray. But whichever one you hunt, you are likely to find him educated, wary of man, forever on guard and ready to flatten on a branch or dive into a den

A hunter uses the weapon that many squirrel fans like best, a scoped .22 rifle. Although most squirrel hunting is done with a shotgun, the hunter with the patience to wait in the right place can enjoy exciting and productive sport with a .22. Some rely on binoculars to spot the squirrels in trees.

at the first hint of danger. That makes waiting them out one of the surest ways to get the best of them.

This method has one other advantage, especially for the pheasant hunter in country where there are woodlots that harbor squirrels. By midmorning there is almost unfailingly a lull in pheasant hunting, one that lasts until the middle of the afternoon or later. The ringnecks have finished their morning feeding and retired into thick cover for a midday siesta. That's an ideal time for the hunter to find a spot in the nearest squirrel woods and rest his own legs.

Squirrels have filled in the lean hours of bird hunting for me more times than I can remember. They have also supplied an excuse for me to take a breather after two or three hours of tramping through the heavy cover of swales, marshes and ditchbanks.

The waiting method is one that pays off only after nuts and acorns have begun to fall and corn has ripened, however. In southern Michigan, where I have done most of my squirrel hunting, that means October. Squirrels are on the ground then, gathering and storing their food supply for winter.

I have known a few hunters, but no more than a handful, who used a scoped .22 and good binoculars for that kind of squirrel hunting. They find a natural blind at the edge of woods or build one—a little brush stuck into the ground around a stump, in front of a log or in a fence corner is all that's needed—sit quietly and wait for the squirrels, alerted when they approached the place, to resume normal activities. They glass the surrounding trees until they spot one, and pick him off.

Often it means waiting for up to an hour, and the bulk of the shooting is at seventy-five yards or more. At least a 4x scope is needed, plus limitless patience. But the rewards are very satisfactory. Even small woodlots, farm groves and open patches of timber often hold a surprising number of squirrels if they have a supply of food, den trees and water nearby.

One of these wait-'em-out hunters once told me, "Once a fox squirrel has heard gunfire a time or two in his home woods he turns into one of the wariest small-game animals alive. The average hunter, walking through a woodlot and seeing no squirrels, is likely to conclude that they have been shot out, but the chances are he's wrong. More often they're still there, sitting quietly at the door of a den, watching him go by." Waiting in a blind with a scoped rifle is one way to fool these smart ones.

Earlier in the year, when squirrels are "cutting," that is feeding in the trees on green hickory nuts and other mast, stalking is a more productive way to hunt them.

Many states open their squirrel season in August now, on the theory that most of the young are out of the dens by that time and hunting is at its best. In the past some states in the southern squirrel range have opened as early as June, to enable hunters to take young animals from the early litters. Those are the ones that supply the best makings for a squirrel pie.

Many sportsmen object to the early seasons, however, on the ground that females with late litters still in the nest are bound to be killed, leaving suckling young to die of starvation. The charge is well founded. A study by the Indiana Department of Conservation twenty years ago indicated that as many as eighty-five young gray squirrels were lost for each one hundred killed legally by hunters. Some died when pregnant females were shot, the rest starved in the nests. In the case of fox squirrels the ratio was sixty-eight young lost for each one hundred harvested.

The early seasons are something I have never liked, for that reason and also because the weather is too warm and the foliage too heavy for good hunting. To me squirrel shooting in July or August involves too many objectionable consequences.

State game men counter, however, by pointing out that there is not a month between late winter and fall where there are no young squirrels dependent on the females. The Indiana study revealed that litters were born from February through October in that state, making it difficult if not impossible to set hunting seasons that would not involve the taking of some nursing females.

The ideal time for a season is after summer litters have been weaned but before mast is on the ground, concluded biologist John Allen, who conducted the study, but he admitted that dates must be a compromise. He pointed out that a late season, not opening until October, tends to reduce squirrel hunting to a secondary sport.

Not every hunter is aware of its popularity and importance. The bushytail harvest in many states averages from one to two million animals a year. But at that the squirrel population today is no more than a patch on that of pioneer times. Squirrels were so plentiful then in the woods of the eastern United States that they were a serious pest, destroying corn and other crops of the settlers. Many states paid a bounty on them, and it was not unusual for a hunter to take a hundred scalps in a day or for up to two thousand to be killed in an organized shoot.

Early writers tell of squirrels so plentiful that a hunter could kill twelve or fifteen in one tree, of twenty thousand shot in a week, of incredible migrations in which animals by the hundreds of thousands moved from one area to another, crossing streams and rivers on the way.

Those days are long gone and the squirrel population has suffered a tremendous decline since the bounty days, but it is still sufficiently large to put squirrels close behind the cottontail rabbit in importance as game.

The two that supply this hunting, the gray and the fox, are not found in abundance in the same habitat, although their ranges overlap to some extent in many states.

The gray squirrel is an animal of forested country, fond of big woods or densely timbered river bottoms, and spending most of its life in trees. The fox squirrel prefers the edges of woods, farm woodlots and other small tracts of timber, and does more feeding on the ground.

In Ohio, Indiana and Illinois, for instance, gray squirrels are confined largely to the timbered hill country in the southern half of each state, while fox squirrels are found in farming country wherever there are enough food and den trees to meet their requirements.

The gray is the smaller of the two,

averaging a pound and a half in weight. A big fox squirrel may weigh two or even three pounds.

As for black squirrels, they are not a separate species but rather a color phase of the gray, common in some areas. I have hunted in places in northern Michigan, notably around Petoskey and on Beaver Island, where the chances of killing one in the black phase were better than taking a gray. Authorities say, incidentally, that the blacks occur very rarely south of a line drawn across the country from St. Louis to about the vicinity of New York City.

Another color phase of the gray, the white, is found in a few places. The city of Olney, in southeastern Illinois, has a colony of about one thousand, descended from a pair of albino grays released by a saloon keeper in 1902. White squirrels are found in limited numbers widely scattered over that state, protected from hunters wherever they occur.

For the squirrel hunter who likes to do his hunting early, August can be a productive month. Through the spring and early summer squirrel diet consists chiefly of nuts stored in the ground the previous autumn, tree buds, berries and wild fruit. But once hickory nuts and walnuts are big enough the bushytails turn to them and the presence of cuttings, gnawed chips of the green hulls, strewn on the ground under the food trees are a sure giveaway.

Early morning and late afternoon are the prime times to hunt, especially for grays. The gray is abroad shortly after dawn, feeds for an hour or two, retires to his den and is not likely to move out again until two or three hours before dusk. The fox squirrel does not get up as early and often remains active all day, especially when he is gathering and storing food on the ground. That is the time when the hunter who plays a waiting game is most likely to be amply rewarded for all his patience.

The most successful hunters scout their hunting grounds ahead of time for signs of squirrel abundance. Newly built leaf nests in the trees and small holes in the ground where the animals have dug for last year's cached nuts are sure evidence of a population.

In addition to stalking, and waiting quietly for a squirrel to show up or betray its presence by barking, there is another way of hunting that can pay off for two partners working as a

The gray squirrel (left) is found in forested country, spending most of his life in trees, and is more wary than his next of kin, the fox squirrel (below). The latter likes farm woodlots and the border of woods, and does considerable feeding on the ground. These differences call for different hunting techniques.

team, especially after the leaves have fallen in the autumn. They move quietly through a squirrel woods, fifty to seventy-five yards apart, alternately walking and standing. One moves ahead, then stops and watches while his partner overtakes him. Often a squirrel will rivet its attention on the hunter who is moving, and flirt around a tree in plain sight of the other member of the team. This is hardly more than a variation of the old trick two hunters resort

Hunter and his dog watch a squirrel sail across an open space from one tree to another. Both the gray and fox are accomplished aerialists, able to travel through the treetops at top speed, and hard to see when the woods are in foliage.

to if they tree a squirrel but are unable to spot it. One stands quietly while the other makes a commotion on the opposite side of the tree. Nine times out of ten this will bring the squirrel around for a shot by the partner who is not moving.

One of the most interesting and productive methods of squirrel hunting I know about is one I have not tried. It's warmly recommended by Bill Scifres, a top-notch Indiana outdoorsman of my acquaintance. He calls it squirrelishing, and as the term suggests, it's a combination of squirrel hunting and fishing.

Squirrel season normally opens in mid-August in Bill's home state and runs until about mid-October. That's a period that also sees some very good Hoosier bass fishing, and as a result Bill frequently found himself in a quandary. If he went after bass wind or weather might make him wish he were hunting squirrels instead, and vice versa. Finally he decided to wrap the two up in one package. It can be

176

done any place squirrels and fish are found together, and since the bushytails frequent timber near water picking the right spot is usually not difficult.

Scifres chooses a river or stream that he can fish by wading or walking the banks. On streams that are big enough and free of obstructions, it can also be done from a boat, but Bill prefers to wade or walk. He keeps his outfit as light as possible. He needs a rod to fish with and a gun for the squirrels, a shoulder-strap bag to carry lures and tackle in, and an old gunny sack with a drawstring, hung on his belt, to enable him to keep his fish alive. His squirrels go in the game pocket of a hunting coat or shooting vest.

If the weather is chilly he wears the hunting coat and chest-high waders. If it's warm he prefers old trousers, a pair of wading shoes, and the shooting vest worn over a light, long-sleeved shirt.

Because he was brought up handling a single-shot .22 (by a father who had a reputation for killing squirrels where there weren't any) that is the weapon of his choice. For those not accustomed to a rifle, he does not recommend it, however. A single-barrel shotgun is likely to let the hunter hang up a better score. A lightweight .410 is not too much heavier than the .22, and is an ideal gun for this hunting. Bill does not suggest a scope, for the reason that the rifle gets

hard use and may even go under water from time to time.

Whatever gun the squirrelisher chooses, Scifres recommends a single-shot only. For a hunter chest-deep in the current of a stream the muzzle of a gun can be dangerous, and it's easier to be sure that a single-shot rifle or shotgun is not loaded. That should be done only when a squirrel is located and the hunter is ready to shoot. Scifres carries three or four shells in a shirt pocket, where he can get at them in a hurry.

He hangs his rifle on his back by a shoulder strap or shoves it muzzle-down into the back of his waders. To play doubly safe he keeps the action open until he is ready to load and shoot, and after the gun has been fired he checks very carefully to make sure it has not been reloaded, before he returns it to his back.

He prefers to wade upstream, for the sake of keeping behind him any roil or disturbance he creates in the water. He fishes as if that were his sole interest, but keeps an eye on the timber along the banks, watching and listening for a squirrel moving in the trees, cutting on a green walnut or just sitting and watching him.

"It may be hard to believe that a man can hold a rod and shoot a squirrel with a rifle," Bill says, "but if you do it right the rod becomes a rest for the gun. I hold the rod about a foot from the handle in the palm of my left hand and rest the butt on or

177

against my left shoulder. The stock of the rifle is against my right shoulder and the forearm rests on top of the rod in my left hand. Gun, rod and shoulders form a triangle, and by bearing down with my left hand I can hold the .22 as steady as a rock."

He admits that he can't remember ever bringing in a limit of both bass and squirrels on the same trip, but it's a rare day of squirrelishing that does not supply a full platter for the Scifres supper table, fried bass on one end, fried squirrel on the other. And the action while you are gathering those makings leaves little to be desired.

There is one other way to hunt squirrels, and many rate it the best of all. That is with a dog.

I have never owned a squirrel dog but it has been my good fortune to have a few friends who did. At the present time, for example, my neighbor Freeman Peace has a 13-inch beagle named Queen that is one of those once-in-a-lifetime (and not in every lifetime, either) dogs that will hunt whatever her boss puts her on.

Free gathers in an average of fifty coon pelts a fall with that little hound and if a cottontail bounces out under her nose when she is running a coon she doesn't even know it's there. But take her out to a brushy swale the next morning and turn her loose on a rabbit track, and she runs it as gleefully as if she had never smelled coon scent in her life. In the right

place and under the right circumstances, she will also hunt squirrels and do all the right things.

She happens to be the only hound I have known that developed into a good squirrel dog, but that is no more than a matter of chance, for squirrel dogs come in all sizes, shapes and breeds. The first one I knew, when I was a boy on the farm, was a collie that showed equal aptitude for squirrels, rabbits and mink. Most of the squirrel dogs I have encountered since were terriers or small feists.

Whatever their blood line or size, they all had in common the ability to find a squirrel in a patch of timber, track it and run it up a tree, bark underneath until the hunter arrived, and follow the squirrel if it tried to get away by traveling through the branches.

A squirrel treed by a dog is less likely to go for its den than one put up by a man, incidentally. Apparently it reasons that as long as it stays in the tree it has nothing to fear from the dog, and most of the time it makes no real effort at a getaway.

There is special excitement in sending a dog into a woodlot on a warm October afternoon, when yellow leaves and nuts are coming off the hickories together, waiting for the sudden excited yapping, hurrying to the tree and walking slowly around it until the squirrel is spotted flattened in a high fork, with the dog

A squirrel dog trots up to a squirrel he helped the hunter find and kill. Whatever the breed, a dog that will locate and follow squirrels and bark at the tree is the best help a hunter can have.

telling you all the time that you can take his word it's up there.

Although many squirrel hunters, probably a majority in fact, use shotguns today, the squirrel remains a favorite animal of small-bore riflemen.

There is great satisfaction in bringing a fat gray or fox squirrel out of the top of a tall hickory with a .22. It's a tradition that harks back to the days of the Kentucky squirrel rifle, when marksmen avoided putting a ball into the squirrel itself but took the animal by "barking" it instead, shooting away a chip of the bark on which it was flattened and bringing it down by stunning. This kind of accuracy was practiced by Daniel Boone and other noted frontiersmen, and by countless ordinary squirrel hunters in pioneer times.

There are few riflemen nowadays who could bark a squirrel if they tried. But there are many, addicted to the .22, for whom the gray or the fox play the same role the whitetail deer plays for those who hunt with rifles of heavier caliber.

No form of small-game hunting in America has behind it a longer or more colorful line of tradition than squirrel hunting, and none is more deserving of the popularity it enjoys. As an old squirrel hunter of my acquaintance once told me, "You may not kill more than three or four in a morning but it's gosh-awful good fun!"

12

RACCOON

Hounds in the dark of night

No game animal in this country is more completely nocturnal than the raccoon. There are many others that prefer darkness to daylight but they're not as strict about it as he is. Deer do some wandering around the clock, bears prowl and feed whenever they are hungry, even the sly and furtive bobcat and mountain lion hunt in broad daylight if they feel like it. And while the fox does most of his traveling at night he is not averse to an occasional cross-country trot at high noon, nor are the wolf and coyote.

Not so the coon. Almost without exception he stays in his den until early dark, comes out to roam and feed through the night, and goes back into seclusion at the first hint of daybreak. It's close to unheard of to find a coon abroad by day unless he has been disturbed and compelled to move.

As a consequence, coon hunting has always been a nighttime sport. The hunters start out shortly after dark, as soon as coons are on the ground. With the approach of morning

181

the hunt ends, unless men and dogs have played out before that, which is usually the case.

Successful coon hunting depends on three things: good dogs, territory with a plentiful coon population, and hunting that territory to the best possible advantage. The dogs come first, for without them there is no coon hunting.

An ace coon hound has three jobs to do. He must be a strike dog, able to find and pick up coon scent that is often many hours old and as stale as leftover coffee. Next he must unravel and run the track, across dry fields and through wet swamps, in rain and frost, around lakes and streams and ponds, in and out of water, matching wits with every trick the coon pulls. Finally he must be a tree dog with the know-how to decide, when the trail goes up, whether the coon really climbed or changed its mind, sure in his decisions and honest in his announcements, with the sense to let the world know where he is and what has happened, plus persistence to stay and keep on barking until the boss comes along, all night if necessary.

When you get a dog that will do all those things and do them well, and pay no mind to anything save coon, you've got something that doesn't come along every day.

How do you pick one? The first thing is to go to a reliable dealer or breeder. If you're buying a dog old enough to hunt, that's one thing. If you're starting from scratch with a pup, that's something else. In the case of an older dog test him before you put your money down, and then buy on the basis of performance only. Remember it costs no more to feed a top-notcher than a stumble-bum. But don't take him home, try him by yourself, and expect him to do his best. Coon hounds are temperamental. Many will turn in a top performance only for the man they're used to, and it may take yours a month or more to get used to you. So go out with his owner or trainer and size him up under favorable conditions.

In choosing a pup, look first of all for one from a good blood line, with at least three generations of straight cooners behind him. A straight cooner is a dog that will run nothing else. They're not too common and they're worth whatever they cost.

Your pup should be at least eight to ten weeks old before you buy him. That will give you a chance to look for desirable qualities, such as alertness, intelligence, and good head and chest formation.

At about three months start taking him on short walks, teaching him obedience, how to get through fences on his own, and not to molest cattle or other domestic stock. Real training should begin at five or six months if the legal training season permits. It's essential to keep the dog kenneled at all times. Allowed to run loose, he'll chase something and rabbits are likely to be the game most available. Kenneled and properly trained, he never finds out what rabbits are.

Start him hunting by taking him out with old and proven dogs. No young hound belongs in the party when you're breaking in a pup. For the first few nights choose an area where there's little water and where the dogs are likely to tree any coon they strike. It doesn't do to discourage a pup by making things too tough for him at the outset.

Turn him loose with the old dogs and let him learn from them. If he has the right stuff in him don't be surprised if he starts treeing the first or second night out. Then, if the coon season is open, shoot the coon down dead. Your pup has no judgment and he'll dive in and grab the hot end of a crippled coon every time. Don't let him get chewed up at first if you can help it. Some pups will take a split nose or riddled ear without a whimper, but others lose their starch and it takes them a long while to get over it. Better not let it happen to a beginner. Drop the coon, pull the old dogs off, let the pup rassle him, and go on with your hunt.

There is no bigger mistake than to overwork a pup until he plays out and heels. He's likely to get the notion that's where he belongs. Work a pup only when he really wants to go, maybe two or three times a week, until he is a year or more old, try to

keep him out of water and tough country, and if he shows signs of tiring put him in the car and go home.

One other thing to avoid is letting a big, mean coon whip your dogs in water while the pup is along. Get in and tip the scales if you have to. A pup soundly trounced in water is likely never to develop into a really good water dog.

Now and then a promising pup develops gun-shyness. That's a bad trait, but most of the time you can cure it. Take the youngster out with an old dog and a .22 and do a little shooting. Chances are the old dog will give him the moral support he needs. He seems to say to himself, "If it doesn't hurt that character it won't hurt me." But if gunfire still spooks him, take him hunting, tree a coon and have a partner hold and pet him while you shoot. When the coon falls and the old dogs dive in, let the pup join the fun. Two or three treatments of that kind usually turn the trick. Never let a gun-shy pup run away from shot if you can help it. Once that happens you're likely to have an incurable dog on your hands.

By this time, if you are a beginner just getting started, you probably are wondering where you're going to get the old hound to train your youngster with. The answer is that under those circumstances the best investment you can make is to buy an old

On a dark, moonless night, a treed coon stares down from his perch in a scrubby, thorny tree (left). Such nights are best for coon hunting, especially if they are windless and the ground is damp enough to hold scent.

and proven dog at the outset. Go on from there as you like. Acquire and develop a pup to take the place of the old dog when he outlives his usefulness, or continue to buy trained hounds ready for the field, as you prefer. But unless you start with at least one good, experienced dog your chances of getting off to the right sort of beginning are slender, and you may even get discouraged and give up altogether.

The top problem in the training of a coon hound is to keep him from running other game. Over most of the country today, unless he is rabbit-proof, foxproof and deerproof he's worse than useless, and the real coon hunter wants his dogs possumproof, skunkproof and housecatproof as well. That's a big order, but the perfect coon dog runs nothing but coon.

How do you go about developing the straight cooners that are the hope and pride and joy of every coon hunter? There's no secret about it, no magic formula, and it's easier than many hound owners think.

As the young dog gains age and

A sure-nosed tree dog bawls the announcement that he has put the coon up. A good tree dog, correct in his decisions and persistent enough to stay and bark until the hunter comes to him, is essential.

185

experience, take him into places with more off-game, but take him only with your best dogs. Let him profit from their example. They don't fool with rabbit or possum or fox and if he comes from the right stock the odds are he won't either. If he does take a rabbit or deer track, when the old dogs refuse to join him he's likely to give it up and come back after a very short run. Such training, plus keeping the youngster in nothing but good company until he is three or four years old, is the key to proofing against off-game.

But if you hunt territory where deer are plentiful, as they are over much of the best coon range in the country nowadays, the problem is tougher. Deer leave strong scent, are big and exciting, and offer temptation it's hard for a young dog to resist. So if you have a pup that promises to be all right in every other way but persists in running off-game (chances are that deer, not rabbits or other small fry, will be his downfall) better fall back on an electric shock-collar.

Next comes the training that produces a good tree dog. It's the theory of the most successful hunters I know that the best ones are born; you have no need to train them. They tree very young, on anything that climbs, and get better at it as they go along.

But there are ways to train the youngster that isn't a natural. If he comes in on a tree where a coon has climbed and is still there, but goes horsing off on other business, get hold of him and chain him just out of reach of the spot where the coon is going to fall. Leave the other dogs loose and shoot the coon down. When they dive in for the final fracas and he can't join them he'll go nuts. Don't give in. Keep him out of the affair, bag your coon and go looking for another. A few frustrations of that kind and if he's ever going to be a tree dog he'll be ready to bark as loud and stay as long as any hound in the pack. Once he is treeing well, make things up to him by tying the rest of the dogs and letting him have a few coons all to himself. That will clinch the deal for keeps.

Don't expect a straight cooner and perfect performance before your dog is six or seven years old, at least not in states where the coon season runs for no more than two or three months a year. If you can hunt legally the year around you may develop him to perfection sooner than that, maybe in three or four years. Much depends on the country and the coon. Any pup can tree a kit in flat open farmlands, but it calls for a lot of savvy and experience to unravel the trail of a tough old boar through water and force him to climb. The really infallible coon hounds I have hunted behind have been, without exception, not less then seven years old.

When you've got the dog you want and it comes to the actual hunting, pick good territory first of all. Look for a fertile, productive farming area. Coons, like any other animal, are most numerous where their food is most plentiful. They also like water and if you can find a place that combines corn with streams, lakes and bogs you're in clover.

Finally, don't overlook the acorn crop. Given their free choice, coons probably prefer acorns to corn. The reason you find them in cornfields more often than in oak woods is that corn is always available, while acorns aren't. But in good acorn years any patch of timber is worth a visit.

In the North your best bet is fields of standing corn. In the South, where coons do not hibernate and so have no need to fatten, you rarely find them in such fields. The favorite areas for southern coons are creek bottoms and swamps, where wild fruit, acorns, frogs and crawfish are plentiful. In prairie country cornfields and river bottoms share honors as the hotspots.

It's a good plan to go out ahead of hunting season and look for sign, tracks along creeks and ponds, places where coons have been feeding. Also ahead of season the hunter should call on farmers and ask permission to hunt. Coon hunters are welcome on most farms if they behave themselves (it's a good idea to invite the host along now and then) but the farmer is likely to want to know when they are going to pay him a visit. Awakened in the small hours by strange hounds tearing the night apart in his front yard, he's not going to like it. Better introduce yourself and make your arrangements in advance.

Den trees mean little in sizing up the local coon population. The animals den in too many queer places for trees to tell much. They prefer a hollow tree to any other site if they can find one, but they'll settle for such oddball locations as drain tiles, woodchuck, fox and badger holes, crevices in cliffs, hollow logs, muskrat houses, and small caves under upturned stumps, hummocks and bogs. In early fall, before the weather gets bad, they like to sun themselves in squirrel nests or the empty nests of hawks and crows. They'll even live at that time of year in dense cattail thickets in a swamp. They often shack up in barns, sheds, abandoned buildings, or the lofts of country churches and schoolhouses. A barn coon is a toughie to run, incidentally. He takes off for home like a housecat and if he makes it and the dogs start raising hell around the place before you can get there you're usually in trouble.

Hunting methods depend on the area, the dens and feeding places in it, weather, time of year, location of the nearest water, wind direction,

A young coon goes to the top of a small tree to get away from the hounds. Bigger and wiser coons like bigger trees, and once they are sheltered in a high fork they are often canny enough to avert their head so the light of the hunter cannot shine their eyes.

and size and age of the coon you are after.

Coons are animals of habit, but they change the habits as winter approaches, at least in the North. In early fall they leave their den at deep dusk, go for water first of all, then mosey to a feeding area and get their fill of fruit, frogs, corn, acorns or whatever they happen to fancy. In a field of uncut corn, where food is plentiful and cover heavy, they'll loaf around for two or three hours. Once their bellies are stuffed they climb and lie up until shortly before daylight, come down, feed again, go back to water and home to the den.

If you are putting your dogs down early in the evening pick cornfields near a swamp or woods, places a coon can reach with a minimum of travel. Fields a mile or more from cover should be saved for later in the night. You're likely to find big coon in those far-from-home spots, especially if the area hasn't been hunted previously, but you have to give them time to get there.

There's an added advantage in putting your dogs down in corn. You're likely to surprise coons at supper, and any track you strike is fresh. The hunter who starts in timber, guided by den trees, often has a job of cold trailing to do and by the time he catches up the coon may have climbed for its midnight nap.

In areas of marsh, lakes and bogs, where the hunting is likely to be tough, it's best to start near water and give the dogs a chance to push the coon away from it rather than toward it. For the same reason, seasoned hunters often put down close to farm buildings, hoping the chase will wind up some distance away, and in drain-tile country they start near the places where they know coons are denned. Sometimes a coon will circle

Hounds close in on a coon they have overtaken on the ground. Outweighed and outclassed, he is still ready to give a good account of himself. An old coon that has been treed and shaken down is likely to take his chances on the ground.

back and hole up in spite of all you can do, but your chances are best that way. The rule is simple: Begin where you don't want to finish.

If you want an easy chase look for a cornfield with timber or a tree-studded fencerow along one side, start the dogs at the opposite side and let things take their course. Most of the time there'll be a coon up a tree within ten minutes in such a place.

Whenever possible, hunt into the wind. Hunting downwind the dogs are likely to miss coons in corn and other places of heavy cover. Also, if the chase is a long one, it's far easier to keep the dogs in hearing if you have the wind in your favor.

Weather has everything to do with success. Plenty of hunters think a wet rainy night is best, but the best men I know do not agree. They say that on misty nights after rain scent tends to wash out and the dogs turn in a poor performance.

The best conditions are a dark, moonless night, cloudy but with no rain that day, with the ground wet enough to hold scent. Coons travel far and wide in such weather and the dogs can run a track like greased lightning. Shun nights of full moon, but if you do go out at such times hunt the thickest swamps you can find. Coons like to stay in heavy cover when the moon is bright.

In dry weather lowlands not too far from water are the best bet, and in exceptionally dry periods hunt along creeks and the borders of ponds and lakes. Coon are reluctant to leave water in time of drouth.

On nights of high wind, better stay home. Good coon dogs range widely. They're likely to strike beyond hearing at such times, and it's also hard to follow them once the chase is under way. Other nights to avoid are those when the ground is freezing or there's a hard, black frost. Coons are hard to trail then. And don't hunt on snow, for every ringtail in the country heads for home as soon as even a wet fall starts.

Once the first snow or hard freeze comes, they lie up until the weather breaks. They'll resume feeding then but are far less active than they were earlier, coming down only every two or three nights, avoiding the cold crisp, nights of moonlight altogether, and traveling little. If they can no longer find standing corn they'll feed on shocked corn, but they dislike the open fields, fill up in a hurry and get out. And once winter arrives for good they den up. They'll move now and then on a thaw, even in January and February, but in the north the best of the fun is washed up by December.

Here and there around the country a few dedicated coon hunters have proven that, given the right conditions, coon can be hunted by daylight about as successfully as

Two hunters take a breather at the end of a successful chase. The true coon addict counts his sport worth all it costs in lost sleep, hard chases that sometimes last until daybreak, and the expense of keeping and training good dogs.

after dark. It's a novel sport, packing action and excitement of an unusual kind.

The right conditions mean two things. First, coon dogs that are sure-fire on a cold track and will do enough barking that they can be followed. Second, country and timber where at least a fair share of the coon population does not den up in hollow trees during hunting season.

The first time I sampled this method, a number of years ago, I accepted an invitation to hunt with a pair of dog men, friends of mine, at the northern Michigan town of Gaylord. That area has extensive evergreen swamps and coons frequently climb a thick spruce or cedar at daybreak and curl up among the branches for the day. Lacking a suitable evergreen, they may settle for a high fork in any tree, or an abandoned hawk nest if they can find one. Many take shelter in hollow stumps or stubs, or even dig a daytime nest in the top of an unused muskrat house.

For daytime hunting in such country, the dogs are put down shortly after first light, while scent is still fresh from coons that have fed or traveled back to their home dens during the latter half of the night. With luck, the dogs pick up a cold track in short order. If, when they unravel it, it ends in a hollow tree that winds things up, at least in Michigan, for this state's game laws

A cornered coon snarls defiance at the dogs. A tough old boar is able to put up a fight that wins the respect of hounds and hunter, and some dogs lose their reluctance to tackle one single-handed.

prohibit cutting or molesting such dens. But if the hounds track the coon to a hideout in the open, say in an evergreen, a stump or an empty nest, the rest is as simple as in after-dark hunting.

In my opinion, in general this daytime hunting does not match after-dark coon chasing for excitement, and it's done by no more than a handful of hound men. But the hunter can see where he's going and what's happening, and wherever the right conditions prevail it's an interesting way for coon-dog owners to get extra action of an entirely different sort.

So far I have talked only about the hunter's tricks. What about the coon's? He has a bagful. He's not as crafty as a fox, but he's not stupid either. He can't outrun the dogs, so he figures to outsmart them instead, and a fair share of the time he succeeds.

He'll circle and run in his own track, duck into grass or other thick cover, let the dogs run by and go back the way he came. If he crosses the track of another coon he'll follow it until he reaches a suitable place to fork off. One of his best tricks used to be running the top rail of a fence, maybe jumping to a tree without coming back on the ground. But there aren't enough rail fences left nowadays to make that profitable.

Water is his favorite ally. If he can get into it there's an even chance he'll throw the dogs off his track altogether. Failing that, there's also a chance he can whip the whole pack, maybe drowning a dog or two in the process. Not more than about one coon in twenty is big and savage enough to kill dogs, but you have to watch out for that one, especially if the chase leads into the vicinity of a river or small, narrow lake. The coon will swim across and the dogs are likely to be lured after him. Once they're in the water he turns back to meet them, climbs up on a hound's head, gets a good grip and forces the dog under. That hound is a goner unless you get there in a hurry.

Coons do clever things around water. On Washington Island, on the Wisconsin side of Lake Michigan, they have been known to run along shore at the very water's edge, where breaking surf washed out their tracks and left the best dog stymied. They'll get into a brushy pond, climb up and travel through the tops of the brush, back and forth and around and around, until they drive a dog

Water is the coon's natural ally. He swims readily, and often takes to a pond, lake or stream to shake the dogs off his track. Cornered in water, a big coon is capable of fighting off the hounds, even of holding one down until it drowns.

Tracks resembling those of a miniature bear show that a raccoon has prowled here, in the mud of a stream bank, looking for fish or frogs.

194

crazy. One November night a few falls ago a friend of mine, who lives on a small lake, was awakened at daylight by two dogs barking tree in his front yard. He found them tearing up shrubbery and raising cain generally under a big dead stub near the water. There was no coon on the stub but one long branch that overhung the lake furnished a clue, and sure enough, over by the opposite shore a V was spreading across the water and my friend looked that way just in time to see a big coon swim out of sight in the rushes.

Taking to a tree from water is a common coon trick, and so is climbing a tree some distance away and then traveling through the tops to the home den. They'll go up on a grapevine or clump of brush to gain time, jump and run again. In slashings where timber has been cut or in a big windfall they'll take to the tops and stay there, to the confusion of the most experienced dog. And once in a while you encounter one that seems to have wings. I recall an old boar that friends of mine ran five years in vain. His route and method of escape were the same every time. He'd take to a certain rail fence, run it, and vanish. There were trees near enough to the fence for him to jump onto, but he was never in those trees and nobody ever figured him out. So far as I know he died of old age.

The best chase you'll ever have is on an old coon that has been treed, shaken down and allowed to get away from the dogs. One lesson is all he needs and it's next to impossible to tree him thereafter, that night or for many nights to come. I know hunters who play that trick whenever they get a big buster up a tree, holding or tying the dogs while they shake him out, giving him enough time to get into cover—the start he needs depends on the territory—and then striking up the music all over again. There's little chance dogs will ever put that coon up again. He'll go into a dense swamp, a big cornfield or bog and marsh around a lake and play ring-around-the-rosy until they catch him on the ground or give up. The odds are he'll outlast the dogs, too.

But before you try that make sure your coon is old enough and big enough to take care of himself, for it's a sure-fire way to murder kittens. They'll run off a hundred yards or so and stop in grass or brush, where they're sitting ducks when the dogs are turned loose again.

The true coon hunter hunts for fun, not for pelts. It's the chase, the good dog work, the cunning and tricks of the coon that count, rather than the size of the kill. To the men who follow it, coon hunting is the greatest of all field sports, worth what they spend on their dogs, the sleep they lose, the weariness when they trudge home sometime toward dawn. Worth all that and more.

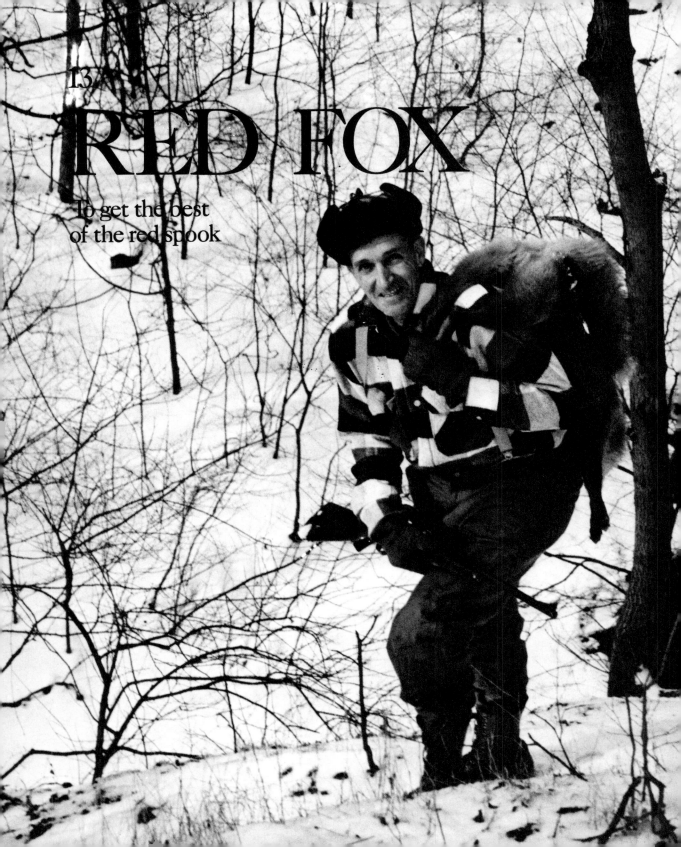

13

RED FOX

To get the best
of the red spook

As far back as I can remember, in our farm neighborhood in southeastern Michigan, there was a little handful of hunters who killed red foxes regularly by a method that everybody considered out of the ordinary and difficult in the extreme. They found a fresh fox track, preferably on new snow, and followed it on foot and without dogs until they got a shot.

It's a method you won't encounter in too many places, somewhat like stillhunting and driving deer, and the trophy, when you take one, is about as hard to come by. It's done only by sturdy and stouthearted characters, for without those qualifications they'd give up after their first hunt.

I remember Tuck Lake, who ran the last country store in our area, telling three of us one winter morning when we were ready to start out on a hunt of that kind, "Just remember one thing. A fox can walk farther in a day than a man can, and stand it better. When I see somebody go traipsing off on a fox track, I always wait to see who's going to hang whose hide on the side of the corncrib."

It started in our neighborhood close to a hundred years ago, the tricks and know-how handed down from one generation to another. It began with a woodsman named Pittenger, who moved to Michigan from Pennsylvania about the time of the Civil War. My grandfather used to relate a yarn about him coming home for supper, weary and famished after an all-day fox chase, and eating a whole pan of hot biscuits his wife had just taken out of the oven. When he finished he turned to her and complained, "Sairy, I wish you wouldn't make them things no more. You got no idea how they hurt my stummick."

Pittenger passed his hunting methods along to two sons, Clarence and George. They hunted foxes that way until they were nearing eighty, and they taught two or three neighbors what they knew about it. It was with that little group that I did most of my fox walking.

Although less than twenty miles from the sprawling outskirts of the automobile cities of Flint and Pontiac, ours was, up to a few years ago, a half-wild country of hills, lakes, woods, swamps and marshes, with many abandoned farms. Rabbits and pheasants were in fair supply, and there are still enough deer to keep a man's hopes up. And since the 1930's, in common with many other places, we have had more foxes than

we need. The men I hunted with accounted for an average of ten to fifteen a winter for more than twenty years.

The method is one I recommend wherever foxes and tracking snow are found in combination. It's a tough way of killing a fox, but it affords a lot of action while you are doing it and a wealth of satisfaction when it's done.

The hunter who takes a fox track needs to remember every minute that he is up against one of the wariest, craftiest and best equipped animals he will ever hunt. The word foxy didn't creep into our language without good reason.

A red fox can stand half a mile downwind from a farmyard and take inventory of everything that's going on, relying on his nose alone. He can sleep with one eye open and catch movement if you poke your hat brim over a rise of ground two-hundred yards away. He can hear a mouse squeak in the grass at forty paces. And his mental equipment is every bit as good as his nose, eyes and ears.

His kind has been matching wits with men and hounds for countless generations, and coming out ahead a fair share of the time. He's smart and suspicious, and takes very few chances. The hunter who claims his pelt by walking him down can figure he has earned the trophy, one way or another.

On top of that, the fox is a very

Trotting across an opening in snowy woods, a red fox is a picture of alertness and cunning. His wet and bedraggled tail reveals that he has been chased by dogs or men. When he is not driven, his brush is dry and fluffy. The fox hunter goes up against one of the wariest and craftiest animals in the woods.

199

Two hunters lead their hounds along the border of a woods,
a place where foxes like to travel and hunt. If they find a
track and run the fox, the chase will be exciting and long.

200

The telltale track of a fox in light snow, a straight line of footprints much like those of a small dog. The hunter who follows such a track, especially without hounds, is likely to be in for a long walk, but he can also expect the unexpected and plenty of excitement.

exciting animal to hunt, especially if you walk his track without dogs and count on taking him by stealth or ambush. I know of nothing else in hunting that beats the sight of a freshly jumped one streaking down a steep hill at top speed, with his tail fluffed out like an angry cat's, rotating round and round to help him keep his balance. He runs like red smoke in a high wind, and he's both a spine-tingling spectacle and a tough target. You can count on him to make the skin crawl on the back of your neck every time.

Once the hunter finds a fresh track, especially on new snow, he is not likely to have to follow it too far before putting the fox up. Usually a walk of less than a mile will do it. Left to himself, the range of Mr. Red is smaller than many hunters think. He is likely to live out most of his life in an area not more than three or four miles across, often less than that, and unless driven by dogs or pushed hard by hunters on foot he may not

201

cross the boundaries once a month. He has his home territory, knows every foot of it, and prefers to stay in it. Walk his track and drive him out of it, and almost every time he will work back into familiar country sooner or later. He may line out for a while or run a big circle, but a yearning for the swamps and hills of home finally overtakes him, just as it does a driven deer or rabbit.

The ideal time for track walking is when snow has fallen in the night, preferably up to two or three hours before daybreak. The hunters who come on a fresh track under those conditions can be sure that the fox is not far ahead. Most of the time he lies up for the day as soon as it begins to get light

Occasionally, although not often, hunters starting out on such a track are able to spot the fox bedded in the open before he realizes he is being hunted. If the day is sunny, he may be lying on the southern exposure of a hill, just over the crest where he is sheltered from the wind. He may also curl up in the lee of a haystack well away from farm buildings, or in the sun on the south slope of a plowed field where he can keep watch in all directions.

In such cases, if someone in the party is carrying a flat-shooting varminter rifle with a good scope, there is a fair chance of gathering in a fox pelt the easy way. Or there is even the possibility that the hunters can stalk within shotgun range if they watch the wind carefully and take advantage of hills, ravines and brushy fencerows.

Far more often, however, the track they are following leads into thick cover, maybe a weed-grown ravine, a tangle of sweet clover, a swale, woodlot or cattail marsh. If no track comes out on the far side they know where the fox is.

There are two ways of proceeding then. One hunter can wait where the track enters the cover, while one or two others, depending on the size of the party, circle around the area and come in from the opposite side, barking like hounds and making plenty of racket. If things go according to plan, which they don't always do, the fox will take his own track back and barrel out of his hiding place almost exactly where he went in. When that happens, the hunt is a short one.

The second technique, and it's the better one if only two hunters are working as a team, is for one to circle ahead, keeping out of sight, scent and hearing, and take a stand on the most likely crossing place. The partner then follows the track and drives the fox out.

That calls for intimate knowledge of the country and fox ways. The hunter who scores consistently must be familiar with every fox crossing for miles around, and be able to pick the right one a fair share of the time.

Killing the fox the first time he is jumped is anything but a sure bet. If he gets away the hunters stay on the track, outguess him if they can, or outlast him if there is no other choice.

"You just walk 'em up and then walk 'em down," George Pittenger told me when I first started to tag along with him, as a boy in my teens.

A ten-mile walk is routine, half again that far is not uncommon, and if the chase lasts all day twenty miles sets no record. Once or twice the winter dusk has found me a dozen miles from home, with no fox pelt to show for the long day, the walk home still ahead and supper hours away.

Mr. Red displays caution and cunning every minute he is traveling. He'll keep the wind behind him and pause for a look back as often as he comes to a vantage point on a hilltop. He'll pick the easiest going, across open fields, down drifted lanes, in the lee of fences. If there is bare ground at the edge of a woods he'll turn aside and follow it, trying to shake the hunters off his track.

While they walk, they have to watch ahead for places where he is likely to lie down and keep an eye on his back track. It may be in the open, but it's more likely to be in thick cover. Most often I have seen them jumped in swamps, brushy fields, under the tops of fallen trees, or from ditch-banks and weed-grown fence

corners. If the track leads into such a place, the hunting party deploys and repeats the performance they used the first time.

If the fox eludes them again, the best thing they can do—although not everybody has the patience for it—is to give him time to drop his guard before they take the track once more.

Almost every fox jumped on such a hunt, even if he is put out more than once, will give you a chance to overtake him if you play your part. He needs at least an hour, not followed or disturbed, to allow his nervous system to quiet down and let him decide that you are not really after him, after all.

When spooked, most of the foxes I have tracked ran full tilt a quarter mile or so, then stopped to look back, usually on a high place such as the top of a hill or on a stonepile, log or stump. Trail one on that first spurt and you are almost sure to find where he halted, sat down, got up, turned around, tramped the snow, itching to know whether a man was coming along on his track, reluctant to move on until he was sure.

If he sees you he's off again, maybe for another quarter mile or so, there to repeat the performance. And he's quite capable of keeping that up for the better part of a day without bedding if you crowd him and compel him to. As Tuck Lake said, he can travel farther than you can and stand it better.

If you give him time to get over his scare, however, if you stay out of sight and convince him that you just blundered across him and he has nothing to fear from you, he'll move on in no great hurry, maybe running for a short distance, then slowing to a trot. And not too far ahead, amost certainly within a mile or two, he'll lie down and give you another chance to sneak up on him.

There are various ways of putting in that vital hour while you wait. I know one highly successful hunter who, once the fox is up and going, turns and walks the other way, out of sight behind a thicket or over a hill. There he sits down, maybe eats his lunch, kills time somehow until he figures Mr. Red has forgotten all about him.

When he takes the track again he finds the same signs of alarm and hurry where the fox lit out, the place where it sat and watched, and the slowing down when it moved on. Nine times out of ten, not long after that the track will veer toward likely bedding places.

I know one hunter who practices this track walking by himself, without the help of partners. It calls for great skill and caution, but he makes it pay off. Not infrequently he is able to catch the fox in its bed and kill it before it is aware of his presence.

Weedy ravines are good places for that. When the track enters one, the hunter leaves it and walks parallel to it, just below the rim, watching the wind and taking advantage of weeds, brush and tall grass. My friend has even surprised the fox asleep a few times and shot it before it opened an eye.

For all his wisdom and cunning, there is one chink in Mr. Red's armor. He's a Nervous Nelly, too high strung and jittery for his own good, and if you push him hard enough and long enough he cracks under the pressure.

As long as things are going his way he stays crafty and cool. He can stand the travel and never bat an eye. After all, he often trots as far in a night of his own hunting as you drive him in a day. But relentless, dogged pursuit is another matter. It worries him, and the longer you follow him the more likely he is to panic and make a mistake.

I recall one fox, tracked the better part of a day, that broke out of a brushy fencerow when three of us came over a low rise of ground and spooked five deer feeding in a field of

A hunter lures a fox astonishingly close with a predator call. This technique has gained much popularity in recent years, in hunting both red and gray foxes. No other method will bring the fox within point-blank range.

picked corn close by. He was too far away to reach with BB's, but one of the party threw a shot at him anyway.

The deer bolted in the right direction, away from us. Not so the fox. He lost his head at the shot, scared out of his senses, and wheeled and ran blindly our way. We killed him at fifty yards as he streaked across the open field. He literally committed suicide.

Sometimes, if shot at beyond range, they race in crazy circles for minutes, rattled and trying to locate the shooting. One of my partners, Lee Caswell, in his early days of hunting missed a shot but scared the fox so badly that it plowed headlong into a woven wire fence. It bounced back, flat on its back with all four legs in the air, and Lee had plenty of time for a second shot before it could collect its wits, regain its feet and get going again.

I have even known one, harassed by day-long pursuit, to curl up and sleep so soundly that a hunter was able to pussyfoot up within a few feet of him before he took alarm.

This method of fox hunting has one added advantage. It's at its best in midwinter, when seasons on most game are closed and the shotgunner finds time hanging heavily on his hands. A day of fox walking is sure to cure that ailment.

There is another method of fox hunting that has gained a great deal of popularity in recent years. That is the use of a predator call. Both the red and gray fox come to a call readily, either on snow or bare ground, and it is one of the most exciting and suspense-filled field sports available to hunters wherever foxes are found. It is described in greater detail in Chapter 17.

Somewhat surprisingly, foxes are harder to hunt after the mating season arrives. You are likely to find two or three together then, but they travel farther, often moving by day as well as at night. Although the hunters I know keep at it as long as snow conditions are right, the best period is from the time of the first snow, in November or early December in our country, until about the end of January. The breeding season is at hand then and the chases are likely to be longer and less productive.

Often the fox hunter on a stand gets unexpected help from other wild creatures. Smaller birds and animals distrust and fear Mr. Red, for good reasons, and it's not unusual for them to give him away.

I sat one morning on a stump at the rim of a brush-grown ravine, while two hunting partners followed a track through a thick woodlot, hoping to push the fox past my stand.

It was a cold January day, the wind set me to shivering and the wait tried my patience. I was itching to move but I knew better. I had learned long before what it's likely to cost a man if he quits his place before a drive ends, whether he is hunting foxes, rabbits or deer.

A fox squirrel finally livened things up by frisking down off a tree to dig for snow-buried acorns. He was the right color, and the first glimpse I caught of him I mistook him for the fox. But the excitement was short-lived.

Another half hour dragged by, and I was fighting the growing temptation to leave the stump, when a hundred yards up the ravine I heard a ruffed grouse flush, its wing thunder startlingly loud in the stillness of the winter day. I knew something had put the bird up. Either one of my partners or the fox was coming.

I didn't have long to wait. A fox leaving a danger zone can travel like a red ghost and make just about as much commotion. I heard a small movement in the brush at the bottom of the ravine, and this one was streaking past. He had come the one hundred yards, from the place where he scared the grouse up, without making the slightest sound. But the bird had alerted me and I was ready for him.

Another time it was a bluejay that gave me a hand. There was a strange chain of circumstances involved that day. One of the hunters in our party disturbed an owl, the owl attracted the attention of the jay as it flew off, and the jay sounded a noisy alarm, calling angrily for a long minute. It hadn't even seen the fox. But the bird's outcry was all the hint Mr. Red needed. He didn't know the reason for the uproar, any more than I did, but he knew it signified an unhealthy neighborhood. He broke from a trot into a full run, on a course that brought him past my stand about forty yards behind me. He might have made it unseen had the jay not alerted me to the fact that something was coming.

I have known crows, and even an alarmed squirrel, to give a fox hunter a boost, too.

The strangest performance I have ever seen on a hunt for Mr. Red happened one day when four of us had followed a track from shortly after breakfast until past noon. It finally led down toward a cattail swale, and we stopped in the shelter of a fence corner to plan our next move.

While we watched the swale, a hen pheasant clattered up out of the cattails in sudden startled flight.

"That's queer," one of my partners remarked. "Pheasants don't get up like that in the middle of the day without a reason."

That was as far as he got. A second bird went flailing out, and close behind her a fox catapulted from the rushes, jumping for her like an excited dog, flipping end for end, all but turning himself inside out with frantic effort. He missed and she kept on going.

A minute later a third pheasant flushed, and again the fox hurled himself into the air behind it in a fruitless try. In all he drove six pheasants out, and after the first one he jumped hungrily for each of them as they cleared the cover. When the show ended he trotted nonchalantly out of the swale and swung off across the fields.

We were puzzled. It was hard to believe that a fox trailed as long and hard as this one had been would have the nerve and impudence to turn aside and fool around in that fashion, even to get himself a pheasant dinner.

Lester spoke for all of us when he said, "If I hadn't seen it with my own eyes I wouldn't have believed it."

Not until the fox was out of sight and we went into the swale did we learn what had really happened. It wasn't the one we had tracked that had tried to catch a meal on the wing; his track led around the border of the swale and across the fields in another direction. The fox that had put on the act for us was smaller, probably a vixen. Her tracks showed that she had come into the marsh earlier, maybe before daylight, and was lying curled on a dry bog when her nose picked up word of the pheasants and she went after them. She had no idea there were hunters anywhere in the neighborhood.

Then there was the fox my friend Walter Lentz encountered while he was hunting deer in cutover country in northern Michigan a number of years ago.

Walt had started to make a drive for two companions. The day was overcast and there was tracking snow on the ground. After about an hour, when he should have been coming out at the appointed meeting place, he cut a line of footprints. So far as he knew he and his party were the only hunters in the immediate vicinity. When a second look revealed that the tracks were his own he decided it was time to take inventory. He wasn't really lost, but he was sufficiently mixed up that he needed to get his bearings.

He was in an old slashing where logging operations had been completed years before. The place was pocked with stumps and grown up with thickets of young fir. Walt pulled out his compass, leaned his rifle across a log, stepped away a couple of paces and took a reading. When he looked up a red fox was standing in front of him about ten feet away, staring him straight in the face.

He had no idea how it got there. He had heard nothing and seen no movement. He had been making enough noise himself, crashing through the brush and trying to move deer ahead of him, to scare any normal fox out of the township. Yet there was Mr. Red, looking surprised and curious but not at all afraid.

Walt had never killed a fox. Not many hunters in our part of the country have. He decided instantly that he'd rather have that red pelt for his den than the biggest rack of deer antlers he'd ever take home. But his rifle was out of reach.

He stared at the fox for maybe a minute, trying to decide what to do, and neither of them moved a muscle. Then Walt took a cautious step backward and put out a hand for his gun, and the fox vanished in a thicket like a rust-colored spook.

That surprise encounter proves two things. First, nobody knows what Mr. Red may do. Second, although he is smart and wary, fast as forked lightning and elusive as a wisp of fog, every now and then he drops his guard and displays about as much gray matter as a porcupine.

Well, it's the unexpected that makes hunting exciting. Measured by that yardstick, fox walking can be very good indeed.

14

BOBCAT

The little cat that's big stuff

One of the least appreciated and most under-hunted game animals in the United States is a small bundle of dynamite wrapped in spotted fur, weighing an average of only twenty to thirty pounds but able to lick three times his weight in dog meat any day, with the disposition of a buzzsaw, the stealth of a shadow, and the guts and endurance to run ahead of hounds from daylight to dark if the circumstances make it necessary. I'm talking about the bobcat.

If I were making a list of American game worth hunting with hounds, I'd put the black bear at the top. For suspense and thrills nothing quite matches bear chasing in my book. Second place would go to the wild boar as I have hunted him in the mountains of eastern Tennessee, but his range is too limited and his numbers too few to make him of interest to sportsmen in general. Third would come the bobcat.

He is far easier to hunt than the bear, and his pelt doesn't begin to match a bearskin rug as a trophy. But in many states bear hunting is handicapped by the shortness of the season and the fact that by November or December most bears in the north are in winter quarters. In contrast, bobcat chasing is an all-winter sport, at its best when other gunning is at a standstill.

As for the coyote, also a good bet for the houndman, he's an altogether different animal. When dogs take his trail he lines out and travels. It's not unusual to run a coyote twenty-five miles in a day, and even its followers concede that coyote hunting yields more exercise than kills.

The bobcat is not that kind of traveler, either of his own accord or ahead of hounds. Except in the breeding season when the toms roam in search of romance, his range is small. In his total yearly wanderings an average cat may cover an area the size of a township. Rarely does it take more than thirty minutes to an hour of cold trailing to jump him. And once he is up and going, he's likely to get into the thickest patch of cover he knows about and run there for an hour or two, often in smaller circles than those of the showshoe hare or even the cottontail. The result is superb hunting, laced with suspense and excitement.

Many hound men will balk at the idea of ranking the little short-tailed cat so high, especially of giving him a place ahead of mountain lion or red fox. But with few exceptions, those who fail to appreciate him have never tried him.

He's shy and secretive in the extreme, but not hard for good cat dogs to find and run. Once they take his trail, he knows as many tricks as the smartest coon. He'll run in his own track, go up on a windfall and travel without touching the ground, get into the shallow water of a swamp to throw the dogs off, run along a log and jump off going the opposite way. He's light-footed and long-winded, with fantastic staying power. He is often reluctant to tree, which means that unless the dogs can bring him to bay on the ground—and he's no soft touch for that, either—the hunter has to intercept the chase and do his shooting as the cat is driven past, usually in the thickest kind of cover. And for all his small size, he's hell on wheels in a fight. As an old Iowa hunter once commented, "Ain't nothing can comb burs out of a hound's coat like a big bobcat."

Not many hounds want to wade into one single-handed, and not many hunters are willing to have their dogs take that risk if they can help it. Whatever a bobcat weighs, it's all whalebone and dynamite. There is hardly a tougher customer walking the woods. He's pure poison in close-quarter combat, and there are very few dogs, even big hunting hounds, up to killing a full-grown one without help.

I have never known an instance of a

hound being killed in a fight with a cat, maybe because the dog always has the good sense to back off in time. Certainly the bobcat is capable of killing the biggest hound exactly as he does a deer, by ripping open the jugular vein with his teeth.

If two or more dogs are teamed up, however, and if they have the guts to sail in and the experience to know where and how to take hold, they can make short work of the kill. But even then there's likely to be dog blood mixed with cat blood, and sometimes in fairly copious quantities.

Experienced dogs know what to expect and not all of them relish the assignment, even when the odds are on their side. The late Tom Koboski, a Michigan conservation officer at Petoskey who hunted bobcats all his life, told of watching two of his hounds drive a medium-sized cat on deep snow, all three traveling at a trot. The dogs were not more than three jumps behind and could have closed the gap in a second, but didn't choose to.

The bobcat is so widely distributed that there are only a few states where sportsmen couldn't do some hunting if they wanted to. He's found in every state except Alaska and Hawaii, and in southern Canada and over most of Mexico. Liking wild and rough country and dense cover, he reaches his greatest abundance in New England; the mountains of Pennsylvania, West Virginia and Tennessee; northern Michigan, Oklahoma and Texas; and the mountain states of the West. He does not require large blocks of unbroken wilderness, as the mountain lion does, and can make out nicely in places where wild land is mixed with farms and crossed by roads. Even such farming states as Ohio, Indiana, Illinois, Iowa and Kansas still have a scattered bobcat population.

Stubtail is not averse to living close to people as long as he doesn't need to have too much to do with them, and he gets along all right on the fringes of civilization. Not many years ago a stray cat prowled into the yard of a park ranger at the Proud Lake Recreation Area near Milford, Michigan, about thirty-five miles from downtown Detroit, and licked the pants off the ranger's dog before it was treed and shot. And a couple of springs after that the wife of one of my neighbors surprised what she thought was a big tomcat in her garage. When she went for it with a broom the cat spit, snarled and streaked out like greased lightning. Only then did she see that it had a bobbed tail. That happened just a few miles farther from Detroit than the Proud Lake encounter.

In New England and the Great Lakes states stubtail keeps to evergreen swamps. In the South he likes canebrakes, brushy woods or tangled river bottoms. In the mountains of the West he goes for canyons and rough draws with thickets of sagebrush, juniper and mountain mahogany,

cover so thick a man can hardly walk through. In the rolling, fairly open country of such states as Oklahoma you find him in patches of timber that have plenty of underbrush, thickets or grass.

Wherever he lives, the little cat knows where the most inaccessible retreats are located and if trouble looms he seeks them out. Like all predators, he is found where his food is plentiful, and an abundance of rabbits, squirrels and other small rodents often is the key to a thriving bobcat population.

In many places stubtail is more plentiful than sportsmen realize. His choice of habitat, nocturnal habits and stealthy ways leave little sign of his presence. The average hunter could spend weeks in a good bobcat area and never suspect there was a cat around.

The black bear, unless he's made bold by hunger, is no slouch at keeping out of sight, but you're far more likely to blunder into him than a

Prowling bobcat climbs down a broken rock face. In the mountains of the West this small feline likes canyons and rough draws; in the Northeast he keeps to evergreen swamps; in the South he is found most often in canebrakes or the thick cover of river bottoms.

bobcat. In a lifetime of outdoor activities, except for the times when cats were driven past me, treed or brought to bay by dogs, I have seen exactly one, and that was only a fleeting glimpse of something that vanished like a puff of smoke.

A hunting partner and I sat down one November afternoon on the side of a ridge that overlooked a thick swamp, where we could watch two deer runways. We had sat quietly for half an hour when, out of the tail of one eye, I saw my partner move. I turned my head slowly and carefully, and he was inching his rifle to his shoulder. Then I saw a bobcat walking a fallen log forty yards beyond him.

He took his time and touched off his shot, but with iron sights a bobcat is a small target at forty yards, and he missed. The rifle cracked and the cat was gone. I didn't see it jump off the log, dodge into the brush or run down the hill. It simply disappeared in thin air and I still don't know where it went.

Now and then the little cat discards his furtive ways and turns amazingly bold. A few years ago a husband and wife, fishing Michigan's Au Sable River, ran their boat ashore with a fair catch of trout on a stringer in the bow. They pushed in under an overhanging tree and as the nose of the boat grounded a big bobcat dropped from a branch, grabbed the fish and bounded up the bank.

Treed on the upturned roots of a fallen tree, stubtail looks down at the hound that got him into trouble. In many parts of the country, he refuses to tree, preferring to take his chances on the ground.

Almost unbelievably, there are even a few cases on record of stubtail making a totally unprovoked attack on a man. I know of one that happened in the woods of Cockburn Island, on the Ontario side of northern Lake Huron, in the late 1950's.

Set for a deer drive, Sidney Bacon of Grand Rapids, Michigan, was standing under a tree at the edge of a swamp. He heard the guide fire a pistol, the starting signal, and the drivers began to bark. Then something hit him between the shoulders and knocked him sprawling.

Half dazed, he twisted around to see a big bobcat standing only four feet away, snarling at him. His back had been wrenched in the fall and he couldn't get up, so he reached out for his rifle and touched off a shot to frighten the cat off. But it only backed away a few feet and stood its ground, still snarling.

Ignoring his injured back, Bacon then hauled himself up on one knee, aimed and shot again, killing it in its tracks. It was a forty-two-pound male,

and Bacon was sure it had jumped him from overhead in the tree. His cap was ripped but there were no scratches on him and no other marks on his clothing. Nevertheless, there was no question that the attack had been deliberate and made in earnest.

One of the strangest things about stubtail, to my way of thinking, is his hatred of domestic cats. There are a few authentic cases of matings between the two, but for the most part the bobcat kills any farm cat he comes across, and often eats what he has killed.

Several years back I knew a resort owner on Manistique Lake in the Upper Peninsula of Michigan who had a big yellow tomcat that carried on a running, if somewhat one-sided, feud with a bobcat an entire summer. The tom was caught and mauled two or three times, and two other cats in the neighborhood were killed.

Finally Big Yellow's owner took to sleeping with a window screen open far enough to let his cat sail through in an emergency, and one moonlight night he was awakened by a clatter as that happened. He piled out of bed and saw a big bobcat coming across the yard, trailing the tom with his nose to the ground.

My friend reached for a loaded gun he kept handy, and in doing so moved his face in front of the window. Stubtail must have mistaken that blur of movement for his quarry, for he launched himself at the screen and struck hard enough to bulge and rip it. Luckily he didn't come through.

Now and then, as if to even the score, the bobcat himself falls prey to a bigger cat. There are quite a few cases on record of mountain lions killing and feeding on bobcats.

It is a strange contradiction that an animal found over so much of the country, and capable of supplying about as much action ahead of dogs as anything that wears fur, should be so little appreciated. Here and there a handful of hunters make the most of him, but over most of his wide range, even in states where sportsmen complain bitterly about the shortage of game and the lack of hunting opportunities, and where fox and coon hunting grow in popularity year after year, they don't give him much of a tumble. Maybe it's partly because it takes good dogs to run him, partly because he is not considered edible. In many places too, there is deep-rooted prejudice against him as a destructive predator, believed to make serious inroads on deer and other game. A number of states keep him on the bounty list.

There's no denying that he takes game and, on occasion, poultry and young livestock, especially lambs and pigs. When he turns stock killer he's a bad actor, too. He has been known to destroy more than thirty lambs in a night, and in one instance a cat that gained entrance to a poultry house left fifty-one dead fowls behind. Often, but not always, such killers are old individuals with worn teeth, that look for easier pickings when they have trouble taking rabbits and other wild prey.

Although rabbits are his mainstay, making up as much as two-thirds of his diet over most of his range, the bobcat also takes squirrels, possums, muskrats, skunks, quail, grouse and wild turkeys if he gets the chance, and even an occasional porcupine.

The bulk of the venison he eats comes from dead deer left in the woods at the end of hunting season. One such carcass will supply a couple of bobcats most of a winter, and unless they are driven off by dogs or men they come back to it repeatedly and clean it up to the last scrap. Such a source of food is an ideal place to strike a fresh cat track.

If other game becomes scarce and deer are plentiful, stubtail does not hesitate to go on a venison diet and do his own killing. I know western hunters who rate him almost on a par with the cougar as a deer killer, but there is little evidence to support that charge.

In predator field studies carried out in Michigan's Upper Peninsula over a period of fifteen years, El Harger, a game biologist with the state's Department of Natural Resources, followed bobcat tracks almost five-hundred miles and found only four cases of deer killing. Three of those involved fawns less than a year old.

The victims do not need to be young or crippled deer or individuals made helpless by deep snow, although he kills those by preference. A 25-pound cat is quite capable of doing away with a 150-pound buck. His usual procedure is to hunt in thick cover where he can surprise the deer, creep up on it in its bed or catch it unawares, and pounce from 10 feet away. A bobcat can put on a real burst of speed for 50 yards or so, and if it misses in its initial leap it may overtake the deer in thick cover.

Wendell Copenhaver, a Montana hunter and guide, once told me of surprising a big bobcat on a deer kill, shooting it and then being able to piece together the entire story from the tracks.

The deer was a yearling muley. The cat, weighing just over thirty-five pounds, had jumped it at the top of a timbered hill and ridden it down the slope for two-hundred yards before he succeeded in bringing it to the ground. He had clawed the deer to ribbons in that desperate running battle.

Once he is on the deer the cat fastens on the head, neck and shoulders, flattened down like a leech, with his claws dug in. Many authorities say he kills by biting through the windpipe or tearing out the jugular

Overtaken in snowy woods, a bobcat faces his pursuers, ready
for battle. Against anything like fair odds, he can whip far
more than his own weight in dogs, and not many hounds want
to tackle him single-handed.

A bowhunter brings his bow to full
draw, zeroed in on a cornered bobcat.
The little cat is an excellent target for
this method of hunting, providing the
dogs can bring him to bay or tree him.

vein with a single bite. But Jerry Philbrick, a California hunter who has helped to account for some three-hundred bobcats, tells me he has never found a deer killed that way. In every case he has known of, he says, the cat killed with a hard bite behind the head, severing the spinal cord. They are also capable of breaking a deer's neck by wrenching the head around and back.

An unusual case turned up at Newberry, in the upper peninsula of Michigan, a few winters ago, when a woodcutter found a 140-pound buck and a 25-pound bobcat lying dead in the snow only a few yards apart. The deer's neck was broken, the cat had died from a deep gash in one shoulder, probably inflicted by a front hoof, since the buck's antlers had been shed earlier. That kind of draw between the two is very rare, however.

Once in a while a bobcat pulls down a full grown antelope, but because the pronghorn keeps to open country such kills are not common.

Whatever his misdeeds in killing deer and other game, save under special circumstances stubtail's value as a game animal greatly outweighs them, and he deserves a better deal than year-around trapping and a bounty law.

In general the bobcat is not as big as hunters think, twenty to thirty pounds being about average for a full grown animal. Anything above thirty-five pounds has to be rated big, and young toms and small females commonly weigh only fourteen to eighteen pounds. A tom, fat and in good condition, trapped on Drummond Island at the north end of Lake Huron in 1955, weighed forty-seven pounds. At the time I supposed that was close to a record, but I was far from right.

In his excellent book *The Bobcat of North America,* Stanley Young lists six that were heavier. One killed in Ohio weighed 55 pounds, another from New Hampshire matched that weight. A New Mexico tom weighed 56, two from Nevada 58½ and 59. The all-time champ, so far as Young's record show, was a 69-pounder killed in Colorado in 1951. The second biggest ever recorded officially in Michigan was a 41-pound female killed by Carl Johnson. She was the only female above 40 pounds that I have ever heard of.

However short he may be on weight, the little cat is long on endurance, tricks, guts and temper—the qualities houndmen look for in any game they run—and when he speaks to a dog there's no doubting that he means what he says.

Success in hunting him depends entirely on good dogs, and putting together a satisfactory pack is not likely to be a short or easy chore.

Two dogs are enough, although many hunters prefer to use three or four. Every pack must include at least one good strike dog that is sure on a cold track, a good tree dog or two in case the cat climbs in some out-of-the-way place and it takes the hunter a bit of time to get there, and dogs with grit enough to hold a cat at bay on the ground but not stupid enough to dive in and get taken apart when there is no need.

Fast dogs are less important than those that are slow but sure. It is not necessary to push a cat at top speed but it is essential to stay on him, both before and after he is jumped. As a California hunter once told me, "A dog with a good cold-nose is a lot more important than one that runs like a greyhound."

Because the bobcat shares his range with deer in most of the states where he is found, the cat dog that is not completely deerproof is useless and worse. That requirement may go far to explain why bobcat hunting has never achieved the popularity it deserves. Genuinely deerproof hounds are not too common, and without them cat hunting is a lost cause almost any place where the cats are plentiful enough to make it worth while.

There are many places where stubtail is run on bare ground, but I have never hunted him that way. In our country the best hunting comes in January and February, when the snow is two to three feet deep in the northern swamps.

No matter how long-legged the hounds may be or how much stamina they may have, they can't push the cat very hard when they are wallowing in soft, dry snow of that depth. And while the bobcat lacks the big fur-padded feet that serve his cousin, the Canada lynx, as homegrown snowshoes, he is far lighter than the dogs, doesn't sink as deep, and has easier going as a consequence.

If the dogs have good footing and can drive him, the average cat won't run more than a two-mile circle and the hunt is not likely to last more than an hour or two. But with deep snow in his favor and the hounds forced to set a slow pace, he is close to tireless. He loafs along ahead of the dogs, stopping now and then to listen and look back, and more than one hunter, slogging behind on snowshoes, has followed such a chase from daylight to dark without getting close enough to the cat to worry him.

In the country where I have hunted, more than half the cats run under those conditions are killed on the ground, refusing to tree. The bigger and heavier the cat, the sooner he climbs. It's the youngsters that give the hounds the hardest workout and and are finally shot, if they are shot at all, running rabbit-fashion through thick cover. The cat that carries better than thirty pounds of weight is likely to tree after a reasonable chase. His wind and legs give out, or he gets enough of it. The smaller

ones are whang leather and whale-bone, and unless dogs and men have unlimited staying power they can't expect much success in hunting them.

Because so many bobcats are killed on the ground, a shotgun is about the only weapon for this hunting. Most hunters favor shot not smaller than No. 2, but I have known a few who contend that a cat is as easy to kill as a rabbit and who regularly use No. 6's or 7½'s.

Although not many hunters resort to a predator call in bobcat hunting, it can be a highly successful and very exciting method. As I have related in Chapter 17 on game calling, the little cat comes willingly but also very stealthily and carefully, often unseen until he is a few feet from the caller.

So far as I'm concerned, Ed Star-back said all there is to say about bobcat hunting many years ago. A northern Michigan game warden, Ed died in a plane crash in the 1950's. He and Tom Koboski and I walked out of a north-country swamp one February day when the winter dusk was beginning to thicken. We were carrying a bobcat whose cold track we had taken an hour after daylight that morning, and four very tired dogs were padding behind us in our snowshoe trail. We broke out of the evergreens half a mile from where our car was parked between the high roadside banks left by a county snow-plow, and stopped to unstrap our snowshoes.

Ed gave me a dry grin. "The little cat is big stuff," he told me.

A hunter and his long-legged hound head home after a successful bobcat hunt. In some parts of the country the cats are hunted on bare ground, but the sport is at its best in the North when winter snow lies deep.

15
COYOTE
Gray ghost of the thickets

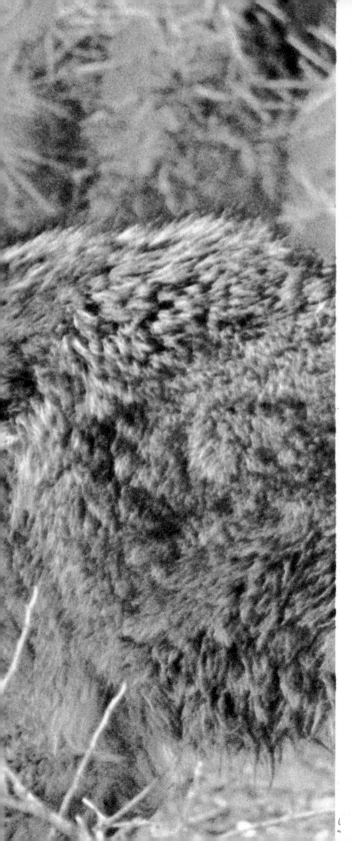

One cold January morning several years ago three friends of mine, Roy Chambers, Roy Vincent and Ham Sheveline, hit a cold coyote track crossing a narrow road that winds through the birches and evergreens of Michigan's Wilderness State Park, at the extreme northwest tip of the state's mitten-shaped Lower Peninsula.

Chambers was a plasterer, Vincent a service station operator, both from the town of Indian River. Sheveline was a fur buyer from Central Lake, forty miles away. One thing the three had in common: They were houndmen and hunters, holding the firm opinion that no game animal in the midwestern United States is capable of supplying better action than the coyote.

They had a homemade prototype of a snowmobile along that morning, big enough to carry three men and powerful enough to tow a wide-runnered sled mounted with two dog boxes. They put Ring and Baldy, their two best coyote hounds, in the boxes, climbed onto the sled and took

227

the track. Snow was between two and three feet deep.

In less than a mile the track led out across Big Stone Bay and onto the open ice of the Straits of Mackinac. Running conditions there were perfect for the dogs, and the hunters let Ring and Baldy go.

Just before they reached Crane Island, land's end at the western entrance to the Straits, the dogs jumped the coyote and he turned into the thick timber of the island. Unless things got too tough he preferred that to the open ice of Lake Michigan. He made one circuit around it, but the snow was feather-light in the woods and he was breaking trail for the dogs. They crowded him hard, he turned out on the ice toward the faint blue line of the Upper Peninsula shore, twenty miles away, and poured on coal. When the hunters got to the place where the tracks left the beach they could see their two hounds, no bigger than specks, a couple of miles out. The coyote was lost to sight among hummocks and pressure ridges.

Vincent and Chambers and Sheveline picked their way onto the ice, fully aware that they were taking their lives in their hands. The north end of Lake Michigan is a huge windswept place, and however solidly it may freeze the ice fields are never still for long. Wind and currents shift and move them constantly. In the sharp cold of a still night the whole white landscape may freeze into one compact mass, with patches of clean new ice where there was open water at dusk. But once the wind stirs the restless floes at daybreak the process of breaking and moving and grinding begins again.

The three men found the ice fully as bad as they expected, and only a firm belief that no houndman ever deserts his dogs, if he can help it, drove them out from the beach.

There were old floes, smooth and covered with wind-packed snow, some of them half a mile across. There were veins of new ice, scoured bare by the wind, clear as window glass, barely thick enough to support the snow sled. There were pressure ridges and jagged upturned pans running off as far as the men could see. Most dangerous of all, there were long cracks of open water.

Some of these were only a foot or so across and the sled slid across them without risk, but others yawned five or six feet wide and had to be followed to a place where currents had jammed the ice back together.

Every now and then, on a patch of snow, they picked up the tracks of the coyote, running a zigzag course for the distant shore. There was no sign that the dogs were gaining on him.

It was almost noon when the hunters ran their sled up on the beach at the foot of a timbered bluff between the towns of Brevort and

Epoufette. The dogs and coyote had gone up the bluff.

Chambers strapped on his snow-shoes and followed. The tracks led toward US 2, a major highway a mile inland. When he reached it, the coyote had turned east, toward St. Ignace. But even a tired coyote—and this one had now run twenty-five miles—has too great an aversion to cars to stay long on a heavily traveled road. This one was sure to go back on Lake Michigan and head for the area where he had been started.

Chambers went back to the sled and the three men drove out on the onshore ice, where the going was better, and turned east. They had gone two miles when they saw dog and coyote tracks leading down across the beach. It was two hours past noon and the wolf was going home, across the almost limitless ice.

For the hunters the return trip was a repeat of the forenoon cross-ing. They followed the tracks, angling back and forth, knowing that even if they lost the dogs they'd have to get off the ice before dark.

They were eight or ten miles off Crane Island when they saw some-thing moving slowly, ahead. It was Ring, still on the track but going at a walk. They overtook him and put him in his box.

It was dusk when they caught up with Baldy, on the open ice to the southwest of Crane Island. They had just enough light left to enable them to watch for cracks as they turned toward shore.

They had traveled not less than sixty miles on the snow sled and the coyote and dogs had run at least as far. Where the wolf finally went when pursuit ended they never knew.

Do you wonder that Chambers told me afterward, "Any time you want to separate the men from the boys just strap on a pair of snowshoes, turn two or three good dogs loose on a fresh coyote track, and try to stay with them."

I still have vivid memories of my first coyote hunt, close to forty years ago. Three seasoned and rugged woodsmen from the Upper Penin-sula of Michigan walked me twenty-three miles on snowshoes between daylight and the time we finally got back to our car, three hours past dark. We killed one coyote.

When I fell into bed in a hotel in the town of Pickford that night, aching in muscles I had not known I possessed, I swore I was finished with coyote hunting for all time to come. I didn't keep the vow, and I learned on subsequent hunts that twenty-three miles in a day is about par for the course.

I know more than one hunter who has followed his dogs up to thirty miles in a day, wound up at dark two townships away from his car, worn out and supperless, and sworn

A line of coyote tracks (left) beckons hunters to start what will almost certainly be a long, hard chase. The maker of the tracks trots through deep snow (right), looking exactly like what he is, a small wolf, with wolf cunning and endurance.

he'd never hunt coyotes again. But I've never known that mood to last longer than a week or two.

A coyote has everything that makes the red fox a prime favorite ahead of hounds, but he has more of it. He's bigger and bolder and tougher, with more speed, more endurance, more cunning and more spunk. His nose is as keen as a deer's, his ears as good, and he has eyes in the back of his head. Although he ranges over a big territory, traveling as far as twenty-five to thirty miles in a night when food is scarce, he knows the location of every swamp, lake, stream, deer yard, beaver pond and windfall in it. Put dogs on his track, he's full of tricks and not likely to make mistakes.

He'll go into a deer yard and circle among the deer, he'll run out on slick ice where he leaves little scent, or take to a highway where the running is good. The dogs that chase him must be big, long-legged hounds, with good feet, plenty of speed and staying power, and no quit to them. They also have to be fighters on land or in water, for a driven coyote will cross big rivers and if cornered near water, is likely to swim out to a log or island, or take refuge in the half submerged top of a fallen tree. Dogs that won't follow can't finish the job.

In our country coyote hunting gets under way when deer season closes, at the end of November, and lasts until the snow goes off in late March or early April. But the best time is from mid-January to late February. Snow conditions are right then and the coyotes, driven by the urge of the mating season, move more and travel farther, making fresh tracks easy to find.

It's useless to go out unless there is enough snow for tracking, and the deeper the snow the better. It's next to impossible to find and identify a fresh track on bare ground. Now and then the hunter can hit a track on a sandy woods road, but there is no way to tell whether it's one day old or ten, and putting dogs down in such cases often means that they run deer instead of coyotes. As for summer hunting, although coyotes can be killed legally the year around—many states still pay bounty on them—I know no hunter who wants any part of it.

Most hunters drive old woods trails or logging roads looking for tracks, using a jeep or snowmobile. (I know some who will not allow a snowmobile along.) If they fail to strike that way they don snowshoes and hike until they find what they are looking for.

Frozen beaver ponds are a good place to find a track. The coyote seems to delight in them, maybe because they are free of deep snow. If he has company they'll play and roll and wrestle on the ice, and they also like to trot up to a beaver house and sniff the warm, appetizing smells

Dogs close in on a cornered coyote. Many hounds are content to hold the small wolf at bay, without closing in and trying to kill him. If they do come to grips, the fight is wicked. Few dogs are willing to attack a coyote single-handed.

drifting up through the ventilation "chimney."

Once the hunters find a fresh track, they put down one or two hounds, the best cold trailers in the pack, and follow on foot with the rest of the dogs on leash or at heel. When the wolf is jumped and the music starts, the dogs take things into their own hands. What happens the rest of the day depends on the speed of the dogs, the stamina of the coyote, how much of a start he has, how deep

the snow is, and a few other factors.

As long as the snow is only a few inches deep the advantage is all with the coyote. He can outrun and out-last the dogs without half trying. But once there is ten to twelve inches of snow in the woods the odds switch. The wolf has to break trail for the hounds then. As they tire they run single file on the track, and if the first one slows down another crowds past him and takes the lead.

Toward the end of winter things

are reversed again. When the snow starts to melt in March it thaws by day and freezes at night, forming a crust that will hold the coyote up but let the dogs break through and cut their feet. They start out fast and eager, but the vim soon oozes out of them under those conditions.

On deep snow hounds may catch and kill in less than half an hour. But that's the rare exception. The average chase lasts three or four hours, and many go all day. The longest run I have ever known a coyote to make, on light tracking snow, was seventy-five miles between daylight and dark. And in the end he got away.

I have not heard a coyote hunter say that he had ever pelted a fat one. They are all bone and muscle, lean and tough as whalebone.

Speed is a prime requirement in the dogs. When first jumped, unless they are close the coyote will loaf along at a walk or trot. But once they start to crowd him he really lights out and a slow dog has no chance of catching him. Staying power is as important as speed, too.

Most hunters prefer a cold trailer that does not open until the coyote is up. Such a dog gets closer before jumping and the chase is likely to be shorter. A hound that bawls on a cold track gives the wolf too much warning.

Wherever coyotes and deer are found together—and that takes in most of the brush wolf's range—the dogs must be deerproof. There are sportsmen living in areas where coyotes are hunted who honestly believe that the hunters spend half their time dogging deer. They couldn't be more wrong. To begin with, running deer with hounds is illegal in most coyote states, and in the second place that's not what the hunters are out to do.

But in the North many coyote chases are run in swamps where deer are yarded, and hot deer scent is a powerful temptation for a hound. Building a satisfactory pack calls for good blood lines, bred for the job and painstakingly trained and broken off deer.

The best of coyote dogs is likely to take a bear track if he gets the chance, and may break on a fox or bobcat, but he prefers coyotes above all. He knows what his boss wants and he wants the same thing. If only one or two experienced dogs are let go on a cold track, deer trouble can usually be avoided. It's when an entire pack is allowed to cold trail that they are likely to be led astray. Once they have hot coyote scent to follow, if they are the right kind of dogs to begin with, they are not interested in anything else.

As long as a coyote isn't crowded and has time to smell, look, listen and think, he makes out very well. But for all his hardboiled cunning, and the fact that he uses his wits every minute he's being chased, right up to the end, he is nervous and high strung and likely to hit the panic button when the hounds close in. He's even a better bet to lose his head when the hunters come up, too, for much as he fears dogs he fears a man far more.

I have known them to take shelter in pole piles, under abandoned buildings, in lean-to sheds. Once when Chambers and Vincent pressed one to the end of his rope he ducked into a barn and sought refuge among a herd of cows. They drove another into a farmyard and he ran around the house in circles until the farmer came out and shot him. I was told of one that even tried to crawl into the basement of an occupied farmhouse through a broken window. The farmer's two big mongrel dogs high-tailed for an open field, sat down and watched the proceedings from a safe distance, but one of the hounds held the coyote at bay until the farmer could take a hand.

One final ingredient is necessary in a coyote pack. That's the guts to fight and hold the wolf once he is overtaken. It isn't essential for the dogs to kill, but they must do enough close-quarter worrying that he will not break bay and run again when the hunters come up.

The brush wolf of the Great Lakes states is a different animal from the coyote of the Southwest. In Michigan the full grown males aver-age around forty pounds in weight, females are about ten pounds lighter. Game men say a big male, carrying fat—a rare condition in a coyote—might go above fifty pounds, but that would be exceptional.

Whatever they weigh, they are wicked fighters, with wolf ways and wolf courage. Very few hounds can kill one single-handed, and fewer are willing to try. Even when three or four dogs bring a coyote to bay they're likely to hang back, each waiting for the others to make the first pass. For that reason you have to have one or two in the pack with enough sand to dive in. The rest will follow as soon as the fight starts.

If the wolf has a chance to back under a windfall or into a stump or hollow log, where his rear is protected, the dog that tries to take him from the front is going to get hurt. A big coyote can cut a hound to pieces in nothing flat in a place of that kind. I have even known of a case or two where a dog was killed.

One thing about chasing coyotes is different from any other type of hunting I know about. In thick swamp cover you may get the chance to shoot one that's almost in your lap. But you also have to be prepared for long shots at a target that's running flat out and very hard to kill. There is no one gun that's better for this than all others, but most of the men I have hunted with vote for a shotgun loaded with buckshot. They also want the gun light to carry and easy to handle in brush.

Buckshot loads are essential. Nothing lighter will do. To begin with, although a running coyote looks big there is really not too much animal under the pelt. You may get only two or three pellets in, and they have to be heavy enough to do the job. In the second place, the fur of a coyote is thick and the skin tough, making it difficult for shot to penetrate. Under sixty or sixty-five yards, buckshot is a pretty sure bet, but much over that there is little use to try.

Finally, the coyote can carry lead. A fox, crippled even with a .22, will usually give up and stop where he is. A coyote, drilled through the body with a .30/06, will keep going until he drops. I know of one shot that way that ran for half a mile and was still ready to fight the dogs when they caught him.

Some hunters prefer a rifle, and I have hunted with one who carried a Savage over-and-under, the upper barrel chambered for the .222 Remington shell, the lower a full-choke 20-gauge shotgun. He used to carry a shotgun, but it seemed that most of the coyotes he saw were at rifle range, so he decided to be ready for whatever happened.

If the dogs are running a coyote in a thick swamp and you get close to them, either they drive him where you could kill him with a club or you don't see him at all. Even if you see

236

A coyote running ahead of a hunter sails over a windfallen tree with effortless ease. Lean and free of fat, long-winded and close to tireless, the little wolf has been known to travel seventy-five miles ahead of dogs, and then escape.

him you don't always hang his pelt on the corncrib wall.

Despite the fact that in the opinion of the men who hunt him the little wolf is one of the top game animals available to hound owners in our part of the country, he is also among the least appreciated and goes greatly underhunted.

Hunters in northern Michigan have demonstrated that with good dogs it is not difficult to hunt a bobcat population down almost to the point of extinction. There is no danger of that with the coyote. Hunters and hounds simply can't cut a swath that wide in his ranks.

He can also be brought in with a predator call, and in some western states coyote calling has a considerable following. In Chapter 17 on game calling, I relate an episode in which a caller lured five coyotes to him at a distance of almost a mile. But with this method, as with dogs, there is no reason to fear that the small wolf will be overhunted. He is too well able to look out for himself.

Probably one of the chief reasons why he is so lightly valued as a game animal is the hostility many sportsmen feel toward him as a deer and stock killer. Bounty systems and poison campaigns grow out of that hostility.

It has to be admitted that in sheep country he is likely to do real damage. But when it comes to deer, there is no evidence to support the claim that a normal coyote population is a detriment to a healthy deer herd. Certainly the little wolf kills deer. Some times he kills full-grown, healthy, even big deer. But far more often those he takes would not live through the winter anyway.

For the most part it's only in late winter, when the snow is crusted hard enough to hold the coyote but let the deer break through, that he attacks full-grown animals in good condition. He can kill about as he pleases under those conditions, but even then he is not often inclined to tackle a big buck. Like all predators, he picks what he can handle most easily.

The brush wolves do work the deer yards in March, but they don't hunt in packs as timber wolves do, and they can't hold a candle to renegade dogs as deer slayers. The dogs slaughter for sport, the coyote kills because he needs food. I have never heard of an instance where coyotes killed fifteen or twenty deer in one yard, as wolves sometimes do shortly before their pups are born. The brush wolf eats what he kills, feeding on a deer carcass as long as it lasts unless he is driven away.

He's an undersized wolf, a gray ghost that can run like the wind and fight like a wildcat. It's hard for hound-men to find a better animal to hunt.

I know one hunter who used to make out very well hunting him by an altogether different method. He is Gene Sherman, a district Enforcement Supervisor for the Montana Fish and Game Department. His technique was to stalk the little wolves in the open or waylay them at places where they were feeding and do them in with a flat-shooting, scoped rifle.

As Gene tells it, when he started hunting them as a kid, in the 1920's, they were as plentiful in the Judith Mountains of central Montana, where he grew up, as quills on a porcupine. At twelve he got a .30/30 Winchester, and went after the coyotes that made regular raids on his family's chicken and turkey flock.

He quickly learned that he had to sneak up and get a standing shot if he hoped to kill, and from then on he scored regularly. He had found a hard-to-take animal that was the last word in challenge, and he has never changed that opinion.

He rates the coyote at the head of the class for wariness, caution and intelligence. It knows instinctively how to take advantage of every bit of cover in the country, and rarely drops its guard.

When Gene first told me about this hunting, he had killed some 125 coyotes. "For a man who likes to match brains with an animal as smart as he is, outguess it, earn it and kill it in a fair game of wits and stealth, there is no better game," he said.

The coyote does most of his moving at night. In the West he travels out from timbered mountains and rough river breaks into open country shortly after dusk, and spends the darkness hunting rabbits, mice and other prey or feeding on dead stock. At daylight he heads back for heavy cover, and by sunup he has gone into seclusion for the day.

That gives the hunter an hour or so of good light for morning hunting. Sherman's method was to roll out before daybreak, walk to a ridge he knew coyotes traveled, belly down and watch the light break over the sagebrush. Many coyotes he caught walking or trotting home. If he saw one mousing he tried to get downwind and stalk it behind whatever cover was available. Many times he was able to crawl within range, even in the open, by moving while the wolf was engrossed in a mouse nest, freezing when it lifted its head.

He also found that if he spooked one in the open, sat down and waited with his rifle leveled, most of the time the wolf would stop and look back within two hundred yards. The pause might last only two or three seconds, but if the hunter was ready that was long enough.

He also did very well by locating the carcasses of steers and other stock where coyotes were feeding regularly, getting into position before the sky turned gray, and waiting for the light to brighten. Hunting that way,

he surprised eight on a carcass one morning and killed half of them in less than a minute.

His favorite rifles were a Winchester .220 Swift scoped with a Lyman Alaskan in 2½ power, and a wildcat on a Springfield action with a .25/06 barrel, with a 4x scope. Most of his kills were made at 200 to 300 yards, but if he needed to reach out farther those rifles were ideal.

Shortly after World War II the poison known as 1080 came into general use in the ranching country of the West, with the blessing of the U.S. Fish and Wildlife Service.

"That ended my coyote hunting days," Gene told me. "The damned 1080 was too much for Mr. Hard-To-Hunt, and there weren't enough of his kind left to make it worthwhile to take a gun out of the cabinet.

"For generations we had thrown everything at him that we could think of, traps, snares, den-digging, dogs, guns and strychnine, and we had never succeeded in killing off more than his annual increase. The coyote population held its own in spite of all men could do. But 1080 sent 'em down the drain in a hurry.

"They were a menace to sheep ranchers and turkey growers and did some deer and antelope damage. But I don't like the idea of taking advantage of anything as smart as the coyote with a poison as deadly and unfair as 1080. Hunting him with a rifle was awfully good fun."

16

RATTLE-SNAKES

These are the deadly ones

"See that one?" Walter Tucker asked me.

He was pointing his snake hook at a tuft of winter-dead grass hardly big enough to hide a ground sparrow's nest, only four or five feet from the soles of my boots.

The grass was dust-gray, totally without color. So were the sand and rocks of the desert around it, and the scattered, parched, dead-looking clumps of greasewood and other shrubs. And coiled in the shelter of that small tuft of grass lay a yard and a half of western diamondback, also dust-gray, exactly the color of its surroundings.

The only bright color on the snake were the sharply contrasting rings of black and white on its tail, the marking that gives this rattler the common name of coontail. But the tail lay almost completely hidden under the sullen looking coils of the heavy body. I had never seen a better —or more hair-raising—example of natural camouflage.

"I see it now that you point it out," I told Tucker.

He grinned, turned the other way

241

and stabbed with his hook toward a slab of flat rock the size of a man's hat, that protruded out of the ground leaving a miniature cavern under the overhang.

"One there, too," Walter grunted.

The snake fitted and almost filled the spot where it lay, but to the untrained eye it was no more than rock and sand and dust.

Without moving out of our tracks, Tucker showed me five diamondbacks, lying in hiding places within sight. None had moved or rattled, and none had I spotted, in spite of careful looking, until he brought them to my attention one by one.

That experience serves perfectly to illustrate the danger involved in hunting the most deadly animals on the North American continent. It also goes far to show what makes that hunting such an exciting and fascinating sport.

There are four kinds of poisonous snakes in the United States and southern Canada, the rattlers, copperheads, water moccasins or cottonmouths, and the coral snakes.

Rattlesnakes of one variety or another are found in every state except Hawaii, Alaska, Maine and possibly Delaware, and the big ones stand among the most dangerous reptiles on earth. The copperhead is scattered from New England to Kansas and from Georgia to Texas. The range of the water moccasin extends from the Carolinas and Florida west to Texas, and up the Mississippi Valley as far as the southern tip of Illinois. Coral snakes are limited to the South, from North Carolina to the Gulf and west to the Rio Grande.

A painstaking and comprehensive survey, the first of its kind, carried out some ten years ago by Dr. Henry Parrish of the University of Missouri, revealed that an average of sixty-five hundred to seven thousand people are bitten by venomous snakes in the United States each year. If a tenth of that number were attacked annually by bears, mountain lions or other wild mammals, the American outdoors would be considered a very dangerous place indeed.

Although the death rate from snakebite is extremely low, only about fifteen victims a year on the average, the ordeal is a dreadful one, accompanied by extreme suffering and often resulting in the loss of a hand or foot, or permanent crippling. Yet despite the risk, the men who hunt snakes for sport rate it the greatest hunting of all.

I have never seen a coral snake outside the reptile house of a zoo, and never known anyone who hunted them. Nor have I hunted moccasins. But I have gone out quite a number of times after rattlers and copperheads, with some of the top hunters in the country, men like Walter Tucker.

At the time I hunted diamondbacks with him in the Texas desert, a few miles west of his home at Pyote, he was a civilian guard at the Pyote Air Base, putting in a fair share of his spare time snake hunting.

Among other things, he hunted rattlers for the annual Rattlesnake Roundup at Sweetwater, a carnival-like, nationally famous event, sponsored by the local Jaycees, that saw an average of some four thousand live snakes brought in each year.

The Roundup was staged in March, when the snakes were coming out of winter quarters. That is the most productive season for hunting snakes anywhere in the country, the exact time depending on weather and the arrival of spring. When the snakes first leave their dens they congregate in numbers in the immediate vicinity and are easily found. In summer, after they have dispersed to their feeding areas, the hunting is far leaner, but when they return to the dens shortly before cold weather comes in the fall there is another productive period.

Some years ago a rancher friend of mine in Montana took a partner to a den location that his sheep herder had discovered. The time was October, shortly before the first snowfall. The two men did not make an exact count, but they were sure they shot more than five hundred rattlers in one forenoon.

It was March when I went out with Walter Tucker. The snakes were emerging from crevices and from among the loose rocks of a shallow quarry pit where material had been removed for a nearby highway fill, along Interstate 80 between Pyote and Pecos.

We parked Tucker's pickup truck on the shoulder of the highway, climbed a two-strand barbwire fence and walked into the desert.

"The big ones don't seem to be out yet," he told me, "but we'll find a few big enough to be interesting." That proved to be a complete understatement. Before the forenoon was over we looked at between twenty and thirty diamondbacks, most of them between three and four feet long, and we trudged back to the pickup with a carrying box that buzzed like a nest of angry hornets.

Tucker's method of hunting was to poke carefully around crevices, rock piles and low cliffs, keeping his eyes open and his guard up. "You have to do that in diamondback country if you want to live to draw your old-age pension," he said with a dry grin, and went on to tell me about a big one that gave him a hard time when he undertook to drop it into his carrying box with his snake hook. He had all his attention on what he was trying to do, and wasn't even aware that there was a small bleached log on the ground at his feet. He stepped back and forth over it half a dozen times in battling the snake. Not until it was boxed did he remember to look down. A second diamondback, fully as big as the first one, was lying in the shade of the log three feet away.

"I broke my first rule," Walter admitted. "I let my guard down. He broke the rules, too. He didn't rattle, strike, or pay the least attention to me. But you can't count on that. I just don't advise outsiders to prowl around in the desert when the snakes are out."

Rattlesnakes, both in the desert and in the sandy flatlands of Florida and Georgia, where the even larger eastern variety of diamondback is found, leave sign as easy to spot as deer or rabbit tracks, once you know what to look for. Where they crawl in and out, and where they lie and bask in front of a hole or under a rock, they smooth the sand and pack it down. The experienced snake hunter quickly learns to recognize such places, and if he visits them at the right time of year he is almost sure to find the snake at home.

The rest is easy, again for the man familiar with the hunting. He walks up quietly and carefully, reaches in with his snake hook, and yanks the reptile into the open. They come out mad as hornets and try hard to get back into shelter, but they can't move fast enough to get away.

In looking for those that were back in rock crevices and small caves, Tucker used a hand mirror that would throw a beam of reflected sunlight like a spotlight. If the snakes were near enough to the entrance, as they were that day, he hauled them out one at a time. When he spotted one beyond reach, he told me, he sprayed gasoline back into the hole with a garden spray can, and the fumes drove the snake out.

I remember very vividly one he took just before we quit hunting that morning. We walked up to a pile of loose rock at one end of the quarry pit, and while we were still forty or fifty feet away he stopped and said in a low undertone, "There's a big one. See it?"

For the life of me I could not make out the snake, coiled in an open place among the dust-colored rocks.

"Stand over there if you want a picture," Walter said, indicating a spot at the edge of a patch of open ground half the size of an average livingroom. "I'll flip him right in front of you."

He inched in, slowly and silently, reached and swung his hook all in one motion, and five feet of thick-bodied rattler came sailing through the air to land almost at my feet. It started back to its lair in the rocks, buzzing furiously, but Tucker kept it at bay with his hook until it quieted down. Then he lifted it gingerly and dropped it into his carrying box.

Another snake hunt I'll probably never forget happened in the broken, rugged hills above the river town of Harper's Ferry, at the northeast corner of Iowa.

The hunter who took me out that day was Joe Martelle, a tall, wide-shouldered professional who hunted

Rearing head and body in a striking pose, a prairie rattler is ready to deal his lethal blow, while his sprung rattles sound their incessant dry buzz of warning. Found throughout the plains country of the West, from the Canadian border to the Rio Grande, this is not as big a snake as either the eastern or western diamondback, but is hardly less dangerous.

snakes for the fifty-cent bounty and also for the fun of it. The snakes we were after were timber rattlers, the kind that bear the appropriate scientific name of *Crotalus horridus*. Men bitten by them, back in rough country a mile or two from the nearest road, have died before they could get out for help.

I suppose that day around the limestone outcrops and in the tangles along the ledges stands out in my mind because I walked within two feet of a big snake before I knew it was there, in tall grass at the base of a rock.

I saw movement just ahead of my boots, saw a big, thick, brown-and-tan body coming out of a round coil in no great hurry, sliding back under a ledge of limestone. I glimpsed a flat, wicked looking head, and then the snake sprung its rattle and the dry, insistent buzzing rang in my ears.

That snake was about ready to shed its skin. The old skin was lusterless, the eyes milky and opaque. The transparent, scale-like covering of the eyes had loosened, and all probability the rattler was nearly sightless at the moment. Perhaps that was why it had allowed me to come so close before it rattled or moved away. "When they're blind they'll lay till you step on 'em," Martelle told me.

Whatever the reason, two feet is too close to approach such a snake, and I don't suppose I'll ever forget the encounter.

I also recall that day because Joe told me of an occasion when he reduced the local rattler population by thirty-three in three minutes. He came across three pregnant females in a bunch. Young rattlesnakes are born alive. One of those females was carrying nine, the second ten, and the third eleven.

Martelle had a set of safety rules worth passing along for the benefit of anyone who plans to hunt venomous snakes.

"Take your time and look where you are putting your feet," he said. "Be especially careful around rocks and logs. Never step over anything until you have looked for a snake on the other side, and never put your hands on the ground or on a ledge until you are sure the coast is clear.

"Above all, don't count on hearing one rattle before he strikes. You get too close, and he'll strike first and rattle afterward."

If he is watchful and cautious, the hunter who goes after snakes only to kill them, or even to pick them up with hook or tongs, does not expose himself to undue danger.

There is of course always the chance that he will get too close to one without knowing it is there, or put a foot, a hand or even his face in the wrong place. And one rule he must remember is never to pick up a weathered board, an abandoned carton, or even a flat rock or piece of firewood under which a snake can hide. If he avoids those mistakes he is safe enough.

I went out early one summer with Dick Jacoby, in western South Dakota east of the Black Hills, country that swarmed with prairie rattlers. Jacoby was hired by the state of South Dakota and had the official title of rattlesnake eradicator.

He hated the snakes for the colts, cattle, sheep and even dogs he had lost to them while he was ranching in his earlier years. He carried a deep-seated grudge against them, loved his job, and had hung up the fantastic score of fifteen thousand rattlers destroyed in ten years.

"They averaged better than three

A hunter, having pinned a big prairie rattler with his snake hook, grasps it firmly just back of the head, in readiness to bag it (above). This is the most dangerous moment of the hunt. For more than one hunter, a slip at this point has resulted in the dreadful ordeal of snakebite or even in death. The snake is then dropped tail foremost into the bag (right). Most hunters take their deadly catch home alive, for sale to reptile gardens or zoos.

feet long, too, so I figure I have killed between eight and ten miles of snake if they were laid snout to tail," Dick told me proudly. "That's not bad payment for the stock I lost when I was ranching."

Jacoby was not a snake hunter in the true sense of the word. Rather he was a snake trapper. He had devised a rattler trap, the most ingenious and effective thing of its kind I have ever seen, and he ran a far-ranging trapline. The trap took advantage of the fact that snakes gather by the hundreds in their winter dens. Prairie-dog towns are a favorite den site with the prairie rattler if they are available. Rock crevices and crannies are about as good, and even fox and badger holes are used.

Dick's trap consisted of an oblong box roughly a foot square and twice as long, built of weathered boards, with a hinged lid on top. An opening about six by six inches in one end was screened to let in light, and a round hole two or three inches in diameter was bored in the other end for an entrance.

Over this hole, on the inside, he attached a wooden tunnel about eight inches long, with the open end cut off at a 45-degree angle, and over this slanting opening he hinged a piece of thick plastic to make a trapdoor that a crawling snake could push up with his nose, but that would drop shut behind him of its own weight once he was in the box.

The trap was set over a prairie dog or badger hole or the entrance to a rock crevice, in a place where signs showed snakes were present. A small entrance box was attached vertically over the round hole in the end, like a chimney on a house, to lead the snake up into the trap itself.

Dirt was packed all around the sides and ends, so that the trap was completely lightproof save for the screen. The snake, crawling up out of its den, entered the tunnel, saw light through the plastic trapdoor, nosed it up, slithered into the box and could not get out.

Jacoby often had more than a hundred of these traps out at one time, in the fall when the rattlers were assembling at their den sites and again in spring when they were coming out of hibernation. It was not uncommon for him to take a catch of a hundred or more in twenty-four hours. In summer, when the trapping was no longer productive, he turned to orthodox snake hunting, but his catch taken that way was never heavy.

When the Oahe dam on the Missouri above Pierre was completed and the big impoundment behind it began to fill, for example, the rising water drove rattlers by the thousands out of their haunts on the river bottoms and along the bluffs, and there was a rash of calls for help.

The snakes scared fishermen, invaded school yards, moved into the vicinity of farm and ranch buildings, and showed up in all sorts of places where they were not wanted. The result was requests from frantic people for the state's snake eradicator to come a'running.

"I did what I could," Dick said, "but there wasn't much a snake hunter could do about it, for it happened in summer and you can make a dent in a rattler population only when they're gathered at their winter den."

Some of his emergency calls he was able to do better by. One came from the daughter of a woman past eighty, who was living by herself on a Dakota farm. A bunch of rattlers was worrying the old lady, the daughter reported.

Figuring that a woman of eighty was no match for rattlesnakes in her yard, Dick hurried to the farm. Even he was a bit shaken when he learned that the snakes were not in the yard. They were under the floor of the house, and the woman heard them rattle in response to her footsteps over their heads.

Jacoby found a hole in the foundation of the house, set one of his traps, and took eight rattlers in a week — plus a five-footer he killed in the yard.

In disposing of fifteen-thousand rattlesnakes, he had never had an accident and did not consider himself in any danger. He had never picked up a live snake and didn't intend to. He wore protective cloth-ing, cowboy boots reaching halfway to his knees, heavy leather chaps that protected his legs, and tough leather gloves. He handled his snakes with an ingenious homemade combination of hook and tongs. And he watched where he was putting his hands and feet every second.

It's the hunter that picks up his snakes alive in his bare hands who risks an accident. Sooner or later, almost every man I have known who handled venomous snakes of any kind has been bitten. The hunter in the field is no exception.

A big rattlesnake ready to do battle is an impressive and frightening sight. As Jacoby once remarked to me, "You have to see one coiled in fighting pose before it really soaks into you what you are dealing with."

The body of such a snake lies in thick coils, the neck is reared and arched like a big S, the evil, triangular head is leveled and trained, ready for its lightning stab. The lidless eyes follow every movement, the black, forked tongue flicks in and out, and the rattles sound their ominous buzzing song. The whole performance is something to chill the blood, and you know there is not an ounce of bluff behind it. Back of the eyes in that flat head two venom sacs are waiting to squeeze shut like rubber bulbs, and a pair of fangs as sharp as any hypodermic needle — and in the case of a big diamondback, a full inch long — lie folded against the

Using a pair of snake tongs, a Florida hunter lifts a heavy-bodied eastern diamondback. Native to the Southeast, from North Carolina south to Florida and west along the Gulf coast to Mississippi, this is the biggest of the thirty kinds of native rattlesnakes, and also the largest venomous reptile found in North America. Attaining an occasional length of seven feet, it ranks among the deadliest snakes of the world.

upper jaw, ready to spring into position and be driven deep into the victim's flesh. Men have died from the bite of such a snake within an hour or two. The hunter who confronts a rattler under those conditions is facing as deadly an animal as he will ever see. Yet if he spots it first and stays out of range he is entirely safe.

The snake can strike a third to half its length at the most, and does not leap at or rush its victim. It will lash out at anything that comes within reach, and it can deal death in the flick of an eye. The person bitten feels the fangs almost before he sees the head move. But the snake he sees is not the one to fear. It's only if he goes too near that he is in mortal danger.

The most productive snake country I have ever hunted is in north Florida, the region of live oaks and Spanish moss just south of the Georgia border. I've had some memorable days there. The rattlers are eastern diamondbacks, biggest of the poisonous snakes of North America, reaching a length of more than six feet and rivaling the terrible tiger snake of Australia and the cobra of Asia for deadliness.

Most Florida hunters use a highly effective method. They drive the rattlers from their dens with gasoline. The diamondbacks do not hibernate because of the mild winters. But they do spend the time from fall to early spring in dens, although not in large numbers, and most of the time the dens are holes excavated by the land tortoise locally called the gopher, resembling a woodchuck burrow in the North.

The rattlers leave tracks in sliding in and out of the gopher hole. When the hunter finds telltale sign, he pushes a length of garden hose down into the burrow—it may extend thirty feet or more—and when he reaches the end he listens for the buzzing of an aroused snake.

If he hears it, he pours a little gasoline into the hose, forces it through by blowing, pulls the hose out and steps back to wait for the snake to emerge. They cannot tolerate the gas fumes, and most of the time they slither forth within two or three minutes. It's almost a sure way of taking the big diamondbacks.

One highly successful Florida hunter of my acquaintance is Paul Allen, who lived near my home in Michigan until he moved to Sarasota in 1965. His father and mother ran a roadside reptile house in southeastern Michigan until the father died in an hour from the bite of an Indian cobra, and Paul has hunted snakes of all kinds since he was a small kid.

He does not like the gas method of taking diamondbacks, for the reason that, as he says, he hunts for sport. "I want to take my snakes the hard way," he told me once, "like still-hunting deer or jump-shooting ducks."

Like the hunters who use gasoline,

Paul relies on finding his rattlers in gopher holes. He captures them by slipping up to the hole very quietly, approaching from the side opposite the sloping ramp of sand left by the gopher, so that the snake will not see him.

Usually he can count on a broad belly track in the sand to betray its presence. If he finds such a track but can't see the snake, he falls back on a flashlight to look for it deeper in the hole. Often, however, he finds it lying just inside the entrance, no more than a foot or two down. Reaching in with a hook and pulling it into the open is then an easy matter.

"It's when you have your diamondback outside the hole that the real excitement begins," Paul says. That is something of an understatement, for he is the kind of snake hunter who pins the reptile's head with his hook, grasps it behind the jaws and drops it into a carrying bag with his hands.

I have seen him hold the head of a six-footer less than a foot from his face, its fangs dripping straw-colored venom, while the powerful body twisted and writhed in his grip, studying it at what he mildly calls close range. He has been bitten once, but that was while handling rattlers in the reptile house, not while hunting them. Nevertheless, he takes chances I would not take for all the gold in Fort Knox.

Allen finds some of his best hunting in recently burned areas where fire has destroyed the cover and the snakes are easy to locate when they have to take refuge in gopher burrows.

Some of the most dangerous, and easily the most spooky, snake hunting I know about is a method I have never tried and don't intend to. That is wading the black pools of a southern swamp in the darkness of night with a headlamp, looking for water moccasins.

Paul Allen and his partner Hank Hall are the only hunters of my acquaintance who do it. I have known them to take almost seventy cottonmouths in an afternoon and night of hunting in the Big Cypress Swamp, in south Florida between Alligator Alley and the Tamiami Trail, capturing the snakes with tongs and bringing them home alive.

"I realize there are many hunters who would face an enraged grizzly without the slightest feeling of fear, but could not be compelled to wade into one of those moccasin pools," Paul admits. "They are spooky places, with sawgrass, slippery logs, stumps, Spanish moss, and water black as ink and three or four feet deep. I've seen more than a dozen cottonmouths in such a pool at one time, my headlight picking them out as they swam or crawled. But Hank and I just aren't afraid of snakes, and hunting those moccasins is great sport."

My reply to that is that when it

252

comes to hunting them chest-deep in the mucky water of a swamp pool after dark, somebody else can have the sport.

There is one rattlesnake performance that few snake hunters, even professionals, ever see and that most of them are totally unaware of. It is the strange sparring match that reptile authorities call the combat dance, staged by two rival males.

The snakes rear as far off the ground as they can, sometimes as high as three feet in the case of big ones, facing one another, often with the tail and back part of the body of one lying on or across the other. Then they weave back and forth in a slow, rhythmic dance. Sometimes, in addition to this strange swaying, they twine around each other.

Nobody knows what starts the argument. One snake may wrap its neck around the other and throw its opponent forcibly to the ground. But they do not rattle or use their fangs, and usually nobody gets hurt.

Snake experts long believed it was a courtship performance, until it was discovered that it occurs all through the summer and fall and that it always involves two males.

It's a ritual not often witnessed. The only person who ever told me of watching it was a Montana homesteader. The snakes that time were prairie rattlers. The dance has also been reported for canebrake, timber, Pacific and diamondback rattlers, and for the sidewinder.

I can't say that I like dangerous snakes, any more than any other man does. But I have to rate them among the most interesting wild creatures I know about, and hunting them under the right conditions is as exciting as anything a sportsman can do.

I once heard a Pennsylvania hunter who had hung up a respectable score on timber rattlers and copperheads state the case very well.

"I've seen more than one spectator come close to heart failure just watching the proceedings," he said. "I'm sure I'll never have a chance to hunt tigers or lions or elephants. Probably I'll never even go after a big bear. But as long as there are copperheads and rattlesnakes on the mountain ledges within a dozen miles of where I live, you'll never hear me complain. They give me all the action I need."

17

THE ART OF GAME CALLING

Make like a rabbit

My friend Frank Heidelbauer said
it as well as anybody ever has.

"There are no words to describe
the eyes of a stalking fox," he told
me. "They're tan-yellow, big and
dilated, almost like the eyes of an
owl, and they watch with an intense,
hypnotic, terrifying stare. Every
time I've had one come real close
I've had the feeling that this must
be about what a human experiences
if he is lying helpless in the jungle
and watching a man-eating tiger pad
in for the kill."

When Frank said that, many years
ago, he had killed about a dozen red
foxes that he called in with a predator
call, all of them within thirty feet.
Four he did in with a .38 caliber
sidearm, the closest exactly twenty
inches from his face.

That was in the early days of predator calling. He ran his score con-
siderably higher later on.

He was the first fox caller I ever
hunted with. An aircraft pilot and
special enforcement officer for the
Iowa Conservation Commission at the
time, he was also a born outdoorsman

255

and hunter, one of the most skilled I have ever spent time with. He was one of the first in the country to take up fox calling, too.

Back in the early 1950's he began to hear more and more stories about hunters who were using a call that imitated the squeal of an injured rabbit to bring red foxes within gun range.

Frank had been interested in game calling since boyhood. He had used a duck call since he was big enough to lug a gun, had tolled a lot of crows to their death, and for two years in a row had won the National Goose Calling Contest at Missouri Valley, Iowa, the first of its kind held in the country.

The idea of calling foxes fascinated him, and he bought two or three of the commercial calls then coming on the market. But he wasn't satisfied with the sound they made, so he

256

A red fox, feasting on a rabbit it has killed (left), hears a call and turns toward the sound. Hidden behind a log, a hunter sounds his call (right) and brings a fox into range (below).

finally cobbled up a homemade device from old duck-call parts and pitched it to mimic the groaning squeal of a badly hurt jackrabbit. He also discovered that toy jumping frogs from the dime store emitted a squeak that sounded like a mouse, and he purchased a supply of the frogs.

He got a chance to test his new equipment on a cold January day when he spotted a fox curled in a tight ball in the center of a big plowed field, without a blade of grass or stray tumbleweed to hide him. Frank managed to get within three-hundred yards, but he was carrying a 12-gauge shotgun and he might as well have been a mile away. So he bellied down in a little hollow, reached out for a few clods of dirt and built a low parapet in front of his face, and then blew a series of agonized rabbit squeals. He was ready to blow a second series when he saw the fox coming across the field at a hard gallop.

Mr. Red was neither suspicious nor cautious. Frank kept blowing and he kept coming. When he was forty feet away Heidelbauer fell back on one of his toy frogs. The fox slowed to a walk, cocking his head this way and that to locate the sound. When he stopped he was just seven feet from the hunter.

Frank rolled to his knees then and the fox jumped back his own length, astonishment written all over him. He backed away, but didn't bolt until the man stood erect. Then he ran like a red streak, but it was too late.

I went out with Heidelbauer toward the end of that winter to see how he did it.

It was during the mating season, when lovelorn foxes are often seen on the move in the middle of the day, walking or trotting across open fields. We sat in Frank's car and watched one cross two stubble fields and an old pasture, in plain sight the whole time on the flat Iowa prairie, before he finally bedded down. The place he picked for that was a small abandoned gravel pit, grown up with brush, in the middle of a plowed field.

There was a larger pit about two-hundred yards downwind from him, a perfect spot for calling. We made a wide circle and reached it without showing ourselves. Next we bellied down on the slope of the pit, about fifty feet apart, stuck a thin fringe of sweet clover in place on the rim in front of us to hide our faces, and Frank started to call.

What followed was as exciting to watch as any hunting experience I had ever had. It took three or four series of rabbit squeals, spaced a couple of minutes apart, to move the fox. He poked his head out of the brush for a look and Frank coaxed him along.

He covered sixty yards on his belly, creeping ahead a foot at a time,

The agonized squeals of a dying rabbit, imitated with a predator call, brought this red fox almost into the lap of the waiting hunter. The fox probably realizes now that he has been suckered, but discovery of the man has come too late to save his skin.

A camouflaged caller lures a bobcat astonishingly close. Stubtail seems particularly susceptible to the lure of a call. Often he will approach within a few feet, and then sit down and look around, waiting to pinpoint the injured rabbit.

stopping to peer and listen. When he was about thirty feet away Frank stopped calling and went over to mouse squeaks on the toy frog. He had decided to kill this fox with his .38 service revolver, and he wanted it close.

There was a little sag in the ground in front of him, and when the fox went down into it he brought the .38 up, cocked and ready. He took the shot at ten feet and the fox never knew what happened. If I hadn't seen it I wouldn't have believed it.

Heidelbauer's experience in fox calling in the level and open country of Iowa was somewhat different from that of other callers I have known since.

He considered that it was important to keep the fox in sight the whole time, from the place where it started coming until it was within range. The sites he liked best were plowed fields, stubbles and old grassy pastures. Once he spotted a fox in a place of that kind, if there was a spot in which to hide within three-hundred to four-hundred yards with the wind in his favor, he considered the fox as good as his.

It doesn't take a great deal of cover to hide a caller, especially if he is wearing camouflage gear or an old faded hunting coat, the kind he would use in a duck blind. And most callers agree that natural cover is better than a blind. A fence grown up with weeds or grass does nicely. So will a ravine or ditch or creek bed where the caller can lie on the bank and peer over the edge through a screen of grass. One of the most important rules is that he must not be silhouetted on the skyline. If he is calling from the slope of a hill he should have the crest behind him.

Frank Heidelbauer never had much luck bringing foxes within range in timber, even in an open belt of trees along a stream. If Mr. Red had that much cover available his natural wariness asserted itself. He was likely to circle and try to get the wind before he approached closely, and if he smelled man at close range he cleared out.

One thing a caller learns quickly is that farmland foxes do not show much fear of human scent at a distance, probably because they are accustomed to it, just as they are used to seeing and hearing people and farm machinery in operation. But if the man smell drifts near them they pay attention in a hurry. I have known them to approach a caller, coming into the wind, within three-hundred yards, but then they stop, take note and shy off.

Frank Heidelbauer had no luck picking a calling spot at random and sitting down to call, although I know other callers who do that regularly in good fox country. Frank liked to locate his fox, get within four-hundred yards of it without alerting it to the fact that he was in the neighborhood, and go to work with his rabbit squealer.

I saw him call one other fox that I'll never forget. He coaxed it across a field and brought it within two paces of where he lay hidden in thin grass and weeds beside a fence. While it stood there, turning its head this way and that in an effort to locate the mouse it had heard, he yelled in its face, "Get the hell out of here!" That one swapped ends in a blur of motion and was running when it hit the ground.

Although the red fox was the first predator to attract the attention of callers, it wasn't long before coyotes and bobcats were being called with as much frequency as foxes, and in a few places hunters were doing well calling gray foxes, sometimes at night with the help of headlights. The gray, incidentally, is far less wary and cautious than the red, and easier to call.

Wherever the caller is located and whatever the animal he calls, the technique is much the same. He must find, first of all, an area that has a good population of whatever he hopes to take. In brush or timbered country he will not be able to locate an animal in advance, stalk close to it and start calling. Nor does he need to. If he chooses the right stand and has mastered the sounds made by an agonized rabbit, he is likely to get action with little delay. Predator calling is no more difficult than duck or crow calling, but the more terror and agony the caller puts into it the better his chances of success.

There are a number of commercial calls on the market, some of them very good. For the most part they mimic the death squealing of a cottontail, but a few are pitched to imitate the harsher gravel-voiced screams of a jackrabbit. The beginner should look for one that he finds easy to use, that has a good tone and carrying power.

One of the best ways to learn to call is from a record. A number of call manufacturers put them out, and they allow the beginner to practice as long and often as he likes. When it comes to perfecting the technique, if he has an experienced caller with whom he can spend time under actual hunting conditions, he's in luck.

As for the mouse squeak that most callers fall back on to bring a called animal the last few yards, there are various devices that will produce that sound. I know one caller who found that a picture postcard made in France, with a small mechanical squeaker laminated between two layers, was hard to beat. But best of all, for the hunter who can master it, is the squeak produced by sucking on the skin on the back of the hand or on a joint of a finger. This can pro-

A western hunter positions himself in front of a thicket that will break his outline but afford him a clear view in front and to both sides. In many places in the West a caller can expect to attract a fox, coyote or bobcat, possibly an elk or deer, or even a black bear or mountain lion if there are any in the area.

duce an extremely lifelike imitation of mouse noise, and is high pitched and far carrying. I have seen Cree Indians on the goose marshes of James Bay—they are among the world's most expert callers, imitating just about anything that walks or flies—lure an owl within arm's length of their campfire with that hand squeak.

The approach to the calling site is all-important. If the animal gets the slightest warning of the hunter's presence, by sight, sound or smell, calling is a waste of time. In open country a rise of ground that has to be crossed or a fence that must be climbed can put a quick end to the hunt. Even in brush or timber, if the caller lets himself be silhouetted

A called coyote slinks close, eyes ablaze with the lust to kill the helpless rabbit it believes is waiting. Bringing such an animal up within arm's reach is a hair-raising experience.

against the sky at the top of a ridge there's a good chance he will give himself away.

The most successful callers, hunting in an area where they have reason to believe there is a fox, coyote or bobcat in front of them but where they have no chance of seeing it, usually pick a calling site on an elevation where they will have a clear view ahead and on both sides. Knolls overlooking swamps, swales or marshes are good spots. So is the head of a draw or gully, or a place on a hillside close to a deer runway or other game trail, if tracks indicate that predators are in the habit of traveling there.

The caller leaves his car out of sight, preferably in a spot behind a hill, and he is careful not to talk, slam a door or make any other noise. He climbs the hill, walking into the wind, but does not cross the crest in a standing position. Instead he gets down, crawls over, and moves far enough down the opposite slope that he can sit and call without being silhouetted on the skyline.

He calls from the shelter of thin brush that will break his outline, from beside a rock, or in tree shadows that will camouflage him, and from a sitting position. Animals pay far less attention to a sitting man than to one standing erect.

If he draws a blank he moves ahead to the next ridge or to some other promising spot, and repeats the performance.

One of the most important rules is for the caller to remain completely motionless from the time he begins calling until the animal is close enough for the shot and he moves to raise his gun.

The kind of gun he needs depends on what he is calling and on the type of country. In areas of heavy cover, where foxes, bobcats and coyotes are likely to come close without being seen, a shotgun is the preferred weapon. In open areas many callers prefer a varminter rifle with a good scope that lets them reach out if they spot an incoming animal that refuses to come all the way. The scope can be a handicap at close range, however, and some stay with iron sights instead and count on getting their shots close enough that a scope is not needed.

Although calling is a year-around sport, some of the best of it comes in winter when the ground is snow-covered. The right camouflage then is a pair of white coveralls, large enough to fit over heavy wool clothing, a white hat or cap, white gloves and if the weather is cold a white parka hood. Many hunters also wrap their guns with white tape at that time of year. For keeping dry while sitting or lying in a snowbank, some winter callers carry a cloth-backed, white rubber sheet.

Foxes, bobcats and coyotes are by no means the only predators that will respond to a call. Badgers, coons, mink, weasels, skunks, house cats, hawks, owls, eagles and even deer have been reported by many callers.

Some of the strangest calling I have heard about was done by Murry and Winston Burnham, two Texas hunters who pioneered in the use of predator calls twenty years or more ago. They devised a call that imitated the squalling cries of a seagull in trouble, and used it to bring in more than one-thousand coons in a period of three or four years. They started calling shortly before dark, and often took ten or a dozen coons in a night.

I know a few hunters in the west who have had marked success in calling bears and mountain lions, and for bigtime excitement that is hard sport to match.

Much of the thrill comes from the behavior of the animal called, whatever it may be. One will come in at a dead run, intent only on the meal he expects to find. The next will take advantage of cover, creep in furtively, circle beyond gun range, stop every few yards to size things up.

Bobcats are especially adept at approaching unseen. They move from one clump of brush to another, follow gullies, stop often to look and listen. I have been told of instances where a bobcat crossed an open sagebrush flat for a couple of hundred yards without showing itself, and the caller had no inkling it was there until it stepped into sight fifteen feet away, ears laid back, eyes blazing, every muscle tense with lust to kill. Cats, and occasionally coyotes, failing to locate the dying rabbit that has lured them, sometimes lie down and wait for it to scream again, often no more than three or four paces from the caller. At such times, hard as it is to believe, bobcats have even been shot at and missed without taking alarm.

Bob Henderson, an expert South Dakota caller (he brought in seventy coyotes, sixteen bobcats, twenty-five red foxes and six grays in one four-month period), told me of calling five coyotes from a distance of almost a mile, from a stand overlooking a dry river bed. They covered five-hundred yards, coming five abreast and running like the wind, and went out of sight in sagebrush. The next he saw of them they were on top of him. The nearest one jumped across his legs as it rushed in to nail the injured rabbit. He killed two of the five, only yards away, missed shots at the other three, and confessed that when it was all over he had the worst case of buck fever he could recall.

It was also Henderson who sat down one day in front of a clump of brush in a cattle trail at the top of a bluff overlooking a big flat, and blew three series of agonized rabbit squeals. He waited a minute then to see what would happen.

What happened was that without the slightest warning, no sound or hint of movement, he felt hot breath on the back of his neck!

He swiveled his head around very slowly and looked a snarling coyote in the face at arm's length. It had come up behind him and arrived ready for a kill. Its hackles were standing, its ears laid flat, its eyes blazing, and the bared teeth were just thirty inches from Henderson's face.

One was probably as surprised as the other. They stared each other down for a few seconds, then the coyote took a few steps back and turned to slink away. At that point Bob rolled around and made the kill with one shot.

That was an unusual encounter, but it serves nicely to illustrate the kind of hair-raising excitement a hunter can expect if he buys a predator call and learns to make noises like those of a rabbit dying by inches.

RIFLES FOR SMALL GAME

Savage Model 65 bolt action, chambered for the .22 Long Rifle or .22 Magnum cartridge, is patterned after a high-powered rifle. The 5½-pound rifle, with 20-inch barrel, takes a 6-round clip magazine.

Savage Model 340 bolt-action rifle is chambered for the .22 Rem. for varmints, and the .30/30 for larger game. The varmint model has a 22-inch barrel, weighs 7½ pounds, takes a 5-round clip magazine.

Winchester Model 310 is a single-shot bolt-action rifle that shoots .22 Shorts, Longs, or Long Rifles. It weighs 5⅝ pounds, has a 22-inch barrel.

Savage/Anchutz Model 54 Sporter combines an accurate small-bore action with a sporting stock for the small-game hunter. Chambered for either the .22 Long Rifle or Magnum; receiver is grooved, tapped and drilled for scope mounting.

Remington Model 582, a bolt-action tubular repeater, is chambered for the .22 Short, Long or Long Rifle cartridges. Tubular magazine holds 20 Shorts, 15 Longs, 14 Long Rifles. Weight: 5 pounds.

Remington Model 700 BDL Varmint Special, a heavy-barreled version of the big-game rifle, comes in .222 Rem., .22/250 Rem., .223 Rem., 6mm Rem., .234 Win., .25/06 Rem. Barrel and receiver are equipped with scope bases.

Savage-Stevens Model 72 Crackshot, a single-shot falling-block action modeled after the 1894 version, features an octagonal barrel like the original. Chambered for .22 Long Rifle, Long or Short cartridges.

Savage Model 24D is a combination rifle/shotgun. Comes in .22 Long Rifle/20 or .410 gauge; .22 Magnum/20 gauge. Barrel length; 24 inches; weight; 7½ pounds.

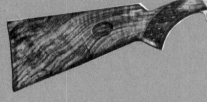

Winchester 9422 is the .22-caliber version of the famous lever-action .30/30. Available for the .22 rimfire or the .22 Win. Magnum. Barrel length, 20½ inches; weight, 6¼ pounds.

Browning .22 Automatic takes down in three seconds to a compact 19 inches. Magazine holds 11 Long Rifle cartridges or 12 Shorts. The rifle loads through stock, ejects through trigger plate.

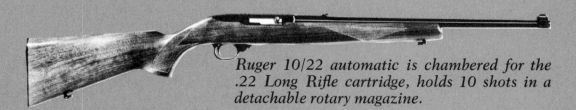

Winchester Nylon 66, an automatic chambered for the .22 Long Rifle cartridge, has a stock of structural nylon. Tubular magazine holds 14 cartridges. Barrel length, 19⅝ inches; weight, 4 pounds.

Ruger 10/22 automatic is chambered for the .22 Long Rifle cartridge, holds 10 shots in a detachable rotary magazine.

269

Part III

FLYING GAME

18

CROWS

Challenge for the shotgunner

The grove was small, covering less than three acres, with farm buildings close by on one side. The trees stood in straight rows, four or five yards apart. It had begun as a shelter-belt planting, to fend the snow and cold winds of the Dakota prairie away from the house and barn.

I pulled off the road beside it in the early dusk of a winter evening, stepped out of my car and blew a harsh squall of distress on my crow call.

Crows boiled up out of that small stand of trees in an angry black cloud as dense as a swarm of overgrown bees. They filled the sky above the treetops, circling, swooping, diving, cawing and yelling in wild turmoil. It was hard to believe that a three-acre woodlot could spew out such a feathered mob.

That patch of timber, close beside what was then US16 but is now Interstate 90, in the southeast corner of South Dakota twenty-five miles east of the Missouri, held a winter roost of more than eighty-thousand crows. I had surprised them just after they had settled down for the night,

273

and they leaped into the sky to the last bird when I sounded my alarm cry. It was one of the most astonishing spectacles I have ever witnessed.

In midafternoon the next day I was crouched in a blind at the edge of a cornfield a mile west of that shelterbelt grove, in company with one of the most skilled crow hunters I have ever met. Chuck Kilburn was at that time a conservation officer with the South Dakota Department of Game, Fish and Parks, doing little in his spare time except hunt crows. He passed up fishing all summer long and just about quit hunting ducks and upland game in the fall, to learn all he could about crows and hunting them. In twelve years he killed more than ten thousand, all singly, by calling them in and dropping them one at a time. He had never fired a shot into a rookery flock and never killed two with one shot.

He had friends who believed he had hung up a national record in crow shooting. "I wouldn't know," he told me, "but I do know I've had an awful lot of action and excitement, and I'm convinced I have given the pheasant and waterfowl population of South Dakota a boost." He believed that the crow does serious damage by destroying the eggs and young of pheasants, ducks and songbirds. Record holder or not, one thing was certain. I learned quickly that what he did not know about crow hunting was hardly worth knowing.

Our blind that day was made from a discarded minnow net, draped over standing cornstalks and held in place with clip-type clothespins. Tumbleweeds placed around it and woven into the meshes of the net camouflaged it. It fitted into its surroundings the way a skulking bittern loses itself in tall rushes. That is the first requirement of a crow hunter's blind.

I had done a fair amount of crow shooting prior to that day, but Kilburn was introducing me to a new wrinkle that I had never seen tested. We had put out nothing in the way of decoys. There was no stuffed owl, no crow profiles in front of the blind or in the nearby fence border.

"If you can call you don't need decoys," Chuck had told me.

By four o'clock that afternoon a flock of a thousand crows had assembled on the far side of a big prairie slough, half a mile from our cornfield, and more were arriving by the minute. Off to the northwest, over the village of White Lake, they were stringing along in broken flight, some so low they barely cleared the farm fences. From the northeast and southeast similar flights were drifting in, converging on the general area of the roost. These were the first arrivals, flying back after a day of foraging over the countryside.

The mob that was building up across the slough was restless, cawing, milling, settling to the ground, jumping back into the air. Every now

274

and then a few broke away to drift toward the shelter-belt grove. In another half hour that movement would increase to a steady traffic.

"When they really start to go to the roost we'll be in business," Kilburn promised.

A dozen lifted off the prairie, climbed lazily and turned toward the grove. They were not making any commotion. They were going home for the night, silent and crafty, as they usually are at that time.

The wind was from the west, blowing hard, and they were riding it. They wouldn't be able to hear Chuck's calling until they had passed us and were downwind, and then in all likelihood they would pay no attention. Crows are reluctant to turn and fight their way back against a high wind.

This little band went by, and Kilburn didn't even try for them. But trailing them a hundred yards behind was a pair of strays, and they flew within range of his call. He spoke to them and they came around like two black kites pulled by strings, pumping their wings, rising and falling, cawing to the bird they had heard down in the corn.

One came in low, almost hanging in the air over our heads, trying to locate the crow that was doing the groaning. The other stayed forty yards up, bucking the wind. I took the low one, Chuck the other. We shot together and two dead crows came tumbling into the cornfield.

That was the start of an hour of as good wingshooting as I can recall. As roosting time neared, the flight turned into a steady stream of crows, singles, pairs, little groups of four or five, big bunches up to a hundred.

Not all of them could be called. Some were too far away, others too tired from a long day of flying to care what was happening to a brother crow. But the lull between shots was brief and when the light began to fail and the flight dwindled, despite the wind and the poor conditions for calling we had between twenty-five and thirty dead crows down in the corn. It had been a very convincing demonstration of the fact that the crow hunter does not necessarily have to rely on decoys — provided his skill with a call is sufficiently great.

Two things happen over the northern half of the United States each autumn that hold great possibilities for shotgunners. One is the fall flight of waterfowl, the other the southward migration of crows that takes place at about the same time.

The ducks and geese need no press agent. Hunters in every state count the days until they are due and cash in when the time comes. On the other hand, crows by the millions come south from their Canadian nesting grounds to winter roosts scattered across the northern and central states from the Atlantic seaboard to the Missouri River and beyond, but only a small number of dedicated crow shooters hunt them.

The fall crow flight in many states, for reasons no one can explain, is no longer as heavy as it was ten to fifteen years ago and the populations in the winter roosts have declined accordingly.

In Pennsylvania, for example, I knew of roosts in the late 1950's that held not fewer than fifty thousand birds. But there has been a steady decline the last fifteen years, both in summer crows and winter migrants, a spokesman for the Pennsylvania Game Commission tells me. The same is true in New York, Ohio, Indiana, Illinois, southern Michigan, Wisconsin and other states. The winter buildup is not what it used to be in any of these areas.

The Missouri Conservation Department estimates that the winter population in that state is down by at least 200,000 birds, although game men think the drop is accounted for in part by the fact that crows in the Bootheel, which once held some of the largest roosts in the state, may have moved across the Mississippi to new locations. But the states on the east side of the river report no corresponding influx.

The big roosts in South Dakota have declined in comparable fashion and only a few have good populations today. Even those are far smaller than they once were. State game men put part of the blame for the slump on the fact that there has been considerable roost shooting done, driving the birds to other locations.

One thing seems certain, however. Although the winter crow supply has dwindled sharply in many states, there are still more than enough crows to warrant sport hunting and furnish firstclass action.

The Missouri Conservation Department, for example, continues to put out an annual list of the location of winter roosts for the benefit of sportsmen (some fifty roosts are presently listed, the larger ones holding an estimated twenty-thousand crows) and Missouri hunters still account for about 200,000 of the birds a year.

In Oklahoma one of the biggest winter roosts in the country, near Ft. Cobb, is still populated by an estimated two million crows each winter and shows no evidence of a slump. And in Kansas state game men report that the winter populations are about the same as in the past, particularly in certain central counties. One of the largest roosts in the state, in Reno County near the town of Medora, has largely disappeared as a result of the clearing of large groves of catalpa trees, but wildlife officials believe these birds have moved to other locations. The neighboring counties of Stafford and Kingman,

Three crows feed in an open field. In winter they leave their roost shortly before full daylight and scatter over the surrounding countryside in search of groceries, sometimes flying as far as thirty or forty miles. In late afternoon they return to a massing area, and then, just as darkness falls, they fly silently into the roost. It is these morning and evening flights that supply lively sport for the crow hunter.

for example, still harbor winter flocks as big as ever.

In general the winter crows follow a fixed routine, using the same roost night after night as long as they are not driven out. Shortly before daylight each morning they leave the roost, usually trickling out to a massing area in an open field nearby. They fly out in singles and pairs, bunches numbering from ten to two-hundred, and now and then big bands of up to two-thousand. They stay on the ground in the massing area, making no commotion, until full daylight or a little later. Then they string out along their flyways and scatter for the day, to rove and feed. The bulk of the flock will stay within ten to fifteen miles of the roost as long as food holds out. But as their groceries grow scarce they range farther away, and before the end of winter many birds may be flying about forty miles from the rookery.

They feed mostly in cornfields, around dumps, or in fields where farm fertilizer has been freshly spread. A garbage dump of the old type is a particularly good place to look for them in times of deep snow.

You rarely see a crow around the roosting area in the middle of the day, but you can get fair shooting by locating feeding birds, moving in without disturbing them, and picking a shooting location close enough that they can hear you call.

In midafternoon they start to drift back to the roost, reversing the pattern of the morning flight. They settle into fields no more than a mile or so away, loaf there for a time, and as the afternoon wanes move on to the main massing area they left at daylight. There they rest quietly until almost dark, when they fly silently into the roost.

In a crowded roost they spend the night perched in dense ranks, one tier above another, packed so closely they touch, and by morning the birds on the lower branches are usually soiled with the droppings of those above.

The two best times of day to shoot are when the birds are leaving the massing area in the morning and when they are returning to it in the afternoon. Their morning and afternoon behavior is altogether different, however.

They come out of the roost at daylight with fire in their tails, rested and full of devilment, spoiling for trouble. For the hunter who wants to use an owl decoy, that's the time to do it. Even without the owl, a few distress squalls on a call will bring crows piling in from every direction, ready to take on whatever they find. Morning shooting on a good flyway is as lively wingshooting as a hunter will ever find.

In the afternoon you are dealing with tired crows. They come stringing in from daylong flight and they

Camouflaged from head to foot and half hidden behind a tree, a hunter uses his call to sound the distress cry of a crow in trouble. Good calling is essential to good shooting, and the more pain and urgency the hunter puts into it, the better are his chances of success.

are not itching for a fight. If they see an owl perched on a post they'll probably swing aside and make a pass or two at him, but their hearts are not in it. Weary as they are, however, the squall of another crow in trouble is something they are not likely to ignore. The caller may have to coax them, and they won't come eager and hellbent as they do in the morning, but if he knows the tricks of his trade they'll come.

Anywhere in a good wintering area, the hunter who does not know the location of a roost can find one with little difficulty by trailing an afternoon flight a few times. That leisurely

movement of the birds home from their feeding grounds is a common daily sight from about three o'clock until dusk, wherever they winter in numbers. Look for crows strung out above the fields, now and then perching to rest, all traveling in the same direction.

Once you spot such a flight stay with it, and sooner or later it will lead you to what you are looking for. If the roost is used by many crows you will have no trouble identifying it. Droppings will lie thick on the ground, broken twigs and branches will be strewn about, and the trees will be whitened with birdlime.

It may take you a week or more to locate a roost, but once you find it you have a full winter of crow hunting ahead. Only on one condition, however. If you want the crow supply to last and the shooting to hold up until spring, stay out of the roost itself. Shooting there, especially if heavy and persistent, is not sport to begin with and is almost sure to cause the birds to move to another location. Leave the place undisturbed and confine your crow hunting to the flyways along which they leave and approach, keeping at least half a mile from the roost.

Study the situation until you figure out the flight pattern by which the birds disperse and reassemble. Wind direction often makes a difference. Given their free choice, crows seem to prefer to come to their massing area against the wind. But at a big roost, where thousands are assembling, they usually come from two or three directions at once, following established routes and using the same flyways day after day, no matter which way the wind may be blowing.

At the White Lake roost in South Dakota, for example, there were three main flights, one from the north, one from the northeast, and a third from the southeast. The birds came along those same flight lanes every afternoon, regardless of wind direction, and Chuck Kilburn told me that they had used the same field, just west of the grove, as a massing area for at least twelve years.

Once you know the flight pattern you're ready to put up your blind. The first requirement for it is that the crows must have a clear approach and you must have clear shooting. Also you should be able to see the flight and watch the birds as they come in. Locate the blind with those things in mind. Look for a spot at the edge of a grove or shelter belt, in a field of standing corn, along a ditch bank or in a brushy or weedy fencerow.

Stay away from roads, telephone and power lines, and occupied farm buildings. Crows are prone to shun such places or gain altitude before they fly over. Even farm machinery parked in a field can be enough to alert them.

You need maximum concealment, for the crow's eyesight is extremely keen and so are his wits, but your blind must blend into the surroundings. Crows will avoid an alien patch of cover even if another crow is begging for reinforcements. So build the blind of the materials around it; weeds in a weedy field, brush at the border of woods, evergreen branches where there are evergreen trees, and so on.

A haystack that's been there a long time is hard to beat. Gouge out a hole in one side, set up a screen of snowfence or chicken mesh in front, disguise it with hay, and you're in business. In a field with cornshocks, open one up and little else is needed. On low ground or slough bottoms make the blind of the grass and weeds that grow there.

When the ground is snow-covered there's nothing better than a shallow cave scooped out of a snowbank, plus a white parka or camouflage suit for the hunter. For some reason crows are not suspicious of a man dressed in..white, and you can get terrific shooting with very little in the way of a blind. They can even be called in while the hunter is crouched in an open field in a white parka, with no blind at all.

Any crow hunter will find it worth his while to carry two items for building a portable blind. With an old minnow net and a pocket full of clip-type clothespins he is ready for anything. Drape the net over brush, weeds, low trees or a fence, clip it in place and camouflage it according to the location. Such an outfit is easily carried, quickly set up, and screens the hunter as well as any blind he can build.

When it comes to calling, one basic call is all you need to use. That's the harsh signal of a crow in trouble. But of course it helps if you can give it variation.

Crows have a language of their own, and understand each other as well as humans do. They can exchange greetings, call the flock together to mob an owl, warn one another of danger. They have yells of distress, growls of anger, and even a death song. There is no better way to learn calling than to study their language and behavior in the field until you can identify and mimic each sound they make.

The most effective cry to bring them to a blind is a blend of excitement and distress. The best callers I have known start with a low note or two, pause, repeat it, pause again and then build up to a climax of long, growling squalls of anger and fright and pain. At the end they sound like a crow whose neck is being wrung.

It isn't easy to describe on paper, but as Chuck Kilburn told me once, the whole performance goes about like this in crow language: "Hi, everybody. There's something wrong around here. I don't like the looks of it. He's after me! He's got me! He's killing me! Help, help!" The more urgency and agony you put into it, the more shooting you'll get.

As for guns, most crow hunters like a 12-gauge full choked barrel that can reach out, and No. 5 or 6 shot is about right. Many use magnum loads.

In addition to his fall and winter shooting from a blind, Chuck Kilburn had another method of crow hunting that I have known no one else to practice. He did it in spring and summer and it provided unusual sport at a time of year when there was no other hunting available. It took advantage of two universal crow traits, endless curiosity and an inborn love of hell-raising.

"Convince a crow that some wild critter is in distress and he's got to investigate," Kilburn summed it up.

281

A *hunter places crow decoys in the branches of a low tree in front of his stand (left). They can be helpful, but are not nearly as effective as an owl decoy. Two crows respond to the lure of a call and the sight of other crows in the trees below, and the shotgunner scores a double (right).*

"Make him think another crow is in trouble and he'll come as if pulled by a string. Or let him know there is crow deviltry brewing and he can't stay out of it."

I spent the better part of a week with Chuck, hunting crows by his special method. It was as challenging as any shotgunning I had ever done, calling for the utmost in caution, patience, effort and skill.

It called for two men operating from a car, one to drive, the other to do the shooting. The team cruised very slowly along country roads until they spotted a crow feeding in a field or perched on a tree or post not more than half a mile away. If the crow was within calling distance they scanned the roadside ahead for a spot to drop the hunter off. It had to be on the side of the car opposite the crow, and chosen for weeds, brush, grass or other cover, or a ditch in which to hide. Always the car had to be between the gunner and the bird. If the hunters spotted such a place in time they were ready for the drop.

Failing that, or if the shooter was on the same side of the road as the crow, they kept going without changing the speed of the car, continuing down the road until they were out of sight of the crow or too far away for him to pay attention to them. There they turned around and drove slowly back to a drop-off place. The crow was now on the side of the car away from the hunter.

The drop was the critical step. The driver kept the car moving, only a little faster than a man can walk. He neither slowed down nor speeded up when the drop was made. The hunter opened the door on his side, jumped out, ran alongside the car for a few steps and ducked down into the patch of cover he had chosen. The moving car had hidden him from the crow.

It was the driver's job, and an exacting one, to reach across as his partner dived for the ditch and catch the door before it could slam shut. He held the door with his right hand, drove with his left, and kept going at the same speed as if nothing had happened. Half a mile down the road he could risk closing the door. A mile away, or out of sight, he could park.

The gunner, secreted in cover or lying flat on a roadside ditch bank, waited a few minutes until the car had disappeared and the crow had had time to forget that it passed. Then he went to work with his call. If he knew the art of calling the rest was routine.

This method of taking crows was hunting in the best sense of the word. You picked an individual bird and pitted your craft and your skill as a caller against his wariness and wits.

But summer crow hunting is now at least technically illegal over all of the country. The long arm of the federal government has reached out to give crows protection as migratory birds.

It began in 1972, with an announcement from the U. S. Fish and Wildlife Service that a new migratory-bird convention had been signed with Mexico, affording additional protection to thirty-two families of birds, including the Corvidae family that happens to embrace ravens, crows, magpies and jays. Under the terms of the convention, the federal agency said, crow shooting would become illegal except in the case of crows committing depredation on farm crops.

Apparently the top brass in the Fish and Wildlife Service had not been aware, when the convention was negotiated, that crows were corvine birds or that crow shooting stood among the leading winter pastimes for thousands of sportsmen in state after state.

The announcement stirred an angry hornet's nest among hunters and in state game agencies all across the country, and the Washington bureaucrats had second thoughts. The new regulations were being reviewed, they announced, and in the meantime crow hunting was still legal. The furor abated, temporarily.

A firm decision to protect the birds during their nesting and rearing time was finally reached. The rules now establish a federal framework similar to that under which water-fowl regulations are set. The crow season cannot exceed 124 days a year. Each state has the authority to control hunting methods, dates and limits within the federal framework, but hunting in nesting season or from aircraft is prohibited.

The only exceptions to these rules are in cases of crows committing or about to commit depredations on crops or other wildlife, or concentrated in sufficient number to constitute a health hazard.

So far, a number of states have indicated that they intend to take every possible advantage of those loopholes. Some say they will set no open and closed hunting seasons on crows if they can wiggle out of it. Others hint that they do not plan to enforce the federal regulations, and still others are permitting year-round crow shooting under the depredation exemption.

"If you see a crow, you see one about to depredate," a game biologist in one midwest state summed up his agency's feelings. Too, many of the big winter roosts, holding up to a million birds or more, fall in the health-hazard category, and the states that have them will not be likely to clamp down on crow hunting unless they are forced to by Washington.

The ban on summer crow hunting is certain to be highly unpopular with many sportsmen, including not only those who practice it but also those who believe, as Chuck Kilburn

At the edge of a snow-covered field, a hunter camouflaged in white scores on an incoming crow from an all-white blind. Winter crow shooting can be fast and productive. Crows flying back to the roost in late afternoon will even come within range of a hunter wearing white coveralls, although he is not hidden in a blind.

does, that the summer crow is a serious enemy of ducks, pheasants, quail, other ground-nesting birds, and young rabbits.

"Crows from the winter roosts feed mostly on waste corn in fields and feedlots," Chuck told me when we were hunting together. "The summer crow, on the other hand, is a crafty and persistent hunter of nests, and if

286

he is numerous enough he cuts a real swath in the population of young game birds, waterfowl and rabbits."

There is, however, a sound reason back of the decision to give protection to nesting crows. Over much of the eastern half of the United States, their numbers have slumped almost to the vanishing point. For that reason, many state game departments probably will approve the action.

In Pennsylvania, for example, the summer crow population has been declining steadily for the last twenty years. In Michigan the birds have fallen so low in numbers that state wildlife authorities were ready to ban summer hunting on their own, regardless of federal action. In my own area in southern Michigan, I have not seen an occupied crow nest in the last five years, and friends in other parts of the state report a similar shortage. Much the same situation prevails in many other states.

No one can be certain of the reasons for the decline, but most game authorities put the blame on agricultural sprays. Because summer crows eat great quantities of grasshoppers, grubs, beetles and caterpillars, they are highly vulnerable to any adverse effects that result from the use of pesticides.

"Normal consumption of these poisons generally does not cause immediate death, and perhaps not even prolonged death," says Paul Taylor, Pennsylvania predator specialist.

"But some of the compounds, taken in even limited quantities by certain birds, result in thin-shelled eggs or no eggs at all."

In one study Taylor located eight active crow nests in April and kept them under observation for four weeks. At the end of that time all eight had been abandoned. Not a single young bird was produced. Taylor calls it a rare occasion to find a nest of young crows anywhere in Pennsylvania today, and points out that while summer crows have been disappearing the winter crow population of the state has remained essentially constant. The winter crow nests in Canada, beyond the reach of heavy pesticide spraying, and because it finds little insect food when it comes south it is not exposed to pesticide residues in its food chain at that time of year.

Farm spraying is highly suspect, say many wildlife authorities. And while sportsmen are not greatly worried about the disappearance of the crow for his own sake, they and state game departments alike are bothered by a nagging question: As the crow has gone, so will quail, pheasants, rabbits, waterfowl and other game species go in a few more years? No one knows the answer.

But at least the present scarcity of nesting crows supports rather strongly the decision of the Fish and Wildlife Service to give them the benefit of a closed season.

19

RUFFED GROUSE

Thunderwings, the magnificent

The first time I shot at a ruffed grouse I was a kid on the farm, sixty years ago. Note that I said *at*.

It was a Saturday afternoon in October, and dad and mother had gone into town to dispose of our modest weekly crop of eggs and home-made butter and spend the money for the few staples we needed. On such a day town held no charm for a boy whose life was centered around hunting, fishing and the trapline that supplied his spending money.

I stayed home instead, and went for a walk with the 12-gauge hammer double that I prized above any other possession. It had so-called Damascus twist barrels, cheaply made but adequate for the black-powder shells of that day. I had acquired it because of the low price and the fact that even a scrawny kid could tolerate the light recoil of the cylinder-bored right barrel and the very slightly choked left.

It was a bright autumn day, sunny and blue-hazed. I crossed onto a neighbor's farm, hoping to see a fox squirrel or jump a cottontail, those two being about the only species of small game in our neighborhood then. I came to an old rail fence hung with wild grapevine and climbed over. As I jumped to the ground a grouse thundered into flight only two rail lengths away. He had been dusting there in the dry sand of a fence corner.

I jumped almost as high as the bird, and when my feet touched earth again I shot. I scrooched down to look under the cloud of black-powder smoke, a standard procedure with that ammunition. The grouse was nowhere in sight, not because I had killed him but because he had rocketed off unharmed.

Whenever I have hunted this magnificent game bird since, I have repeated that same performance an embarrassing share of the time. In other words, I am no dead-eye Dick where Thunderwings is concerned.

Given a good grouse dog that affords fair warning he has found a bird, allowed sufficient time to prepare myself for the flush mentally as well as physically, I do well enough. But the grouse that roars off the ground without a hint in advance, and puts a tree between himself and me in two or three yards of jet-fast flight, does not have a great deal to fear at my hands.

I'm not alone. Michigan game men kept score over a number of years, and came up with some revealing statistics. Michigan hunters were then accounting for upwards of 300,000 grouse a fall. But the study showed that a third of the 100,000 grouse hunters did not kill a single bird and that only one gunner in five killed as many as five in an entire season. The ones who made a real showing were seasoned, dyed-in-the-wool grouse addicts, most of them hunting over good dogs.

Over much of his range, which covers mainly the eastern half of the United States and is centered in the north from Minnesota to New England (although the bird is also found as far west as Oregon and Washington, south to Georgia and Alabama and north to the limit of trees in Canada and even in Alaska; in all he is native to forty-six states and provinces) this grouse goes by the common name of partridge. Often that is shortened to patridge, and much of the time hunters simply use the term pat in speaking of him. Occasionally he is also miscalled the ruffled grouse. There is no such bird but ruffled, and rattled, grouse hunters are common.

The hunter who can rack up a consistently high score on this fast-flying master of trickery is rare. As A. C. Bent, sportsman and dean of bird writers, put it in his *Life Histories of North American Game Birds*, published by the Smithsonian Institution in 1932, "There is no bird that so tests the skill of a good wingshot as this grouse. If a hunter takes his shots as they come, there are very few who can put a bird in the pocket for every three empty shells."

That is one of the major ingredients that give grouse hunting its great charm. The ruffed grouse has been called the king of American game birds so often that the title has become trite, and the fact that he is so hard to gather in accounts for much of the tremendous respect and affection that sportsmen have for him.

There are several factors that make him hard to hit. One is the thunder of his flush, a sudden explosive sound that unnerves many a hunter even after years of grouse hunting. Another is his speed of flight. He threads his way through trees and thickets like a brown, feathered rocket. The thick cover where he is most often found is greatly in his favor, too, and his ability to put a tree instantly between himself and the gun is close to uncanny.

No game bird seems to have a better idea of what to do and where to go when flushed than Thunderwings, and none can execute exactly the correct maneuver more swiftly.

Jumped within reach of a cedar or other evergreen, he bores his way behind it the instant the roar of his wings reaches the hunter. In the early part of the hunting season, when foliage is heavy in the grouse woods, he takes advantage of every leafy thicket. Later he is likely to get in the lee of a tree trunk in the shortest possible time.

One other trick he has that is highly disconcerting to the hunter. I have seen him do it often enough that I am convinced it is deliberate on his part and no accident of flight, either. That is to flush headlong, straight at the man with the gun, and pass overhead so close he could be swatted down with a tennis racket.

I remember one such bird that went by my face at a distance that let me feel the rush of his wings. He jumped no more than four or five yards in front of me and was passing me at head height almost before I knew what was happening. I attempted to swing on him as he rose, failed, twisted around in a 180-degree turn and got off a shot as he rocketed out of sight in the brush. It did him no damage. The hunter who can score in the face of that trick is exceptional indeed.

I know grouse hunters who, for one reason or another, hunt without a dog. In places where the behavior of the birds is right, some even prefer that method. Others go dogless out of necessity, some because of the expense and work of keeping and training a bird dog the year around in return for the few weeks of hunting permitted by the regulations of many states.

My friend Bill Scifres, Indiana outdoor writer, does most of his grouse hunting without a dog for still another reason. He keeps a top-notch setter and revels in her work. But during much of the Indiana grouse season, rattlesnakes and copperheads are still above ground in the places where Bill hunts. They are about as numerous as birds, and he will not risk putting Sugar down at that time of year.

The hunter who does not use a dog does best if he pussyfoots through grouse cover slowly and quietly, cocked mentally and physically and always ready for a shot. Brush-busting puts too many birds up out of sight. The stealthy approach is far more likely to let the hunter get close before the grouse takes alarm.

Good grouse dogs are not exactly plentiful, and many hunters are forced to dispense with them for that reason. It was Hal Sheldon, the New England sportsman and writer, an authority of some repute, who commented many years ago, "A good grouse dog is a highly desirable assistant to the shooter. A poor one is a damned nuisance."

On the other hand, Bill Schaldach, hunter, artist and writer, also of New England, and also an authority on grouse hunting, put things this way: "I am thankful for any small glimmering of ability and sense a dog may have, and I charitably overlook his faults."

I have hunted over a few great grouse dogs, but only a few, and I am indebted to them for some of the most splendid days I have spent afield with a gun and good companions.

In general, the behavior of this bird in front of a dog is close to ideal.

A male ruffed grouse poses on the log where, in all likelihood, he does his spring drumming. Proud, handsome, wary, fast in flight and hard to hit, this grouse is regarded by many hunters as the king of upland game birds.

Although now and then he may run and squat and run again before he is forced to flush, most of the time he lies to the point, especially if the dog comes in fast and spikes him down in the classic fashion of all pointing breeds, and the hunter can take his own sweet time about walking in for the flush.

Perhaps nothing is stranger about grouse behavior than the great difference between the birds in places where they have been hunted for generations and other places where they have been hunted almost not at all. Twenty-five years or so ago, that difference was demonstrated spectacularly in my home state of Michigan, where I have done the bulk of my grouse hunting.

In the farm woodlots of the southern counties, and in the cutover timberlands north as far as the Straits of Mackinac, the birds had grown wise in the ways of dogs and men. They were wily and tricky, as hard to

A hunter sends his setter into a patch of thick cover to search for birds. The ruffed grouse (some hunters miscall it ruffled) is a denizen of thickets, vine tangles, stream-bottom undergrowth, stands of low-growing evergreens. The dense cover where he is found often makes it easy for him to elude the gun.

hunt as the grouse of New England.

But in the state's Upper Peninsula, very few bird dogs were owned at that time and grouse hunting in the classic manner was rare. As a result the birds were almost completely un-tutored and unwary. The common method of shooting them was to walk old brush-bordered logging roads, spot them strolling in the edge of the brush ahead, and kill them either on the ground or as they flushed (which they were in no hurry to do), depending on the sporting ethics of the hunter. Some of the more unscrupulous varied this technique by driving slowly along woods roads and shooting from the car instead.

Those Upper Peninsula grouse were then hardly more difficult to kill than the smaller spruce grouse, the handsome dark bird of the northern swamps that has never been able to learn the lesson of fear and is most often called by the derisive name of fool hen.

Many times I have seen a spruce grouse, surprised on the ground, fly up into the low branches of a tree, perch there and watch the approaching human with total unconcern. They are as easily shot as pigeons in a park, and woodsmen short of food and having no gun have on many occasions gotten a meal by dropping a noose over the head of one of the perching birds and yanking it down.

More than once I have seen Upper Peninsula partridge behave almost as stupidly. But that was quite a few years ago. In the last two decades or so more and more hunters living there have come to use dogs, and more and

In part it grows out of the pleasure of good dog work, of outwitting a wild and beautiful bird. And in part, I suspect, it comes from the fact that he is hard to outwit and far harder to kill. Many an old grouse hunter has told me that nothing he has done in the woods affords more satisfaction than a clean kill on Thunderwings as the bird rises and bores away through the underbrush. As one once said, "The grouse knows by instinct what to do and how to do it. The hunter doesn't have time to think about it, and usually he doesn't know afterward what he did."

Like all wild things, the grouse has a home range where the individual bird lives out his life. Probably it does not often exceed twenty acres. But you are not likely to find birds simply by walking at random through such a place.

Again like all wild creatures, Thunderwings has certain fundamental requirements, and they govern where he is likely to be at any given time of the year. The foremost and most basic is food, of course.

When winter comes and deep snow covers the ground in the north woods, the grouse turns almost exclusively to a diet of tree buds. One of the prettiest sights I can remember was watching a flock of about a dozen fly quietly up from a north-country evergreen swamp one winter afternoon, settle silently in the top of a big yellow birch, and walk about on the

more Lower Peninsula dog owners have gone north with their setters and pointers. It does not take Thunderwings long to learn, and for the most part today the behavior of his kind is about the same on both sides of the Straits.

The charm of grouse hunting is something not easily defined. In part it depends on the setting, the brilliantly colored autumn woodlands, the dark evergreens, the frost-killed ferns underfoot, the roads and trails and deer runways where fallen leaves lie in a thick carpet and their bittersweet fragrance fills the nose like incense.

branches for the better part of an hour, garnering the fat winter buds.

But at the time when most hunting seasons are open and most grouse hunters go afield, the feeding habits of the grouse are totally different. In autumn he depends on beechnuts above all if he can find them, on such wild fruits and berries as wild apples, cherries, thornapples, dogwood, wild grapes and the viburnum known as the highbush cranberry. He is also very fond of clover if it is available, which it is likely to be along old logging roads. Wherever these foods are found in abundance, the hunter can expect to find grouse.

I recall an October when Jim Hacquoil and I took his two pointers (they were among the great grouse dogs I have known) into the wild, roadless country along the Tahquamenon River in northern Michigan. We went in by boat, landing about a dozen miles above the Big Falls.

We put in the better part of a half

A hunter approaches a grouse hidden under a windfall. Few birds are better served by protective coloration than Thunderwings. As a result, the hunter who is not using a dog seldom is aware of the presence of the grouse until it explodes from the ground with a nerve-shattering roar.

day hunting hardwood timber, the edges of balsam fir thickets, and the borders of alder bogs. There were no beechnuts that fall, at least where we looked for them, and we could find no birds on the beech ridges or in the other places.

Then we came into a brush-grown clearing on the river, that had been a hay meadow in the logging days. Clumps of thornapple grew in profusion around the edges and along the river bank, and every clump hung heavy with red fruit. In half an hour in that clearing we moved enough grouse to make the hunt a very satisfactory one.

Water apparently is another requirement of grouse, at least to the extent that in our country they are often found along the borders of cedar and alder swamps. Dust-dry upland woods are rarely good grouse areas.

Andy Ammann, upland-bird expert of the Michigan Department of Natural Resources, has a few rules about where to find Thunderwings that are worth passing along.

"Grouse live in young forests, and they're seldom far from streams, swamps or moist lowlands," he says. "Don't waste time in heavy timber stands where most of the trees are thirty feet or more in height. Except for slashings and thornapple thickets you'll have better luck in or near lowlands. Keep within sight of tag alder and you'll be likely to find birds. Stands of young aspen and thickets of

A setter finds a fallen grouse (above) and brings it proudly
back to the hunter (right). In the thick cover where most
grouse are shot, and where they blend perfectly with the colors
of the woodland floor, a retrieving dog is the hunter's best
friend. In fact, good dog work is one of the chief pleasures of
grouse hunting.

wild berries are productive spots, and small openings with clover and dandelions are the best of all."

The importance of clover as a grouse food is pointed up by the fact that in some state and national forests in Wisconsin old logging roads have been closed to vehicular traffic and seeded to clover for the benefit of grouse hunters. Many of them are laid out so that they provide an easy hike of two or three hours and bring the hunter back to his starting point at the gate. They offer some of the state's best hunting.

In addition to the typical grouse woods of the north, in my home state of Michigan farm woodlots yield a surprising number of birds, and they are fairly easily hunted in such places.

One highly encouraging development for bird hunters is the comeback the ruffed grouse has made in recent years as a result of stocking, in states where he had long since disappeared. In the Midwest, Indiana and Illinois are prime examples. Seven counties in southern Indiana now have a grouse season more than thirty days in length, and there is some excellent hunting. The state opened its first season in modern times only half a dozen years ago, after releases of live-trapped birds had taken hold.

In Illinois, where grouse have been

absent since the early 1900's (the last open season was in 1902), thirty-one birds livetrapped in southern Ohio were released on the eastern side of the Shawnee National Forest in 1967. In the summer of 1972 more releases were made on the west side of the forest. State game men say the stocked birds are doing well, and they look forward to controlled grouse hunting in a few more years.

At the present time grouse season in Michigan opens in mid-September. But I would not give a wooden nickle to hunt grouse or anything else at that time. To begin with, the weather is still too warm to turn on my hunting instincts. And as for Thunderwings, the foliage is still too thick to afford the hunter anything like fair odds. It's in October, when the leaves have begun to come down and something akin to visibility sets in, even in brush, that I start my grouse hunting.

For that same reason, poor visibility, I have never done well in cedar swamps and thick stands of young balsam fir, although I have often found birds plentiful in such places. They either get up out of sight, or rocket around a tree before I can get my gun to my shoulder. I have shot more holes in the evergreen foliage of such trees than I can remember— and I have killed few grouse in the process.

In recent years, grouse seasons have been greatly lengthened in a number of states, and winter hunting, with snow on the ground, has come into vogue. Ohio, for example, has opened its season in early October and allowed it to run as late as the end of February. At more than 140 days some years, Ohio game authorities believe their grouse season the longest in the nation. Nor has the bird supply suffered as a result.

Grouse hunters are relatively few in Ohio, and the birds are found chiefly in rugged, densely timbered counties, in the southern hill country or at the northeast corner of the state. The ridges are steep, the tangles of brush and catclaw afford perfect protection, and the toll taken by guns has remained light despite the long season.

Wherever it is permitted, winter hunting has certain advantages. Snow makes it easier for the hunter without a dog to find birds and allows him to track them and put them up. If the snow becomes deep, they follow their custom of diving into the soft blanket of it to roost at night, and now and then the hunter can find such a spot, put the bird out and get a shot.

Whether you hunt him in October or December, Thunderwings stands very tall. As one hunter put it many years ago, of all the birds that ever swallowed a cherry stone, he gets the loudest applause. And that's in large part because of the superb challenge he offers, to men and dogs alike.

An oldtime grouse hunter once summed it up for me, when I asked him, at the end of three days in a season of extraordinary bird abundance, how he and his partner were making out.

"We're moving a lot of birds," he replied. "We're not seeing all we move, we're not shooting at all we see, and we're not hitting all we shoot at."

That is the essence of grouse hunting.

20

PHEASANT

A crafty target

I have hunted pheasants since the first open season on them in my home state of Michigan, in 1925. For many falls the ringneck season was the big red-letter event of the year on my calendar. In recent years my enthusiasm has waned, in part because it has become increasingly hard to find a place to hunt. No-trespass signs have proliferated in the places where I did my hunting, as housing developments and rural residences have grown in numbers. And also, the birds have plummeted in numbers to a point where they no longer present an irresistable temptation.

The ringneck was an imported alien when we started hunting him in the southern farmlands of this state. The first experimental releases had been made by individual sportsmen a number of years before. In 1917 the state Conservation Department began operation of a game farm, and substantial stocking was carried out each year after that.

Hunters waited, more or less patiently, for the population to build up to a level that would justify an open season. It took eight years, and when it happened it came with almost explosive suddenness.

I hunted pheasants in the cornfields of South Dakota when the birds were at their peak abundance, in the 1940's, and their numbers were hard to believe. I saw them rocket out of the weedy corn ahead of drivers in clouds that must have numbered at least 300 at a time, and I flushed not fewer than 100 to 150 single-handed out of the grass and brush of shelter belts. But at that they were only a little more plentiful than they had been in the best areas of Michigan when that first season opened.

I still remember driving around a square mile of farmland where I intended to hunt, on the afternoon before the first day, and counting more than forty birds feeding in the fields in plain sight. They were as numerous and unwary as barnyard chickens. But starting at daylight the following morning, they shed the quality of unwariness in a hurry.

Driving to the West Coast many years ago, I stopped one May evening in a gas station in the town of Sandpoint, at the north end of Idaho's Lake Pend d'Oreille. When I walked into the place I all but fell over a good-looking springer stretched full length just inside the door. He was a dead ringer for one I had at home, and reasoning that springer men ought to have something in common, I introduced myself.

The owner was a hunter and fisherman named Fay Williford, and the result was an invitation to stay over in Sandpoint the next day and fish the big lake for bluebacks, small landlocked sockeye salmon.

I had as good a morning with a fly-rod as I can recall, and in the middle of it our talk turned to bird hunting. Forgetting that among hunters in that part of the country the Hungarian partridge, grouse and ringneck are all often called pheasants, and wondering whether ringneck behavior might be the same in the grassy valleys of Idaho as in the cornfields of Michigan, I put a question to Williford.

"Are pheasants hard to find out here after the first day?" I asked.

He looked at me with a slow grin. "The Chinks are the ones that get smart," he said.

I knew, of course, which bird he was referring to, and I have never heard ringneck behavior described more accurately. Wherever you find him, once the guns start to thunder the pheasant gets smart, and he has a vast store of natural cunning to draw on.

For many years, at the peak of his abundance, this naturalized alien from Asia by way of England provided more exciting hunting than any other upland bird in this country, and there were millions of shotgunners who would unhesitatingly have named him the greatest game bird we had. To some extent his diminished numbers have changed that in recent years, but they have done nothing to dim his wariness and craft. He is still among the shotgunner's most splendid targets.

Across the northern half of the country, from New England to Oregon, he has long held among feathered game a place that matches that claimed by the cottontail on the four-footed list. He has been everybody's bird. For a long time no other was hunted by so many or caused so much powder to be burned — and few caused it to be burned in vain more often.

He requires neither wilderness nor big tracts of wasteland to satisfy his needs. A ditchbank, a swale, a patch of grass in a fence corner, with plowed fields all around, suits him nicely. He thrives best where the corn grows tallest, and reaches peak numbers at the edge of town or city as readily as on the most remote farm.

And when the blue chips are down, when the dogs have him pinned in the weeds and the showdown is at hand, his greatness shows to best advantage. He has then what a game bird needs most of all, the guts and cunning to skulk and dodge and get away. Even in the most heavily hunted country, the cock pheasant population is never quite shot out. Always a few smart old roosters are left, to come out of hiding after the season closes, no matter how often and thoroughly the covers have been combed.

As I have already hinted, the behavior of cock pheasants on the opening morning of hunting season is one thing, but the behavior of the same birds two or three days later, when they have had a chance to wise up to what men and dogs and guns are all about, is something altogether different.

I remember that on the first morning of that first Michigan season, back in 1925, we didn't make our shooting count as we should have, likely because it was new to us. But six of us, hunting on one eighty-acre farm, collected our legal limit of twelve birds, drove forty miles back to our jobs, and were only an hour or two late for work. Pheasants, we agreed, were pushovers.

But four or five days later we went back to the same farm for a second hunt, and things had taken a dramatic turn. The ringneck population had all but vanished. What we didn't realize was that they were still there but we didn't know how to find them.

As the years have gone along, the pheasant, always fast on his feet, clever at skulking and matchless at hiding, has if anything sharpened his skills, too. He stands up to an army of hunters that would wipe out a less resourceful character, and does it by wits alone. Long before hunting season ends, in the heavily gunned areas where the bulk of the ringneck popu-

Handsome, arrogant and crafty, knowing when to run and when to fly, tough for a dog to handle and by no means easy to hit, the pheasant ranks high among the game birds of this country. No matter how heavily his range is hunted, there are always a few canny cock birds like this one left at season's end.

lation is found, men and dogs have combed every square yard of cover, most of it many times. Only a bird that knows what to do and when to do it could stand up to that relentless pressure. Nevertheless, there are ways to get the best of him.

First of all, map your plans ahead of time, contact the owners of the land where you want to hunt, make sure of good bird territory and also of a welcome. The latter is especially important nowadays. Above all, don't trespass where you are not wanted, or without permission.

Second, be in the field on the first day of the season as soon after daylight as the hunting laws of your state allow. Over virtually all the pheasant range, game men report that at least half the year's total kill is taken the first day, and of that kill more than 50 per cent are downed in the first two or three hours, except in states where shooting is banned until noon.

The heavy early kill is only natural.

306

Since the previous autumn the birds have lived completely unmolested. The old roosters have forgotten the lessons of other hunting seasons, the young ones have never heard gunfire. So for a couple of hours they're easy. But by the end of the first half day all their self-protective instincts are aroused. They skulk and hide, run instead of flying, move into dense cover where it's hard for dogs and men to penetrate or into isolated pockets where no one is likely to look. For the rest of the season they get wiser and more wary as the days pass. So take full advantage of the first day and the first hour if you want sure-bet hunting. After that you'll earn any birds you kill.

All through the season early morning is likely to be the most productive time. Pheasants move out from their nighttime roosting places shortly after daybreak to feed, and the fact that the morning air is damp and the ground often wet with frost or dew is a big help to dogs.

The birds are on the move for a couple of hours, then gradually go into seclusion for the middle of the day. By ten or eleven o'clock in the morning there is little use to hunt unless you are willing to tackle standing cornfields and other big areas of cover. An hour or two before sundown they begin to work out to feeding places again, and from then until dusk is another prime time to be afield.

Weather has much to do with success. Wet summers that produce an exceptionally heavy cover crop mean hard hunting. Dry hot days make things tough for dogs, particularly during the heat of the day, and the birds seem especially prone to run in such weather. Damp days following rain provide the best conditions, and plenty of birds are killed while it is actually raining, but I have never enjoyed hunting at such times. Pheasants seek out thick cover and sit tight on rainy days, making them hard to find and hard to flush. Plowing through dripping weeds and grass is not for me. Windy days mean tough shooting, too.

Tracking snow in pheasant season is not common in my part of the country, but when it comes it affords an unusual opportunity. Cold weather is likely to bunch the birds in areas of heavy cover, and the snow makes them easy to find and put up. The hunter who lacks a dog gets his best breaks under those conditions.

Don't hunt by yourself if you can avoid it. Any gunwise ringneck will run circles around a lone man, in heavy cover or light. It takes two to tango with this bird, and three or four are likely to do better. In big fields of standing corn in such states as Iowa and South Dakota it's not unusual for hunters to team up in parties of a dozen to twenty, especially in making drives, but that's not a method of hunting I enjoy.

Size up each piece of cover before you move into it and plan your strategy according to conditions. Don't hunt through a swale, weedy stubble or field of standing corn into a brushy woods or shelter belt. You're encouraging birds to make a getaway if you do that. Instead, work through heavy cover toward a bare field, road, water or some other barrier that will force the runners to take wing. And if there are enough hunters in your party, send standers to wait for 'em when they fly, just as you would post standers on a deer drive.

Unless you are hunting over a good dog, driving is one of the surest ways of taking pheasants, and even with a dog it often adds to the score. It needs only four or five men to do it in average cover, two to drive, the rest to stand, and it's especially productive in standing corn, sweet clover, dry marshes or wherever birds are likely to run ahead. Pushed toward some natural barrier, they are almost sure to give the standers shooting when they flush. Swales and small patches of cover can be driven by two men, one standing, the other working through. Two men also can do an efficient job of hunting narrow belts of cover, such as fencerows and ditchbanks, one on each side to be ready for birds no matter which way they go out.

If you are hunting in the vicinity of farm buildings, safety requires you to keep a reasonable distance away and common sense dictates that you work out from the buildings, not toward them. There's nothing more frustrating than to jump a pheasant and watch helplessly while he sails away over a nearby house or barn. Push him in the opposite direction if you possibly can.

The hunter who goes after ringnecks without a dog is making the greatest blunder of all. No man can match wits with this shifty, ground-hugging roughneck on his own. He'll sit tight while you tramp past two paces away, run out of the country without letting you know he is there, circle around you, play a dozen tricks that you can't hope to cope with. Bird hunting of any kind without a dog is dull business in my book. In the case of pheasants it's close to a hopeless business as well.

What breed? You can get a lively argument on that score wherever pheasant hunters foregather. Maybe the best answer is that all bird-hunting breeds are good and almost any dog is better than none at all. I've known farm collies that did a pretty fair job, and many rabbit hunters work their beagles on ringnecks with satisfactory results. Basically, however, bird hunting calls for a bird dog.

I've had great pheasant shooting over pointers, setters, Brittanys, springers and retrievers. In my judgment more depends on the training,

Three pheasant dogs freeze staunch on point as the hunters walk in. By working away from heavy cover they have forced the bird into the open. But if it's a rooster, and if skulking is possible, the ground-hugging ringneck is more likely to run than to lie to the point. Whatever happens, dog work of this kind adds greatly to the joys of pheasant hunting.

Two cock pheasants explode out of cover at close range, and the dog leaps after them. The hunter's lead looks wrong in the picture, but if he waits until the top bird is twenty or thirty yards away and leveling off, the shot should not be difficult.

experience and ability of the dog than on the breed. But I do have a personal preference and I'll risk criticism by revealing it. For me the springer is the ideal pheasant dog, teaming up with the ringneck as naturally as the beagle goes with the cottontail.

Wherever you find him, the pheasant is ready to travel if that seems the best way to save his skin. That makes him hard for a pointing dog to handle. While the dog is staunch on a ribbon of body scent the bird is likely to be legging it for the next township, and by the time the dog discovers he's gone it's too late.

Many a pointer and setter gets wise in the closing years of life, learns to circle around, head the bird off, come in fast from the opposite direction and slam to a point at close range. Pheasants spiked down that way are likely to lie until the hunter can get there. But not every dog masters that technique, and to me it makes sense to outwit the runners with a dog that will trail them and force them up. For that job a well-trained springer is hard to beat. He'll hunt close, move fast when birds are found, jump them as quickly as possible. Now and then one will be crafty enough to get beyong range before flushing, in spite of all the dog can do, but it's been my experience that that happens less frequently with springers than with dogs that point. Whatever breed you choose, you'll do best with a dog

trained to work close. Above all, you need a dog that will trail and run down cripples and bring them back.

The ringneck has amazing vitality and great capacity to carry shot. Wounded, he'll spend his last ounce of energy in running and hiding, and he can disappear in cover that seems incapable of secreting a bird of his size. A single tussock, a bush, a few sparse blades of grass along a fence— these are all he needs. I've even known cripples to take refuge in brush heaps, a culvert, drain tile or woodchuck den. Only with a good retriever can you hope to salvage such birds as that.

In addition to avoiding the loss of cripples, as well as dead birds that fall in very thick cover, the work of a good retriever is one of the major satisfactions of pheasant hunting.

The questions of greatest interest to pheasant hunters today are what has caused the slump in ringneck numbers in recent years and what is the outlook for the future.

In the late summer of 1965 the Governor of South Dakota called a special meeting of his Game, Fish and Parks Commission. There was good reason to predict fireworks. The air was thick with rumors of bickering in the game department. Biologists and game wardens were at each other's throats, the commission and its staff had fallen out, and turnover in personnel was running abnormally high.

The Governor went straight to the root of the problem. He opened his remarks by saying, "Number one on the list of things I want to discuss with you is the pheasant season. What has happened to the pheasants?"

Whether or not he realized it, the Governor of South Dakota, long acclaimed the ringneck capital of the United States, was raising a question that has bugged hunters periodically and created king-size headaches for state game departments, almost since pheasant hunting began in this country. A lot of people have wondered from time to time, "What has happened to the pheasants?"

There was good reason for concern in South Dakota that year. The ringneck population, that may have stood at a fantastic thirty million in the early 1940's (about fifty birds for each human resident), numbered an estimated ten million and was still providing nationally famous shooting in the fall of 1963. But the next summer a long drouth hit. By the autumn of 1964 the figure had plummeted to less than five million and the fat was in the fire.

Clamor was sweeping the state for the game department to "do something" to bring the pheasants back. The remedy most frequently urged was a return to high fox bounties, which the department had succeeded in cutting from $7.50 to $2 a few years before.

Not only were sportsmen alarmed for the future, but as the Governor reminded the game commission, "People have economic reasons for being vitally interested." They had indeed. In the three previous years between 50,000 and 70,000 nonresidents had paid a fee of $25 to hunt pheasants in South Dakota each fall. That meant as much as $1,750,000 in license money alone. Add what the outsiders had spent for travel, lodging, meals, guides, and the processing of birds, and it was plain that pheasant hunting was one of the state's important sources of income. The decline was hurting in the cash registers, and hurting hard.

Nor was South Dakota alone, by any means. In many states, those years were lean ones for pheasant hunters.

North Dakota closed its 1966 season outright. The 1965 and 1966 seasons in Oregon were the poorest in 10 years, with a kill of about 250,000 as compared with 475,000 in 1958. In Minnesota the kill plunged from 758,000 in 1964 to 220,000 a year later. Ohio's 1965 season was the poorest on record, 1966 not a great deal better. In Michigan the kill fell far below average. Illinois hunters took only about half as many birds in 1965 as in 1963, 533,000 compared with 1,066,000.

That was not the country's first pheasant slump. The birds took their first major tumble in the mid-40's. From 1935 to 1945, all across the ringneck belt, the population had soared, in what game men called the most spectacular eruption of game the country had ever seen. Clouds of birds were getting up before the guns in state after state. The hunters of that generation had never seen anything like it.

The crash came, and it was equally spectacular. States as widely separated as New Jersey, California and Minnesota reported their 1945 kill only half that of a year or two earlier. Ohio, Connecticut, Washington and Pennsylvania suffered a drop of 25 to 35 per cent in one year. In a 3-year period in Michigan the kill plunged from 1,400,000 to 450,000. But within a year the upswing started, and before the end of that decade the gloom was forgotten.

Pheasant populations have been rising and falling ever since, but nowhere have they regained their former numbers. The slump this time appears to be permanent.

Most game technicians insist there is nothing mysterious about the periodic depressions, that their causes are known and fully understood, even though nothing much can be done about them. Whether or not that is completely true, to the average sportsman the pheasant slumps are one of the greatest and most frustrating mysteries of hunting.

What accounts for the nosedives? Among the major enemies of the ringneck are winter blizzards, summer drouth, ice storms, wet springs, the dragline that drains wetlands, the bulldozer that clears shelter-belts and brush-grown fencerows, the sprays that kill weeds and roadside cover (little is known about the effects of other spraying), the raising of more sheep and cattle, and even the farmer who plants potatoes instead of oats.

The mowing machine is one of the deadliest of all. In Ohio at times nearly a third of the hen pheasants nesting in hayfields have been crippled or killed by mowers. The loss in one North Dakota county was two thousand birds in a single season, and two counties in Minnesota reported five thousand hen casualties one summer. Biologists call alfalfa, cut early, a death trap.

Here's a sample of opinion from leading ringneck states as to the chief causes of the pheasant decline.

South Dakota: It has happened because of such things as blizzards, pesticides, weedicides, fertilizers, fall plowing, corn chopping, an increase in alfalfa, more livestock grazing, less cover, predators, cold springs, hot weather at hatching time, and diseases.

California: Habitat is the key to pheasant populations.

Pennsylvania: We have lost 850,000 acres of pheasant range to the encroachments of civilization in the last 25 years.

Wisconsin: In 20 years over half of our 5,000,000 acres of wetlands have

Leveling down on a ringneck rising from cover, a hunter has only a second to get his lead. The cornfield alien does not fly as fast as a grouse, but he is no pushover for the gun.

been drained. Earlier hay cutting, destruction of fencerow cover, pasturing of woodlands, and a trend toward corn and soybeans have all affected our pheasants adversely, too.

Iowa: Federal land-retirement programs provided millions of acres of safe nesting cover, but most of these benefits have now been lost.

Illinois: An increase in row crops at the expense of hay and small grain,

abandoned farms being put back in use, mowing while birds are nesting, hail in June—these were behind our recent drops.

Oregon: The only certain thing is that pheasant habitat is shrinking as human population expands. Subdivisions and freeways are not helpful to farmland game.

Ohio: Summer drouth is a major factor. The pheasant supply depends

315

A hunter scores a solid hit on a rising bird. Moments of triumph like this are no longer as frequent anywhere in this country's pheasant range as they once were. The pheasant, which long supplied many farmland states with unsurpassed bird hunting, has slumped sharply in numbers in the last ten or fifteen years, and the chances of a comeback look slim.

With a pheasant clamped firmly in his jaws, a retriever does his job with dash and style. For no hunter is a dog more essential than for the man who goes after pheasants. It takes a dog to find birds, to flush them, and above all to retrieve dead ones that fall in thick cover and to run down and bring back cripples.

on food, cover and weather conditions, and these are matters of local economics and the will of God.

North Dakota: Weather conditions and the abundance or scarcity of habitat rule the roost. We have lost millions of acres of soil-bank land in recent years, and that went hand in hand with hard blizzards. The combination dealt our birds a knockout blow.

Michigan: Hay mowing in nesting season means a poor hatch. Add drainage, clean farming, housing developments and road building, and it's easy to see why the population falls off.

Minnesota: One severe March blizzard can mean a slump as great as 40 per cent the next fall.

Nebraska: The chief limiting factor in this state is nesting cover. You can have five times as many hens, but if they can't find a safe place to nest the factory will shell out no more young birds.

State after state flatly rules out overshooting as a cause of pheasant slumps. There is no case on record where, under cocks-only rules, long seasons or heavy harvests have had anything to do with a drop in the bird supply. Every state that has weighed that factor has come to the same conclusion.

Says the game director of a leading ringneck state, "Even in a long season, hunters will not hunt hard enough to take more than 60 per cent of the fall population of roosters. A harvest of 90 per cent is safe."

In general, too, state game authorities discount the role of fox predation in the slump.

"Fox predation is dramatic, and one of many factors that limit pheasant numbers," Les Voigt, Wisconsin's conservation director, once told me. "But it has never been shown to be the major cause of declines, anywhere in the Midwest."

Illinois echoed Voigt with the statement that "Predators do little damage in a secure environment."

At its peak, South Dakota pheasants yielded a harvest estimated at 7.5 million birds. Then the bottom fell out, and the fox got the blame. But the dropoff was just as sharp west of the Missouri River, where there were no foxes at that time, as in the best fox counties to the east, and the bountying of 42,000 foxes in the next three years failed to bring about any major comeback in pheasants. When the soil bank was established, fox numbers doubled—and so did pheasants. The two thrived equally, side by side.

Foxes do kill pheasants, and so do hawks, owls, crows, opossums, skunks, raccoons, weasels, minks, badgers, cats and dogs. But if habitat and weather are favorable, they do not take enough to tip the balance, game biologists contend.

Almost without exception, however, pheasant hunters disagree. They equate the lean ringneck hunting of recent years with a continuing surge in the fox populations, and most of them believe that if foxes were thinned out pheasants would come back accordingly.

Which side is right, and to what degree? No one can say.

It would be very pleasant to end this chapter on a note of optimism but I can find no grounds for that.

The pheasant is a great game bird, one of the best the shotgunners of this country have known, and a return to the numbers of former years would bring joy to millions of sportsmen. But the present slump has lasted too long, and the conditions working against the ringneck supply have become too widespread, to justify any real hope of such an upsurge.

To that statement let me add a postcript. Nothing could delight me more than to be proven wrong.

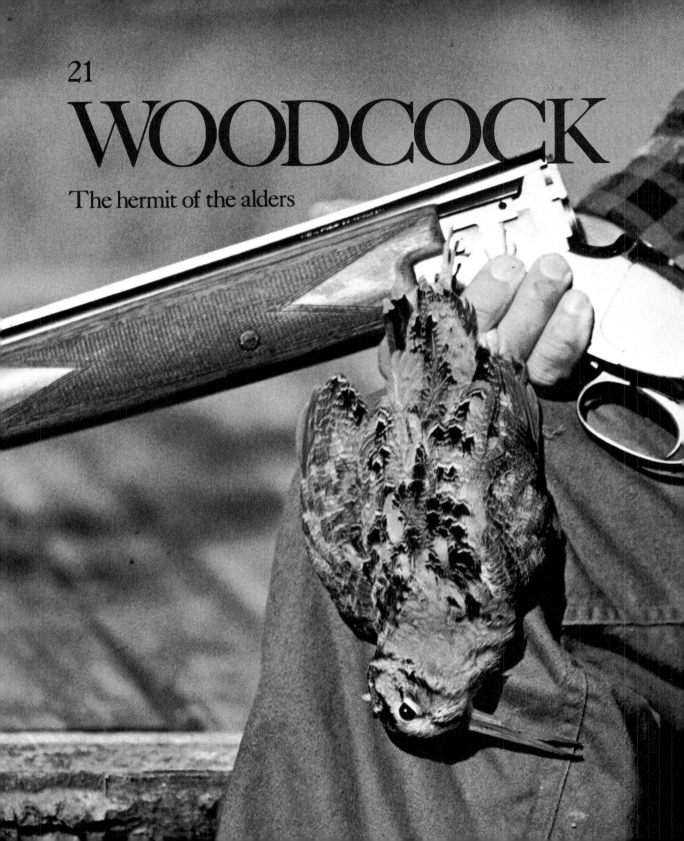

21

WOODCOCK

The hermit of the alders

A few times in my life I have had the good fortune to encounter a heavy flight of woodcock on the nose. The result has been some of the liveliest and most interesting bird hunting I can remember. A few other times, earlier in the autumn, I have found a place where locally hatched birds were abundant. That was good, but not as good as the October shooting, for the reason that I am not partial to September shotgunning, when every thicket still holds its unfrosted summer foliage.

Whether you call him woodcock or by one of his many local names (the list includes such oddities as timber doodle, wood snipe, bog sucker, owl snipe and, among the Cajuns of Louisiana, bec) the bird is an odd character, about which little is known even by hunters.

Science lists him among the shorebirds, along with his near relative, the snipe, and the plovers, yellowlegs and the rest of that fascinating and beautiful clan. Yet he has little more to do with the shore or marshlands than the ruffed grouse. In fact, he is found most often in the same upland covers, although he does show more preference for alder bogs and other low-lying places than the grouse.

That may well be because it is in the soft black soil of the bogs that he finds the most abundant and easily accessible supply of the food that sustains him throughout his life, earthworms.

When he rests through the middle hours of the day, however, he is likely to choose a birch-grown ridge instead of the wooded wetlands. And when his nesting season arrives, the shallow bowl on the ground in which the hen woodcock hatches her four eggs (invariably four, never more nor less) is unfailingly located in a fairly open upland place.

His range takes in the eastern half of the United States and Canada, east of a line drawn from Minnesota to Texas. West of that he does not venture, since the open plains are not to his fancy.

Over all of that range, interest in woodcock hunting is at a relatively low ebb today. Not as low as in the case of the snipe, which is lightly hunted indeed, but few shotgunners are genuinely dedicated woodcock addicts. Those that are reap rich rewards.

In general, this odd recluse, hermit of the alders, is one of the most underhunted birds on the upland list. In state after state, from the Canadian border south to Louisiana, hunters harvest fewer than half the woodcock that is justified by the size of the flight.

It was not always thus. In his excellent book on North American shorebirds, published by the Smithsonian Institution in 1927, the late A. C. Bent called the woodcock a prince among game birds and a delight to the palate of an epicure. Bent wrote very warmly of the pleasures of woodcock hunting, and in his day most bird hunters rated it prime sport.

The number of woodcock harvested by sportsmen at that time was unquestionably large, but it never approached the kill of snipe. On that score Bent had this to report:

Probably more snipe have been killed by sportsmen than any other game bird. Snipe must have been exceedingly abundant 50 or 60 years ago, as the oft-quoted achievements of James J. Pringle (1899) will illustrate. He was not a market hunter but a gentleman (?) sportsman, who shot for the fun of it and gave the birds away to his friends.

During the twenty years from 1867 to 1887 he shot, on his favorite hunting grounds in Louisiana, 69,087 snipe and a total of 71,859 of all game birds; but his shooting fell off during the next 10 years for he increased his grand total of snipe to only 78,602 and of all game birds to only 82,101. His best day, undoubtedly a world's record, was December 11, 1877, when he shot in 6 hours 366 snipe and 8 other birds. On his best seven consecutive shooting days, alternate days in December, 1877, he killed 1,943 snipe and 25 other birds. During the winter of 1874–75 he killed 6,615 snipe. Captain Bogardus, the famous trap shot, killed, with the help of a friend, 340 snipe on one day in Illinois, and seldom got less than 150 on good days.

Woodcock were never killed in numbers that came close to matching those. Nevertheless, forty years ago the bog hermit stood very high on the upland game bird list, and was far more heavily hunted than he is today in most states.

At some point—it seems to me as levels of sportsmanship suffered a decline—interest in both woodcock and snipe hunting tapered off. Likely that was just as well, for there is no question that the kill of both was excessive in the early days.

At any rate, at the present time the local birds depart and the woodcock flight passes through with many hunters never seeing the birds and few bothering with them. There are even those who are hardly aware that they exist.

Yet all of the northern states have substantial nesting populations and good flights move across them from the north each fall. The birds come

and go almost unnoticed, except by a handful of enthusiasts.

As with all game birds, good woodcock hunting depends on a liberal supply of birds to hunt. The season opens fairly early in the autumn, in September in most of the northern states, usually before the flight has begun to move south.

By October the migration is due, and when it reaches its peak woodcock hunting can be a very exciting pastime. The birds pour in in great numbers, and their favorite haunts teem with them.

But if it is exciting, the flight shooting is also likely to be brief. The woodcock is an uncertain will o' the wisp, here today, gone tomorrow. A cold spell can send him scurrying on, and covers that are alive with birds at sundown may be empty by morning.

I recall an October when a friend phoned me from Baldwin, seventy-five miles north of Grand Rapids, Michigan, where I was living at the time.

"I got into a woodcock flight this afternoon," he announced. "Found a few acres of alder swamp along Baldwin Creek where there was a bird under every bush. It was terrific. Can you be here right after breakfast tomorrow morning?"

I could and was. But I made the drive past fields that glistened under

A woodcock flushes almost underfoot, in cover more open than that where the bird is usually found. The woodcock rises more slowly than the grouse, most commonly at close range, fluttering up with no thunder of wings. But once airborne, he turns, dodges and corkscrews, and gets out of sight in a hurry.

white frost so heavy it looked like snow, and the roofs of farm buildings shone equally white in the early morning light.

We walked into the alder bog about the time the sun struck through the treetops, behind two good dogs. Neither the dogs nor we could find a single bird. The cold night had sent the entire flight hurrying south.

There was another fall when a partner and I went to Beaver Island, off the Michigan mainland at the north end of Lake Michigan, for some of the best grouse hunting I can remember.

When we arrived at the island village of St. James, about the first thing we were told was that the woodcock flight was in. For a week the small swamps around Beaver's inland lakes, and the wooded hills as well, had been alive with woodcock. Alas, we were a day or so too late. In a week of hunting we flushed and killed exactly one timber doodle.

The rest were in warmer climes, five hundred miles or so to the south.

That is typical woodcock behavior. The migration can dribble through and last for weeks, or the best of it can pass and be gone in a few days. Usually, however, the hunter who starts early and works his dogs as long as birds are to be found can bank on at least two or three weeks of first-class action as the fall goes along, sometimes more than that.

Even when the flight is in, it is not always an easy matter to find concentrations of birds. Woodcock behavior is sufficiently erratic and their choice of haunts sufficiently unpredictable that, unless the hunter knows of a good place from previous autumns, he may not know where to look for them.

In general, however, they are most likely to be found in damp locations with thick cover. Alder thickets along streams, stands of popple (aspen) at the border of swamp or marsh, lowlands grown up with willow or cedar—all these are usually productive. Now and then you find birds in dry locations on brushy hillsides, especially in the middle hours of the day. For a rule of thumb, good ruffed grouse country is likely to be good woodcock country when the flight is going through, particularly if it is boggy or swampy.

In one of its habits the woodcock is consistent in a way that benefits the hunter. If cover and conditions remain unchanged, he comes back fall after fall to the same places. The hunter who locates the right area one year can usually count on equally good luck the next, provided things stay the same.

As with ruffed grouse, I have had my most enjoyable woodcock hunting over dogs, either pointers or setters that understood how to handle birds. Those were times when the flight was in, the weather perfect and the dog work flawless. That is by far the best way to hunt them, and those are days you don't forget.

I recall one such hunt with a good friend, Karl Kidder, then a Michigan conservation officer, later killed in the crash of a state aircraft. We walked into a tract of swamp along a

Belled to enable the hunter to keep track of him in thick brush, a bird-wise setter brings back a fallen timber doodle. Many retrieving dogs find the smell or taste of the woodcock so offensive that they refuse to pick one up.

creek that warm October afternoon and found that for once we had timed our hunt perfectly. The place was swarming with woodcock. Our two dogs found so many they didn't know what to do with them, and we didn't care whether they handled them or not. Every few steps a bird went fluttering up, and for an hour, until sundown brought legal shooting to a close, we had a woodcock carnival.

But the usual happened. We went back to the same bog before the sun had melted the frost on the grass the next morning, and found the place as deserted as a tomb. The birds had moved on in the night, hurried along by the frost. We went through the alders yard by yard and never raised a single straggler.

The woodcock lies well to a dog, and most of the time flushes at close range. They rise far more slowly than the grouse, and with none of his wing thunder. Instead they flutter up rather weakly, at a speed that would indicate a very easy target. But that appearance is deceptive.

At about the height of the alder tops, just as the hunter finds them over the barrel of his scattergun, the flight pattern undergoes an abrupt and baffling change. They drop abruptly back to the brush, twist, turn and dodge, and get out of sight in an astonishingly short space of time. Most woodcock that fall to the gun are killed at short range, and for most hunters a high percentage of

the birds flushed do not fall at all. Maybe that is what makes woodcock hunting what it is.

Often there is a second or two, just as they reach the top of the brush and before they begin to corkscrew, when they are in level flight. For the shotgunner whose reflexes are fast enough, that is the moment of truth. For that brief space of time the bird is a fairly easy target, provided he can be seen at all. For me at least, woodcock killing is a matter of shooting instinctively, and usually as quickly as I can.

One of the strange things about this extraordinary bird is that few hunting dogs are willing to retrieve him. No one knows the exact reason, but there must be something about his smell or taste that is offensive to the dog. Yet on the table his dark flesh rates close to the top among all the birds that are hunted for sport and food.

The most unusual woodcock hunting I have ever done, and maybe the liveliest, came on an October evening many years ago. I had driven north that fall for a weekend of grouse hunting with three partners, in the Traverse City area of Michigan's Lower Peninsula. My companions were in camp ahead of me, in a snug cabin on the Boardman River. They were finding a fair number of birds, but when I arrived on a Friday afternoon they had news that did not concern grouse. They had spotted an evening flight of woodcock, coming down off the timber-grown uplands to an alder bog that covered an acre or two, close beside the river. The way they described it, it was a sight to see. I had heard of such flights but had never seen one. Bent had described them in graphic words.

"From their haunts on the uplands, where they rest during the day, the birds fly through the open just before dark to their favorite feeding place along some swampy run or boggy thicket," he wrote. "They resort regularly to the same spot night after night. If the shooter knows of such a place, where the birds are fairly plentiful, he can station himself there about sunset and feel reasonably sure of a few shots during the brief time that the birds are coming in. But increasing darkness soon makes shooting difficult."

There it was, all spelled out for us. There was only one thing wrong. The part about difficult shooting turned out to be a classic understatement.

The flight would get under way about the time the sun went down, my buddies said, and continue at least as long as the birds could be seen against the darkening sky.

We walked down to a small open meadow pocked with old pine stumps, between the alder bog and the bordering hills, and got ready. The birds would come off the uplands, flying just above the treetops, cross the meadow and pitch down into the bog, I was assured.

The sun dropped lower, and suddenly the first woodcock appeared, streaking overhead like a small rocket on an erratice course. He zigzagged in above the birches and aspens, twisting and darting in the fashion that is the despair of gunners. Two of us tried for him and missed, and he dived into the alders as if nothing had happened.

That was the start of an hour of action as fast as I have ever had with a shotgun. The flight built up as dusk came on, until woodcock were zigging and zagging across the meadow like bees coming to a hive. They'd come into sight above the trees, twist and corkscrew and make it to the bog almost before you could get off a shot.

That was many years ago, and I do not remember my exact score. But I know I shot well over a box of shells, and I think I picked up either three or four birds. My partners did about as well. As Bent had remarked, the shooting was difficult.

Shooting timber doodles after sundown is illegal now under federal regulations, but at that time it was entirely cricket, and I can recall no other hunting I have done quite like that evening shoot on the Boardman.

One other thing about the bogland hermit is worthy of mention. That is his remarkable natural camouflage. No bird is better served by protective coloration, and none seems to rely on it more completely.

In a lifetime in the outdoors I have seen the nests of something like a dozen woodcock. Always I discovered them by sheer accident or was led to them by someone who had found them that same way. I have never known an instance of a human discovering a woodcock nest with his eyes, provided the hen bird was covering her eggs.

Brooding, her brown and buff and umber colors match so perfectly the frost-killed brakes and odds and ends of forest duff around her that it is almost impossible to make out her outlines on the woodland flood. I have stood two paces away from the spot where I had found a nest a day or so earlier and stared at the bird for minutes before I was able to see her.

I have found nests when I was down on my hands and knees, gathering trailing arbutus or searching for morel mushrooms. On those occasions my first inkling of the bird was the sudden and startling feel of something soft and warm and alive under my groping hand. One nest I discovered when a companion put his foot down into half of the bowl with the bird still there, crushing two of her four eggs. She fluttered off then, doing a fabulous broken-wing act, rolling and tumbling over the ground with trailing feathers, hoping to decoy us from the nest with the curious behavior to which quite a few ground-nesting birds resort. I have watched a hen woodcock stage that same astonishing performance when we found, handled and photographed her brood of four newly hatched chicks, too.

All that I have just said hints strongly at the woodcock's most astonishing trait, the willingness of the brooding female to rely on her camouflage and her almost suicidal determination to stay on the nest. Most of the time, once a nest has been located, a human intruder can sidle up within a pace of it without flushing the bird. Many times she can be gently stroked without taking alarm, and I have known of instances where she was lifted carefully off the eggs and put down on the ground a foot or so away, only to scramble instantly back.

The most amazing instance of this behavior carried to extremes that I have ever heard of happened in Maine a number of years ago. I'd be reluctant to believe the story had it not been attested to by reliable witnesses and vouched for by the U. S. Fish and Wildlife Service.

John Stobie of Waterville, an employee of the state game and fish department, was working near the Lily Bay fish hatchery when he discovered a woodcock on her nest. When he approached and examined the bird at very close range, he decided there

was an opportunity for some unusual pictures. He phoned the nearest photographer, twenty-five miles away in the town of Greenville.

But the photographer hedged. He explained that to get the kind of pictures Stobie wanted it would be necessary to transport a lot of equipment to the nest and the cost would be prohibitive. Undaunted, Stobie concluded that the next best bet would be to try to take the bird to the photographer.

He went to work with a shovel, loosening a square of sod around the woodcock five feet by five. She stayed on the nest, showing no sign of alarm. Stobie then called on some helpers, and they very carefully lifted the chunk of turf into a box big enough to take it and loaded it onto a truck. Still the bird stuck to her nest.

Stobie hauled her, box and all, into Greenville, lugged the box into the studio, and the photographer had a field day. When the pictures were completed the box was reloaded onto the truck, Stobie drove back to the site of the nest, replaced the sod and left the woodcock as he had found her. He kept watch and reported that she hatched her four young as if nothing had disturbed her.

Whether as an elusive and swiftly vanishing target in the multi-colored thickets and alder bogs of October, or as a unique subject for the camera hunter in April and May, hard to find but ridiculously easy to approach, the woodcock deserves a high place on the list of the upland game birds that make their home in the eastern half of this country. He could tolerate more hunting than he gets, and sportsmen miss some wonderful action by neglecting him.

As my friend Joe Stephenson of the Michigan Conservation Department told me years ago, "They're easy to hit, but they're also easy to miss. They're found in beautiful places, and they're delectable on the table. If we have a gentleman's game bird, the woodcock fills the bill."

A hen woodcock broods on her nest, a shallow bowl on the woodland floor. Only her eyes and long bill betray her, against the background of dead leaves, grass and forest duff. No bird is better served by natural camouflage. Mushroom hunters sometimes discover such a hen by touching her before their eyes make her out.

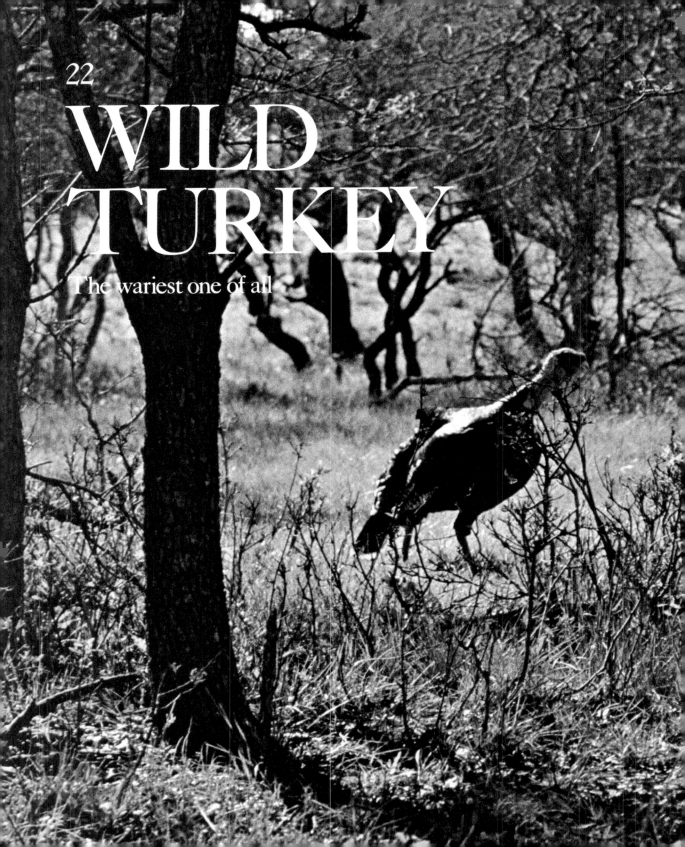

22

WILD TURKEY

The wariest one of all

"If wild gobblers wore horns they'd be the most prized trophies in the eastern half of this country."

It was a seasoned turkey hunter who told me that, in the eastern mountains many years ago. It was his contention that the wild turkey is the hardest game to hunt of anything that walks or flies in the forests of North America. I had no reason to disagree with him at the time, and I still don't have.

This is as good a time as any to say that I have never killed a wild turkey. But I have spent enough time hunting them, and enough time in the company of other men who knew close to all there is to know of turkey lore, that I feel qualified to say that the smartest whitetail buck that ever carried a rack can't hold a candle to a mature wild gobbler when it comes to being hard to outsmart.

The turkey hunt I shall remember longest is one I made in West Virginia about a dozen years back. One of the members of the party was Wayne Bailey, then that state's specialist in turkeys and turkey

333

management. He has since moved to North Carolina, where he is in charge of the turkey research and management program of the Wildlife Resources Commission.

At the time I met him, Wayne had been hunting turkeys every season for twenty years. He had killed ten or twelve gobblers, and in addition had learned a great deal about turkey behavior in connection with his job. The few days I spent with him made the hunt as enjoyable and profitable as any I can recall. I am indebted to him for much of what follows in this chapter.

His story of his first gobbler was about as lively a hunting anecdote as I had ever heard. He was on a turkey and bear hunt with his father and two other partners, camped in the Cranberry River country in southeastern West Virginia. It was his first try for turkeys. The party killed two bears the first day, and getting them out of the woods was a hard job. Wayne was too tired to get up with the others before daylight the next morning. He was still sleeping soundly, around eight o'clock, when a shot rapped out from a ridge above camp. That brought him out of the sack wide awake, and he stuck his head through the tent flaps in time to see a big gobbler go sailing across the valley and light in the timber on a high spur a quarter mile away.

The first turkey he had ever seen, it was all he needed to make him forget he was tired. He wolfed down a few bites of breakfast and headed for the top of the mountain where the gobbler had disappeared. But when he got there, after a fast, hard climb, he could find no turkey sign and he soon gave up hope of locating the bird. He didn't know much about turkeys but he knew enough to feel sure they didn't come that easy.

He sat down beside a tree and was close to dozing off when he heard something coming up the hill below, moving through dry leaves. It made quite a racket, but he quickly decided it was a squirrel. The gobbler was too much to hope for.

If it was a squirrel it would probably come up on top of a log at the brow of the hill directly in front of him, so he trained his shotgun on the log and waited. The noise kept coming until it was behind the log. Then something moved, a quick, small, wary movement, and the head of a big turkey was in sight over the log.

They were looking each other in the eye at about fifteen yards and one look was enough. The gobbler ducked before Wayne could pull the trigger, and started around the hill like a greyhound. The hunter bounded to his feet and took after it, running as hard as he had ever run in his life, and shooting each time he caught a glimpse of turkey through the brush. He didn't take time to aim. He just pointed his autoloader in the bird's general direction and emptied it.

It was still running when he fired the last shot but he didn't see it after that. He kept going and just beyond the place where the gobbler had disappeared he found it, breast-down on the yellow leaves under a big poplar, wings outspread, a twenty-pound gobbler, the most beautiful sight a novice turkey hunter ever laid eyes on.

Bailey set his gun across a log, reached down and lifted it by one leg—and the bird recovered as if nothing had happened!

Wayne had the turkey by the leg in one hand. The other leg and both wings were free. It did its best to fly but he went down on his knees and hung on. It struggled and scratched and pummeled him with its wings, blinding him with blows, and its spur tore his hand until blood was trickling down his wrist, but he wouldn't let go. Finally he pinned it on the ground, straddled it with both knees and finished it off.

When he looked it over he found that a single pellet of No. 2's had creased it along the side of the head just over one eye, and knocked it out. There wasn't another shot in the bird.

"I suppose I'd have been a turkey hunter the rest of my life if that episode had never happened," Wayne told me. "Likely I was born to it. But if anything was needed for a clincher, the excitement and thrill of that first bird did it."

What makes the turkey so hard to hunt? First and above everything else, wildness. He's not called the wild turkey for nothing. The name means more than just a turkey that doesn't live a domesticated life in a farmyard. It means wild in every sense of the word. Wildness is the essence of his nature and being, and he cannot and will not change.

Consider this one fact: Since white man first discovered him on this continent more than three hundred years ago no one has ever succeeded in taming the eastern wild turkey and fitting him to life in a pen. He fights an enclosure endlessly and not even the allurements of the mating season can take his mind off freedom. The early Spaniards found the Aztecs rearing a domestic strain of turkeys. They took those tame birds back to Spain and from them are sprung the domestic flocks of the world today. All attempts to reduce the pure wild turkey of the eastern United States to captivity and breed and rear him in confinement have ended in failure.

Game farm turkeys? Without exception they have a strain of domestic blood. They must have to survive and breed. That is why states interested in bringing back the wild turkey have abandoned the stocking of game-farm birds and sought to repopulate their turkey range with pure-strain, live-trapped wild birds instead. The result has been the re-introduction of turkeys in many places that had not known them in this century. At the present time between thirty-five and forty states have huntable populations.

Above all other traits it is that basic wildness, that distrust of man and reluctance to have anything to do with him, that makes the turkey the great game bird he is.

When it comes to natural equipment you might think a deer out-ranks him—until you've tried them both. The turkey has no sense of smell, and while his ears are pretty good, he doesn't rely on them the way a deer does. In fact, until he sees something suspicious he may ignore strange noises altogether.

Bailey was setting up a live-trap one morning, as part of one of his research projects, at a spot where a flock had been paying regular visits to bait for several days. In the midst of the job he looked up and saw about a dozen turkeys walking down the mountain toward him.

They were the last thing he wanted to see at that minute, for he wasn't ready for them. If they came close enough to see him and spook, the chances were they'd never come back. It doesn't take much to make a turkey avoid a place permanently. So he picked up a hammer and rapped

No bird symbolizes the unspoiled woodlands of America more perfectly than the wild turkey. Wild in every sense of the word, cautious, sagacious, and equipped with the keenest eyesight of any of our game birds, he is rated by old turkey hunters the most difficult game to hunt that flies or walks in the forests of this country.

two or three times on a length of iron pipe, thinking they'd take the hint and shy off.

At the first clank of the hammer they stopped, threw up their heads and listened warily. But when he quit pounding they hesitated only a minute, then came on. The noise was certainly new to them but they didn't connect it with danger. He dropped his work and attempted to crawl into a thicket but they spotted his first step and left the area immediately, never again returning to the trap. The strange noise they could ignore. One glimpse of a man was more than enough.

On the other hand, one false note on a turkey call can send an old gobbler high-tailing out of the neighborhood for keeps. It all depends on what they hear and how they interpret it.

But a turkey relies mainly on his eyes. I know of no other game bird

A turkey flushes at easy gun range. He prefers running to flying, and normally he takes wing only if the hunter crowds him hard or surprises him at close range. More at home on the ground than in the air, he feeds and travels afoot, even in deep snow. But he does fly into a tree to roost at night.

or animal whose vision can begin to match his.

A deer may walk up to you if you sit motionless on a stand, may even come within a few feet without noticing you or making you out. A turkey very rarely. Like all birds, they are particularly well equipped to detect moving objects, but they can also see and recognize a motionless man at distances that seem incredible. Even though you're hidden behind a stump or log or screen of brush and even if you don't bat an eyelid, if you let an approaching turkey get within thirty yards before you kill him he's too close. The chances are, at that range, he'll discover you and be gone before you can get your gun to your shoulder.

And if you move while there's a turkey anywhere within sight you're a dead duck. Many times they flush 100 to 150 yards away when a sitting hunter turns his head ever so slightly or moves a hand an inch or two. Many a stillhunter has come over a ridge in view of turkeys at distances of from 100 to 200 yards, only to have them take alarm the instant his hat topped the rise, no matter how cautiously he was moving. Nine times out of ten, in such cases, the hunter never catches a glimpse of the birds. Only the racket of their hurried departure tells him what has happened.

Crowded hard enough or caught flat-footed at close range, the turkey will fly, but he prefers to run if circumstances permit. He's far more at home on the ground than in the air. He feeds and travels afoot and even in deep snow, when the walking is tough, he still slogs through it, although he does show a greater readiness to fly then.

He's no slouch at flying when the time comes but he does have difficulty in threading his way through thick stuff, which may be one reason why turkeys are found usually in open mature forests, rarely in areas of dense undergrowth. Many hunters think the turkey is not quite as fast as getting into the air as the ruffed grouse. Experienced turkey addicts are not so sure. And once on the wing, if he is in the open and can fly downhill, a gobbler makes better time than any grouse.

As for making a quick getaway on the ground, he has no equal. Game men who undertake to live-trap turkeys with cannon nets find out very quickly just how fast they can move.

The standard net is of nylon, thirty feet wide and sixty long. Ready for use, it is folded back along one side of a baited area. Four cannons loaded with blank shotgun shells fire heavy projectiles that carry it out. It works pretty fast. Yet unless the turkeys are close to the folded net there is no use to fire it. They'll travel five or six yards while the net is spreading and falling, and if they have any kind of a start they get away every time. And they move just as fast when they see anything in the woods they don't fancy, too.

They have none of the curiosity about man that is often the undoing of a deer. They waste no time staring, wondering, coming in for a better look. Their rule is to run first and find out later, and they don't run toward thick cover as a deer does. They just put distance between themselves and danger, as much distance as they can in the shortest possible time.

The first problem on a turkey hunt, of course, is to locate turkeys, and that can be difficult, even in country where they are plentiful. The greatest handicap lies in their unpredictability. They may be on a ridge in the morning, in a cove in the afternoon, at the foot of their home mountain today, on top tomorrow. They roost where night overtakes them, now in a sapling, again in the biggest tree they can find, one night a pine, the next a leafless hickory. You never know just where to look for them.

I hunted hard that fall in West Virginia. For three days our party sat, walked, climbed ridges, combed coves from daylight to dark without seeing or hearing a turkey. The third evening, after we had quit, skunked, another hunter stopped at our camp to show off the big gobbler he had killed that afternoon.

He and a partner had gone out after grouse that morning. They had a poor day, so poor they spent part of it calling crows to pass the time. In late afternoon they put their dog down in a hayfield.

To their amazement a turkey sailed out of a tree at the edge of the field, beyond range. Then the dog made a stand in thick cover and when they walked in turkey No. 2 thundered up. They busted him and went home.

It's rarely that easy, but it can be. You find turkeys where you're not looking for them and they do what you don't expect. But only now and then do they play into your hands as that gobbler did.

It's not hard to find turkey sign in good range. The hunter may locate a roost by the droppings underneath, or scratchings where the birds have searched for beechnuts, acorns and other food, exactly as farmyard turkeys do. A flock will tear up the dry leaves on a ridge a mile long in a day or two, leaving sign that even a beginner can't miss, and an experienced hunter can tell from the scratchings which way the birds were moving. But finding sign and finding turkeys are not quite the same thing. The sign only means that the birds were there an hour ago or yesterday or last week. By now they may be miles away, on another mountain. The wild turkey is a born traveler, forever on the move.

The home range of the average flock covers something like one-thousand to twelve-hundred acres. Many flocks and many individual birds wander over more range than that, and it is not unusual for them to walk three or four miles in a day. That may not sound like much, but you have to take the ruggedness of mountain country into account. They go in and out of coves, through hollows, up and down steep ridges. Turkey hunting is not for men with weak hearts.

Left undisturbed, the birds stick close to their home range, covering it at fairly regular intervals, in big irregular circles. There are still a few oldtimers, in the more remote sections of the eastern mountains, who watch a flock, time its movements, and lie in wait when the birds are due through a certain gap. It pays off, too, but only in areas where the turkeys are very lightly hunted. For nothing that wears feathers or fur is quicker to change habits or pull out when a neighborhood becomes unhealthy.

An old gobbler has a long memory where danger spots and close calls are concerned, too. If you spook him there's not much use looking for him around that same place again, at least for weeks or months.

Basically there are three methods of hunting turkeys. You can still-hunt, wait on a stand, or call. Standing calls for more patience than many hunters have, but if a man knows how to pick a good location it is more productive than stillhunting. In other words, your chances are better if you let the turkey come to you than if you try to get to him.

Turkeys often come to an untimely end by blundering into hunters who are not even looking for them. Squirrel and grouse hunters cash in that way every fall, purely by accident.

Few hunters are willing to spend three days in the same spot, sitting motionless from daylight to dusk, waiting for a turkey to come along. But those who are, and who know where to sit, are almost sure to score. There is hardly a flat or gap in good turkey range that is not traveled by birds sometime within a three-day period. If you take a turkey that way, however, you are likely to earn him.

Most hunters who sit and wait hide themselves in some fashion, behind a log, in a brush heap, or in a hole by the upturned roots of a stump. But the hunter must be able to see on all sides and free to turn if he needs to, and for that reason many prefer to sit in front of a tree rather than behind it.

Success for the stillhunter depends largely on weather conditions. That is a poor method on a dry, windless day, when dead leaves crackle underfoot and a man walking through the woods can be heard hundreds of yards away, no matter how carefully he moves. On such days it is better to find a promising stand, curb your impatience and take your chances that a turkey will come to you.

If you want to stillhunt, pick a rainy day. It may be uncomfortable, but good rain gear will take care of that, and both conditions and turkey behavior are in your favor. The birds travel less in rainy weather. They feed, but they are likely to be found standing around in clearings or open coves or at the edge of woods roads, where the hunter has a good chance of making a silent and successful stalk. In such weather wild turkey behavior is much like that of tame turkeys.

I know of one party of seven experienced hunters that hunted hard for three or four days in dry weather a few falls ago without seeing a bird. Finally there came a day of rain and

As a hunter takes aim, a called turkey spots him and flushes — but too late. It is not often the keen-eyed gobbler can be lured this close, especially with the hunter unconcealed in the open. Turkey calling takes skill and experience, coupled with knowledge of the bird's haunts and habits.

high wind, and when the party returned to camp that night they brought in seven good turkeys. Luck of that kind is rare, whatever the weather, but it will give you a hint as to how much better turkey hunting is likely to be on a rainy day.

The general rules for stillhunting turkeys are much like those for deer. Move slowly, make frequent stops, and look and listen carefully before you move on. A flock feeding in dry leaves makes a lot of racket, and if you take it easy and stop often enough you may hear them before they hear you.

If you locate birds that are out of range, better not try to stalk them, unless the woods are wet. If they're moving your way freeze and let them come to you. If not, wait till they are out of sight, then try to get around them and pick a stand where they are likely to cross. As a last resort you can try calling them back, but don't be surprised if they pay no attention.

Once a stillhunter has reason to believe there are birds in his vicinity, he should work uphill if possible. Turkeys fly uphill with difficulty and prefer to fly down. There's always a chance a flushed bird will come over you if you are below him. And if you are moving through an area where a flock has just been flushed, be ready for a straggler to get off the ground or sail out of a tree. One or two birds often loiter behind the rest.

Snow is a help to the stillhunter, especially in locating turkeys, although it has disadvantages too. The birds are likely to change or restrict their range when snow comes, making them hard to find, and the hunter is under the added handicap of being more easily seen. But if he finds the fresh tracks of a feeding flock he can overtake them, and if a stalk is impossible he may be able to pick a stand ahead of them and get a shot when they work up to him.

One final warning if you want to stillhunt: Go it alone. Two men make twice as much disturbance as one.

As for calling, many hunters who have had no experience with turkeys think it solves everything. They imagine all a man has to do is sit down, yelp a few times, and a turkey is almost sure to come walking up. It's hardly that simple. Calling is a special skill, not easy to acquire. It can be a big help in gathering in a turkey, but only under the right

Camouflaged hunter coaxes a gobbler into the open with a cedar-box call (below). The type of call varies widely, and includes the box, various kinds of mouth calls (left), and a box of thin, seasoned wood scraped with a piece of slate (right). A favorite of oldtime turkey hunters was made from the wingbone of a hen bird. Even such oddities as clay pipes and a leaf between the lips have been used.

conditions and if it is done exactly right.

To begin with, turkeys will almost never reply or come to the call of a strange bird not a member of their own flock. The hunter who merely sits down and starts yelping to the silent woods around him has very little chance of getting a response. The odds are even good that any turkeys within hearing will vamoose instead, especially if he overdoes his calling or is not expert at it.

Calling is a fairly sure bet under one set of circumstances, however. That is when the hunter succeeds in scattering a flock on the first flush. He has to get close to do it, catch them by surprise, force them off the ground and send them flying in all directions. Their one idea is to get together again. Even though the hunter has done some shooting or has killed a bird out of the band, if he or another member of his party will secret himself and call properly, at least part of the scattered flock is almost sure to come back, often within a few minutes.

A stray turkey by itself also is likely to come to a call, especially in the case of a young bird that has become lost from a flock or survived when others of its family group were killed. Such a bird is lonesome and eager for company. How can you tell when there's one around? Usually it will be doing some cautious calling on its own. That's your cue to talk back with your best imitation.

Whatever type of call you use, cedar box or wingbone, master it first and then don't overdo it. Turkeys themselves call sparingly and at long intervals. Sound three or four yelps, then wait about ten minutes before you repeat. If you have no reply or a turkey does not show up within the next half hour you may as well quit for the time being.

Better learn to gobble and putt as well as yelp, too. In short, if you want to fool a wild turkey you have to speak his entire language and speak it expertly. Calling is not for the amateur.

Most of the states that have huntable turkey populations, in the North as well as in the major turkey range of the South and in the eastern mountains, now allow spring gobbler hunting. That is an entirely different ball game from hunting turkeys at other times of year.

Many inexperienced hunters believe that because the toms are in a state of perpetual excitement in the spring, they are less cautious and likely to respond to any call that sounds reasonably like the notes of a lovesick hen. Actually, the opposite is true.

Wayne Bailey thinks the spring gobbler is the most wary of all. That is the only season, he points out, when turkeys, especially the toms, advertise their presence for all to hear.

Because they are gobbling, announcing their whereabouts to hunter and predator alike, their wildness and wariness is increased. And the more they are hunted the more crafty they become.

Too, the tom that gobbles when the hunting season is open is very likely to draw responses from two or three hunters trying to mimic a hen, and of that number one is almost sure to sound a false note. That's all the hint the gobbler needs. He leaves that neighborhood by the shortest route, and is very slow to return.

In fall and winter, the heavier the hunting pressure the greater the kill. In spring the reverse is true. Many states with a spring season limit the number of hunters by a permit system. This is an excellent device to prevent crowding in the turkey woods and maintain a quality type of hunting, but it is not needed to save turkeys. Bailey thinks the spring kill would be even lower than it is if more hunters were afield.

Relatively, it is extremely low. In recent gobbler seasons, for example, close to 1,000 permit holders in Indiana took only 12 turkeys. In Illinois, 1,200 hunters collected 52 toms, and in Michigan 4,600 permit holders went home with 96.

"The harvest is very light but the fever runs high," one state game man told me. That is the case just about everywhere the birds are hunted in spring. The hunter who hears a tom leaves the woods excited and satisfied, even though he is empty-handed.

Although shotguns are close to the universal firearm for turkeys, in a few cases where the law permits spring hunters fall back on rifles so they can reach out farther for an incoming gobbler. More than one sportsman protests that that is taking unfair advantage of the birds. There is also marked landowner resistance to the spring hunts in some states.

"We just don't cotton to the idea of hunters running around in our woods with shotguns when the leaves are coming out and flowers are in bloom," one landowner summed up the feeling.

So far as harming the turkey population is concerned, the spring gobbler seasons are biolgically foolproof. Only toms are killed, and in almost every state the hunt comes after the peak of the breeding season is past, when the male birds have served their purpose for the year and the hens are already on the nest. In the North, for example, the mating period reaches its peak early in April and the hunts are slated for the latter part of that month or early May.

There is hardly a more exciting method of hunting in this country than calling in a spring turkey, or one that requires a higher degree of skill and sportsmanship. The bird may gobble or he may not. He may — if he has not been spooked or shot at

previously—come running, but he is at least as likely to skulk in from the hunter's rear. However he comes, he'll come cautiously, and when he arrives he shakes the hunter's nervous system as few game birds or animals can. The sight and sound of a tom turkey strutting and gobbling just beyond gun range is hard to match for excitement and suspense.

One thing not worth trying is driving turkeys as deer are driven.

You can't tell which way they'll go when they're spooked.

What it all adds up to is that nobody knows what to expect of a wild turkey. Hunting him is a game of wits, in which you pit your patience and knowledge and skill against the wariest and canniest thing you'll ever try to kill. Meet him on his terms and outguess him as you go along—or resign yourself to the fact that you'll never be a turkey hunter.

A gobbler walks boldly into the open in a dry-country setting. The Merriam's and Rio Grande races of turkey, found in the arid Southwest, are rated by most hunters less wary and cautious than the race native to the woodlands in the eastern half of the country.

349

SHOTGUNS FOR FLYING GAME

Winchester Model 37A, a single-shot shotgun, comes in 5 standard gauges, full-choke barrel. Barrel length varies from 26 inches in .410 to 36 inches in 12 gauge.

Stevens Model 311 double-barreled shotgun is chambered for 12, 16, 20 and .410 gauge; barrel lengths are 26, 28 and 30 inches. Choke combinations include Improved Cylinder and Modified, Modified and Full, Full and Full.

Savage-Fox Model B double-barreled shotgun is a lightweight arm with 24-inch barrels, in 12 or 20 gauge. A variety of chokes are available.

Browning B-SS, a double-barreled shotgun, comes in 12 or 20 gauge, 26- or 28-inch barrels. The 28-inch is choked Modified and Full; the 26, Modified and Full or Improved Cylinder and Modified.

Savage Model 330, an over-and-under shotgun, is available with interchangeable 12- or 20-gauge barrels, a 28-inch choked Modified and Full, or a 26-inch Improved Cylinder and Modified. It has a single selective trigger.

Browning Superposed over-and-under comes in 12, 12 Mag., 20, 28, .410 gauge. Single selective trigger, automatic ejection and take-down system are features.

Savage Model 30, a pump-action shotgun, comes in 12, 20 and .410 gauge, with barrels 26, 28 and 30 inches. Chokes include Improved Cylinder, Modified and Full.

Winchester Model 1200 Field Gun, a pump action with ventilated rib, comes in 12 or 20 gauge, choked Full, Modified or Improved Cylinder, with barrels 26, 28 and 30 inches.

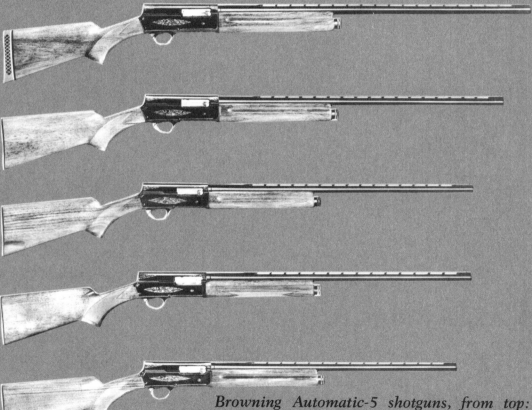

Remington Model 1100 autoloading shotgun with ventilated rib is available in 12, 16, 20, 28 and .410 gauge, in Full, Modified and Improved Cylinder choke. Barrel length varies from 26–30 inches.

Browning Automatic-5 shotguns, from top: 12 gauge, 3-inch Mag.; 12-gauge standard; 16-gauge lightweight; 20 gauge, 3-inch Magnum; 20-gauge lightweight.

PHOTO CREDITS

ERWIN A. BAUER: pages 11, 19, 24 (bottom), 30, 32, 56, 61 (bottom), 63, 68, 70, 78, 80, 85, 91, 98, 116, 123, 124, 134, 139, 142, 148, 152, 168, 175, 180, 184, 188, 191, 196, 205, 220, 230, 257, 259, 272, 286, 288, 296, 302, 307

DAVID BOOKS: page 293

BILL BROWNING: pages 65 (right), 69, 82, 108 (top), 158, 264, 337, 338

PETE CZURA: pages 57, 61 (top), 140, 150, 151, 210, 233, 279, 282, 283

LARRY DABLEMONT: pages 7, 26, 35, 38, 240, 277, 344 (left)

BYRON DALRYMPLE: pages 2, 37, 52, 176, 179, 226, 254, 260, 332, 345, 348

JAMES DAUBEL: pages 4, 5, 170, 294, 295, 298, 299, 317

C. H. DICKEY: pages 10, 250, 311, 324, 326, 342, 344 (right)

D. D. DICKEY: pages 310, 316

BEN EAST: page 76

CHARLES FARMER: pages 42, 96, 138, 165

STEVE GILBERT: page 111

GENE HORNBECK: pages 24 (top), 144, 217, 221, 236, 237

G. C. KELLEY: pages 75, 108 (bottom)

GEORGE LAYCOCK: pages 224, 320

BILL MCRAE: pages 15, 58, 60, 65 (left), 72, 90, 109, 112, 114, 119, 200, 245, 247, 263

LEONARD LEE RUE III: pages 45, 48, 87, 101, 102, 103, 146, 156, 157, 174, 185, 189, 194, 199, 201, 231, 256, 315, 330

JAMES TALLON: pages 50, 100, 192, 214

RICHARD WRIGHT: page 21

INDEX

INDEX